HISPANIC MILITARY HEROES

VIRGIL FERNANDEZ

HISPANIC MILITARY HEROES

Inquiries should be addressed to:

VFJ Publishing
P.O. Box 81976
Austin, TX 78708

E-mail: virgilf@sbcglobal.net

First Edition, April 2006

Cataloging-in-Publication Data

Fernandez, Virgil
Hispanic Military Heroes

p. 224   cm. 21.59 x 27.94

I. Hispanic American–Veterans–History   II. Veterans–United States
III. United States–Armed Forces–20th Century
IV. Hispanic American–Military History–United States

355.008 Fe   E 184 FE
ISBN 0-9675876-1-1   LCCN 2005937318

Book Editor–Virgil Fernandez, AAS, BA, BS
Proofreading and Indexing–Mindy S. Reed, MLIS, MA
Layout and Graphic Design–Michele Mason, BS

Printed in the USA at:
BookMasters, Inc.
2541 Ashland Road
Mansfield, OH 44905

Cover Illustration:
The Borinqueneers, A National Guard Heritage Painting by Dominick D'Andrea.

Dedication

This book is dedicated to Manuel Gonzales Manchaca, Jr.

Following the attack on Pearl Harbor, Mr. Manchaca volunteered to join the Navy at age 17 and proudly served for four years. He is one of a generation of Americans who instantly knew they had a duty to perform and gladly did it; no questions asked. Manuel was one of about 500-thousand Hispanic men who left home during World War II to go fight for America. He was lucky and came home safely.

We proudly salute and thank you Manuel for your heroic deeds then and throughout your life.

Manuel Gonzales Manchaca Jr. was born August 17, 1924 in Kenedy, Texas. His family then moved to Austin, TX shortly thereafter. Manuel attended Austin High School, but decided he needed to earn some money and left to join the Civilian Conservation Corps in Wyoming in August 1941. His work ended on December 23, 1941, two weeks after the Japanese attacked Pearl Harbor.

His brother, Jessie, quickly joined the Navy after the Japanese bombing. Not wanting to be left behind, and wishing to go get his share of *Jap's*, Manuel decided to also join the Navy.

However, Manuel was only 17 years old in December 1941. He needed his mother's signature to enlist. After some convincing by young Manuel, his mother, Ruth G. Manchaca, agreed to sign and allow 'Manny' to go fight for his country.

Manuel was elated and went off to join the Navy on June 17, 1942. He served aboard the

USS Chenango in the Mediterranean and also in the Pacific. He was in charge of supplies aboard the ship as a Storekeeper Third Class.

Manchaca was also an amateur boxer, both while in the Navy, and later as a civilian. He is said to have knocked out or beaten many an opponent in the Austin area. He later decided to quit the dangerous sport and concentrate on raising a family with his wife Orelia Sifuentes Manchaca. They had five children; Vivian, Rebecca, Manuel Jr., Jeannie, and Michael. Following the war, he was discharged on May 18, 1946.

Upon returning to Austin, he enrolled in the Travis County Vocational School and earned a certificate as an Electrician. He worked for several electrical companies before starting his own business a few years later. Manuel wired houses and businesses in the Austin area for more than 40 years before retiring in 1992.

However, every year Manuel managed to call one of his old Navy buddies to reminisce about their war days. Manuel still proudly wears his US Navy hat around his retirement center in South Austin. However, now his wife, Orelia Sifuentes Manchaca, takes care of him as proudly as he did when he took care of his family and country.

Manuel celebrated his 81st birthday in Austin in 2005 with his immediate family, numerous grand kids and many other family members and friends.

Anchors Aweigh y Gracias Manuel as you prepare for your 82nd birthday party.

Table of Contents

We few,
we happy few,
we band of brothers;

For he today that sheds his blood with me
Shall be my brother.

> *Shakespeare,*
> *Henry V,*
> *Act IV, Scene 3*

Foreward

This book is a historical review of the accomplishments made by Hispanic military veterans, as well as civilian Hispanics, who participated in military campaigns undertaken by the United States of America throughout this country's history. Also included, are articles about Hispanics who have contributed their special skills and knowledge in their endeavor to help make this country a special home for us as we move into an uneasy future.

I have compiled the many articles written by various authors and incorporated them into this book. I have also used information from federal government and military publications. Specific details were also obtained from the Congressional Medal of Honor Society and from the Home of Heroes Medal of Honor websites. I wish to thank the many writers, publications, web sites, federal government agencies, and private citizens who have granted me permission, whether directly or through a representative, to use their information, articles, and/or photographs for inclusion in this book. Bibliographic citations for all the articles have been provided in the Bibliography section at the back of this book.

The writers include; Dean Acosta, Carl V. Allsup, Karen Anderson, Libby Averyt, SSG Marc Ayalin, Mike Baird, Judith Bellafaire, Sig Chrisenson, Carol Cohea, Raoul Lowey Contreras, John Culhane, Carmina Danini, Virginia Cueto, Melvin Ember, Lionel Fernandez, David Flores, John Flores, Santiago A. Flores, Roger A. Freeman, Joseph L. Galloway, Alicia A. Garcia, Kevin Garcia, Maria-Cristina Garcia, Jim Garamone, Ron George, Richard Goldstein, Elena Gomez, John Gonzales, Richard Gray, Carlos Guerra, Lucy Guevara, Laurie Hahn, Barry Halvorson, Mark Holston, MSgt Sarah Hood, Scott Huddelston, Terry Hudson, Rene Juhans, Gregg K. Kakesako, Linda D. Kozaryn, George W. Langdale, Art Leatherwood, Linda Lou, Dennis McLellan, James M. Myers, Kae Nelson, Joe Olvera, Cynthia Orozco, SGT Jimmie Perkins, Lisa Harrison Rivas, Ken Rodriguez, Sonya Ross, Mary Scott, Manuel Servin, Edward Simms, Deborah Sullivan, Barrett Tillman, David Uhler, Sig Unander, Lt. Col. Gilberto Villahermosa, Steve Vogel, SPC Felicia Whatley, Michael J. Williams, Rudi Williams, US Air Force, US Army, US Marine Corps, US Navy, and numerous websites.

Specific details are available in the Bibliography at the back of this book.

Preface

As we enter the third year of fighting in Iraq in November 2005, many Americans still question why we went to fight the Iraqis in the first place. Was it to protect their oilfields, to help that country become a democracy, or to show the world we will never back down from anyone.

Regardless, the harsh criticism President Bush has received from many corners may not have been as strong if we would not continue to loose so many of our best and brightest. Then there are the injuries by the hundreds, if not thousands of Americans have endured since this wars' inception. This of course, includes the many Latino soldiers who have also suffered. By October 2005, 1 out of every 10 deaths in Iraq had been by a Latino. This amounts to more than 200 out of the more than 2,000 U.S. soldiers killed in Iraq having been Hispanic. But Hispanics account for slightly less than 10 percent of active duty personnel.

Some military analysts say the reason so many Hispanics have been killed and injured may be due to the fact that many Latinos score low on proficiency exams and are only qualified for the more dangerous front-line combat jobs. But an Army Link News report in August 1999 stated that even when Hispanics score higher, "military recruiters reported that even those Mexican-American recruits who 'tested out of the infantry' opted to enter the infantry anyway."

It is also felt the educational system is failing kids in the Hispanic community and thus their career choices become limited. Therefore they choose the one job with good starting pay and a promise of training and educational benefits: the military. However, once there, their options are limited again by not bringing a strong educational background or having limited English language skills. This is supported by the fact that about 12,000 noncitizens from Spanish-speaking countries are active duty personnel in the U.S. military. Of these, about 20 were killed early on in Iraq, including a young Latina from Houston, Army Pfc. Analaura Esparza Gutierrez. A total of five Latinas have died in Iraq so far.

Retired Brig. Gen. Bernardo Negrete, formerly of the Army Recruiting Command, says Hispanics are attracted to the military by several things: "The military structure is very similar to that of a typical Hispanic family. Respect for discipline, a strong sense of responsibility and bullet-proof loyalty." Jorge Mariscal, a professor at the University of California, San Diego, and a Vietnam veteran, disagrees. "Poverty and lack of opportunities are driving a generation of Hispanics to war," he said. "They can't find a job or pay for college. This is about having no other choice."

In a Feb. 27, 2005 article, the Austin American Statesman cited reasons some experts believe why many Hispanics continue to enlist in the military:

■ Military recruiting is most effective in the poorest schools, where Latinos are often found.

■ The Marines have a reputation as being the toughest and this appeals to those who want to prove themselves to their friends and family.

■ The military is a way to demonstrate a patriotic sense of duty among Latinos.

■ Recent immigrants want to show they are grateful for being in America, or they are drawn by a U.S. policy that allows troops who serve during wartime to apply for citizenship sooner.

In 1969 I joined the service for two reasons: As a patriotic lower middle-class Chicano in San Antonio, I wanted to follow my brother-in-laws foot-steps as a sailor in the U.S. Navy. And while there, I knew I would earn educational benefits I needed to help pay for college. Without the G.I. Bill I would have probably never even considered enrolling in college, and consequently, graduating from The University of Texas-Austin in 1975 with a bachelor's degree in government.

A 2000 survey of young Hispanics prepared for the Department of Defense found that social class and educational aspirations are the most powerful predictors of whether Hispanics will enlist.

"It's really a class issue, then an ethnicity or race issue," said Jorge Mariscal, a Chicano historian and veteran who heads the Chicano studies pro-gram at the University of California, San Diego.

According to the U.S. Census Bureau, in general, Hispanics are significantly less likely to complete high school than whites. In 2002, only 57 percent of Latinos older than 25 had completed high school, compared with more than 88 percent of whites and 78 percent of blacks. Portions of these Latinos include immigrants who arrived in the U.S. as teenagers with little or no English language skills. Therefore, they found it difficult to learn English and just dropped out of high school and got a job.

But the military is still seen by many Hispanics as being a respectable and patriotic career. There are many Latinos whose forefathers joined the service for job security. Other Latinos also see the military as the best way to quickly and easily move up and out of poverty. Today, the military offers good pay and benefits, including medical and retirement. In 2005, not many employers can offer this to someone with only a high school diploma and limited skills.

This all goes back to why so many Hispanics are being killed and injured in Iraq, and previously in Vietnam. Since there is no military draft to worry about, Latinos must be better prepared before signing up for the service.

So is it wrong for Latinos to join the military service and risk being injured or killed? I'll have to say no, it is not wrong. However, all new recruits must be prepared for active duty by perhaps joining their high school ROTC program or working for a year or two after high school. But many of these young Latinos may be too *gung ho*, or perhaps they have a strong desire to demonstrate they are tough and patriotic, and volunteer to go first into a deadly firefight.

Sadly, I had a friend who wanted to go fight and be a hero in Vietnam. All the military branches rejected him due to his low scores. However, the Army eventually opened their door and gladly signed him up. He was then sent to Nam and was killed when he stepped on a landmine a few weeks after arriving. He did not have to go and did not have to prove anything to anyone. However, believing he had no other alternatives, he decided the military was his only way to demonstrate he was more than a high school drop-out.

This book is for all to see that not only are Latinos patriotic, we are also brave, hard-working and care about our family and community. Sometimes Hispanic military personnel want to prove to our family and maybe ourselves as well, that we can succeed and move up and out of our low income existence.

"Hispanic Military Heroes" is not only about all the stories you will read here, but also about all the stories that may have not been told. Stories, which may bring sadness or sorrow about family or friends that were lost, physically or emotionally. I do not mention all the wounded or mentally scarred Latinos who went to war and came back much different than when they left. I do not want to ever forget about the Purple Heart veterans, those veteranos who suffered–or still suffer–from PTSD, and the disabled veterans.

So why is the U.S. still fighting in Iraq, there are many opinions, regardless, young Latinos will continue to join to military to defend and protect us, and we will always honor and salute them.

In the barrio, the anguish caused by seeing their sons and, sometimes, daughters go to war gave birth to songs such as "El Corrido del Padre de un Soldado." Its author is unknown. It can be found in the compilation CD titled "FlacoJimenez; Un Mojado Sin Licencia," produced in 1977.

The following is the original text to the song "El Corrido del Padre de un Soldado."

El Corrido del Padre de Un Soldado

Soy un padre como hay muchos, que no hayamos que pensarpues tenemos nuestros hijosallá peleando en Vietnam, Virgencita milagrosadevuelvelos como se van.

Diosito santo te pidoque tengas más compasiónde nuestros hijos queridosque andan en otra nación. Bien sabes que se llevaronparte de mi corazón.

Virgen divina, Virgencita de San Juán, protege a to do el soldadoque nos defiende en Vietnam.

Adios mis padres queridos, nos dijo casi al partir, dijo no se queden tristesque pronto he de venir.soy purito mexicanoy no le temo al morir.

Se despidió de su novia, de sus hermanos también, le dió un abrazo a su madre, y a mí me dió otro también. Se encomendó ante nosotros, y ante Diosito también.

Diosito santo, tu sabeslo que una madre sufriópara darle vida a su hijohasta la vida arriesgóa cambio de la de mi hijome vida te ofrezco yo.

Virgen divina....

The Lament of a Soldier's Father

I am like many fathers, that we don't know what to think because we have our sons over there, fighting in Vietnam, miraculous Virgin return them as they left.

Holy God, I ask youhave greater compassion of our dear sons that are in another nation. You know that they took with them part of my heart.

Divine Virgin Virgin of San Juan protect all the soldiers that defend us in Vietnam.

Goodbye, my dear parent she told us, just as he left he said don't remain sad for I will be back real soon. I am a real Mexican and I am not afraid to die.

He said goodbye to his fiancée, and to his brothers, too, he gave a hug to his mother, and he also gave one to me. He asked for our blessing and of that of the Lord.

Dear Lord, you know what a mother has suffered to give her son his life she even risked her own life, in exchange for that of my son I offer you my very own.

Divine Virgin...

So, in the end, a combination of patriotism, duty, and responsibility have all played a part in creating

Hispanic Military Heroes!

SGT. RAFAEL PERALTA

■ ■ ■ ■ ■

1

Sgt. Rafael Peralta

Note: This chapter includes articles written by Lance Cpl. Travis J. Kaemmerer, USMC, and Tony Perry and Richard Marosi. For details please see Bibliography.

The war, Iraqi Freedom, had been officially over on November 15, 2004 when U.S. Marine Sgt. Rafael Peralta volunteered to go out with an assault team, seeking insurgents in Fallouja, Iraq. As a scout, assigned to perimeter security, he could have stayed further back. Instead, he took the lead as his platoon stormed a house in search of heavily armed insurgents known to be hiding in the neighborhood.

Along with Peralta, was Marine combat news correspondent LCpl Travis J. Kaemmerer, a 21-year-old native of Taunton, Massachusetts.

The following is CPL Kaemmerer's story of what happened that day in Iraq.

...As a combat correspondent, I was attached to Company A, 1st Battalion, 3rd Marine Regiment for Operation Al Fajr, to make sure the stories of heroic actions and the daily realities of battle were told.

On this day, I found myself without my camera. With the batteries dead, I decided to leave the camera behind and live up to the ethos "every Marine a rifleman," by volunteering to help clear the fateful buildings that lined the streets.

After seven days of intense fighting in Fallujah, the Marines embraced a new day with a faceless enemy.

We awoke November 15, 2004; around daybreak in the abandoned, battle-worn house we had made our home for the night. We shaved, ate breakfast from a Meal, Ready-to-Eat pouch and

waited for the word to move out. The word came and we started what we had done since the operation began–clear the city of insurgents, building by building.

As an attachment to the unit, I had been placed as the third man in a six-man group, or what Marines call a 'stack.' Two stacks of Marines were used to clear a house. Moving quickly from the third house to the fourth, our order in the stack changed. I found Sgt. Rafael Peralta in my spot, so I fell in behind him as we moved toward the house.

1.1 Sgt. Rafael Peralta, USMC.
Photo courtesy of United States Marine Corps (USMC).

A 25-year-old Mexican American who lived in San Diego, Peralta earned his U.S. citizenship after he joined the Marine Corps. He was a platoon scout, which meant he could have stayed back in safety while the squads of 1st Platoon went into the danger filled streets, but he was constantly asking to help out by giving them an extra Marine. I learned by speaking with him and other Marines the night before that he frequently put his safety, reputation, and career on the line for the needs and morale of the junior Marines around him.

When we reached the fourth house, we breached the gate and swiftly approached the building. The first Marine in the stack kicked in the front door, revealing a locked door to their front and another at the right. Kicking in the doors simultaneously, one stack filed swiftly into the room to the front as the other group of Marines darted off to the right.

"Clear!" screamed the Marines in one of the rooms followed only seconds later by another shout of "clear!" from the second room. One word told us all we wanted to know about the rooms: there was no one in there to shoot at us.

We found that the two rooms were adjoined and we had another closed door in front of us. We spread ourselves throughout the rooms to avoid a cluster going through the next door.

Two Marines stacked to the left of the door as Peralta, rifle in hand, tested the handle. I watched from the middle, slightly off to the right of the room as the handle turned with ease. Ready to rush into the rear part of the house, Peralta threw open the door.

'POP! POP! POP!' Multiple bursts of cap-gun-like sounding AK-47 fire rang throughout the house. Three insurgents with AK-47s were waiting for us behind the door.

Peralta was hit several times in his upper torso and face at point-blank range by the fully automatic 7.62mm weapons employed by three terrorists. Mortally wounded, he turned and fell into the already cleared, adjoining room, giving the rest of us a clear line of fire through the doorway to the rear of the house.

We opened fire, adding the bangs of M-16A2 service rifles, and the deafening, rolling cracks of a Squad Automatic Weapon, or "SAW," to the already nerve-racking sound of the AKs. One Marine was shot through the forearm and continued to fire at the enemy.

I fired until Marines closer to the door began to maneuver into better firing positions, blocking my line of fire. Not being an infantryman, I watched to see what those with more extensive training were doing. I saw four Marines firing from the adjoining room when a yellow, foreign-made, oval-shaped grenade bounced into the room, rolling to a stop close to Peralta's nearly lifeless body.

In an act living up to the heroes of the Marine Corps' past, and to the amazement of the other Marines–Peralta–in his last fleeting moments of consciousness and with his last bit of strength–reached out and pulled the grenade into his body.

I watched in fear and horror as the other four Marines scrambled to the corners of the room when the majority of the blast was absorbed by Peralta's now lifeless body. His selfless act left four other Marines with only minor injuries from smaller fragments of the grenade.

During the fight, a fire was sparked in the rear of the house. The flames were becoming visible through the door. The decision was made by the Marine in charge of the squad to evacuate the injured Marines from the house, regroup and return to finish the fight and retrieve Peralta's body. We quickly ran for shelter, three or four houses up the street, in a house that had already been

1.2 LCpl Travis J. Kaemmerer, USMC.
Photo courtesy of USMC.

cleared and was occupied by the squad's platoon.

As Staff Sgt. Jacob M. Murdock took a count of the Marines coming back, he found it to be one man short, and demanded to know the where-abouts of the missing Marine.

"Sergeant Peralta! He's dead! He's fucking dead," screamed Lance Cpl. Adam Morrison, a machine gunner with the squad, as he came around a corner. "He's still in there. We have to go back."

The ingrained code Marines have of never leaving a man behind drove the next few moments. Within seconds, we headed back to the house unknown what we may encounter, yet ready for another round. I don't remember walking back down the street or through the gate in front of the house, but walking through the door the second time, I prayed that we wouldn't lose another brother.

We entered the house and met no resistance. We couldn't clear the rest of the house because the fire had grown immensely and the danger of the enemy's weapons cache exploding in the house was increasing by the second. Most of us provided security while Peralta's body was removed from the house.

We carried him back to our rally point and upon returning were told that the other Marines who went to support us encountered and killed the three insurgents from inside the house.

Later that night, while I was thinking about the day's somber events, Cpl. Richard A. Mason, an infantryman with Headquarters Platoon, who in the short time I was with the company became a good friend, told me, "You're still here, don't forget that. Tell your kids, your grandkids, what Sgt. Peralta did for you and the other Marines today."

As a combat correspondent, this is not only my job, but also an honor.

Throughout Operation Al Fajr we were constantly being told that we were making history, but if the books never mention this battle in the future, I'm sure that the Marines who were there will never forget the day and the sacrifice that was made.

Within days, Sgt. Peralta's heroic act was retold in newspapers across the United States, including the Los Angeles Times. Staff writers Tony Perry and Richard Marosi gave this account on Dec. 6, 2004. Sgt. Rafael Peralta is dead, but the story of his sacrifice to save fellow Marines will live long in Marine Corps lore.

1.3 Rafael Peralta (right) and friends having fun at a backyard party. Photo courtesy of www.blogsofwar.com.

"If he hadn't done what he did, a lot of us wouldn't be seeing our families again," said Lance Cpl. Travis J. Kaemmerer, who witnessed the blast.

Garry Morrison, the father of Lance Cpl. Adam Morrison, had trouble keeping his voice from breaking when he spoke of Peralta.

"He saved the life of my son and every Marine in that room," Morrison said in a phone call from Seattle. "I just know one thing: God has a special place in heaven for Sgt. Peralta."

Family members of other Marines in Peralta's unit who were close to the blast expressed similar gratitude. The unit was Alpha Company, 1st Battalion, 3rd Marine Regiment, 3rd Marine Division.

"The Bible says it all: No greater love hath no man than to give his life for another," Becky Dyer, the wife of Cpl. Brannon Dyer, said in a phone call from Honolulu. "My husband and I both feel that way," she said. "That's how the whole company feels about Sgt. Peralta."

In a modest home, in a blue-collar neighborhood the Peralta family feels pride but also grief, anger, and confusion. Rafael Peralta was the oldest son: strong, a weightlifter and athlete, head of the family since his father died in a workplace accident three years ago. He loved the Marine Corps.

Fellow marines remember Peralta as a squared-away Marine, so meticulous about uniform standards that he sent his camouflage uniform to be pressed while training in Kuwait before entering Iraq.

But mostly they remembered acts of selflessness: offering career advice, giving a buddy a ride home from the bar, teaching salsa dance steps in the barracks.

He joined in 2000 and had recently reenlisted. While in the Marines, he became a U.S. citizen. The only decorations on his bedroom walls are a copy of the U.S. Constitution, the Bill of Rights and a picture of his boot camp graduation. As Peralta waited to begin the assault on the insurgent stronghold of Fallouja, he wrote a letter to his 14-year-old brother, Ricardo.

The letter arrived the day after several Marines and a Navy chaplain came to the Peralta home to notify the family of his death.

"We are going to destroy insurgents," Peralta wrote. *"Watch the news.... Be proud of me, bro. I'm going to do something I always wanted to do."*

"You should be proud of being an American. Our father came to this country and became a citizen because it was the right place for our family to be. If anything happens to me, just remember I've already lived my life to the fullest."

Peralta had left his mother, Rosa, with similar words. She said he told her, "I want you to be strong and take care of my brother and sisters because I don't know if I'll return." His mother added, "I'm proud of him, but my heart is sad."

"Most of the Marines in the house were in the immediate area of the grenade," Kaemmerer said. "Every one of us is grateful and will never forget the second chance at life Sgt. Peralta gave us."

Even in their pain, Peralta's family members are not surprised that he decided to lead from the front.

"My brother was very courageous," Ricardo Peralta said.

1.4 Cmdr. Robert D. Delis gives a cross to Rosa Maria Peralta, after her son, Sgt. Rafael Peralta's body is laid to rest Nov. 23, 2004. Photo courtesy of Cpl. Edward R. Guevara Jr., USMC.

"He wasn't scared of anyone or anything." Still, his older sister, Icela Donald, 24, wished that her brother had not been so brave.

"It doesn't surprise me that he did something like that," she said. "But it kind of makes me mad. He had a family, and we need him." Donald, who lives in Florida, came to San Diego to be with Ricardo, their sister Karen and their mother.

The family has been accommodating to the media, but know that soon attention will shift. "People will forget about him," Donald said. "That's when it will hurt the most."

When Peralta's body returned to San Diego for burial, his family members were unable to recognize him. They identified him only by the Marine tattoo on his left shoulder. Family members kept a two-day vigil next to the casket before burial Nov. 23 at Ft. Rosecrans National Cemetery at Point Loma, CA.

Ricardo Peralta was the first family member to talk to members of the "casualty notification" team. Despite his youth, he knew instinctively why they had come to his house. Among family members of Marines, there is no greater fear than seeing an official car pull up at their house, with Marines in dress uniforms.

Ricardo Peralta called his mother to hurry home from her job as a housekeeper at a hospital. Once home, she quickly became distraught and ordered the Marines to leave. Donald said her mother had only recently begun to recover from the death of her husband and her son's fiancée.

Rosa Peralta's husband, a diesel mechanic, was killed in September 2001, when a truck he was working on rolled and pinned him. In December 2003, Rafael Peralta's fiancée was killed in a traffic accident in Michoacan, Mexico, where she had gone to attend her mother's funeral.

"God is punishing me, but I don't know why," Rosa Peralta said.

Karen Peralta, 13, knows how she will remember her older brother.

"As a hero," she said.

Does his heroism make it easier to accept that he is gone?

"No," she said quietly, her eyes downcast and filling with tears.

California congressman Bob Filner introduced legislation in December 2004 to award Sgt. Peralta the Congressional Medal of Honor. This process may take several months.

Gen. George Washington leading a charge during the revolutionary war. Image courtesy of the National Archives.

HISTORY OF HISPANICS IN THE U.S. MILITARY

■ ■ ■ ■ ■

2

History of Hispanics in the U.S. Military

Note: The following is a compilation of articles written by various writers including; Raoul Lowery Contreras, Lionel Fernandez, SFC Douglas Ide, Pete Normand, Refugio Rochin, John P. Schmal, and Col. Gilberto Villahermosa. For details please see Bibliography.

Sgt. Rafael Peralta is only the latest Hispanic military hero to step forward, but we must never forget that many other Hispanos throughout the years have also sacrificed for this country and its revolutionary beginnings. Many Latinos have made the ultimate sacrifice such as Sgt. Rafael Peralta did.

Latino GIs have also received more Congressional Medals of Honor than any other ethnic group, in proportion to the number who served. In total, 42 Hispanic Americans have received this decoration, the nation's highest award for valor.

Thousands of Latinos and Latinas have also made significant contributions to the United States via the military, starting with the American Revolution, and today in 2005 our brothers and sisters are fighting and dying in Iraq.

THE AMERICAN REVOLUTION (1775-1782)

Although Spain was a strong colonial power in North America in the 1700s, the Spanish defeat in the Seven Years War led to the parceling of land to the English in the Spanish Colony of Florida. Spain, therefore, felt no loyalty to the British Monarchy during the course of the American Revolution.

Despite negotiations with the Continental Congress, both sides could not agree on the fate of Florida and therefore Spain played no overt role in aiding the American colonists.

Nevertheless, several Hispanic forefathers, like the father of David Farragut, provided discrete aid to the colonists. Another such man was General Bernardo de Galvez, a Spanish Army Officer and Governor of Louisiana in 1777.

From 1775-77, de Galvez provided rations and weapons to the Continental Army. In 1777, he arranged safe passage for James Willing, an American agent of the Continental congress, who had led a successful campaign along the Mississippi river harassing British shipping, plantation owners, and military outposts.

2.1 General Bernardo de Galvez.
Photo courtesy of U.S. Dept. of Defense.

Taking advantage of weaknesses in the British defenses and Spanish recognition of American Independence in 1779, de Galvez captured all the British forts along the Mississippi from Lake Pontchartrain to Baton Rouge. He later defeated all British forces in Florida and restored control of this region to Spain. For his contribution, de Galvez has been memorialized on a U.S. stamp and a statue in Washington, DC, and in his namesake city of Galveston, Texas.

In 1781, French and American forces were about to abandon their siege of Yorktown for lack of funds. Women in Havana, however, took up a collection and were able to raise a substantial sum of money. By delivering their gift to the French Expeditionary Force, they were able to insure that the siege would continue.

POST-REVOLUTIONARY WAR

One of de Galvez's officers, Francisco de Miranda, also played an important role in the defeat of the British on the Mississippi and the capture of the port of Pensacola.

Ultimately a revolutionary himself, de Miranda left the Spanish army and led a campaign against Spanish colonialism while living in North America and Europe. In 1805, he led an American-sanctioned invasion of Venezuela and is credited with the title of "Precursor of Latin American Independence."

Hispanic Americans joined General Andrew Jackson in defeating the British during the War of 1812.

TEXAS-MEXICAN FRONTIER (1830s)

The next conflict involving Hispanics in American history took place over territorial disputes between Mexico and the Republic of Texas. When Mexican general and self-proclaimed President Antonio Lopez de Santa Anna attacked the Alamo on March 6, 1835, 183 Texans were killed, six of them Mexicans fighting for Texas' liberty. Of the 11 survivors of the battle at the Alamo, 10 were Hispanics.

Juan Nepomucena Seguin was a Tejano Patriot who was fighting at the Alamo with the Texans when he was ordered to go for reinforcements. Seguin was born on October 27, 1806 in San Antonio, TX.

He was 14 years old in 1821, when his father, the Alcalde of San Antonio, welcomed Stephen F. Austin to Texas.

The Seguin family, and others of the upper class in Mexican Texas, supported Mexico's policy of allowing foreigners to settle the area in the early 1820s. A liberal like his father, Juan Seguin entered politics, and in 1834 was appointed as the chief administrator of the San Antonio district. He was an outspoken champion of the Texans' demand for more self-government, and was very critical of the dictatorial policies of Mexican President Santa Anna.

In September 1835, with the advance of the Mexican General Cos against the rebellious Texans, Seguin recruited a company of Mexican ranchers and joined the Texan forces at the Battle of Bexar. His conduct in the resulting victory was so distinguished that he was granted a commission as a captain of cavalry in the regular Texas Army.

On February 3, 1836, he was among the twenty-five men who accompanied Colonel William Travis into the Alamo. Then on the night of February 25,

2.2 Juan Nepomucena Seguin.
Photo courtesy of Texana Records.

after the Alamo was surrounded, he was chosen to carry an urgent plea for reinforcements to the Texan commander at Gonzales, TX. However, by the time he could accomplish this task, the Alamo had fallen to Santa Anna.

Seguin rode on to San Jacinto where Santa Anna and his troops had marched and served bravely at the Battle of San Jacinto. Seguin was then promoted to the rank of lieutenant colonel, and returned to San Antonio, where he was able to give an honorable burial to the ashes of the Alamo dead. He later served three terms as state senator in the Texas Legislature.

But with independence came many Anglo newcomers to San Antonio who mistreated the native families.

Seguín, the only Mexican Texan in the Senate of the Texas republic, served in the Second, Third and Fourth Congress. Among his legislative initiatives were efforts to have the laws of the new republic printed in Spanish.

Later, while serving as Mayor of Bexar, he was branded a Mexican sympathizer and was forced to flee for his life. He died at Nuevo Laredo, TX in 1889, unappreciated for his service to Texas.

His remains were returned to Texas in 1974 and buried at Seguin, the town named in his honor, during ceremonies on July 4, 1976.

Jose Antonio Navarro was among the truest of all Texans. He was born February 27, 1795 in San Antonio of a prominent Spanish heritage. His father was a native of Corsica, Spain and his mother was descended from a noble Spanish family.

Navarro's early education was very basic, though he later studied law in San Antonio and was licensed to practice it. He was compelled to flee to Mexico because of his support of the Gutiérrez-Magee expedition in 1813, but returned to Texas in 1816. Before Texas independence Navarro was elected to both the Coahuila and Texas state legislature and to the federal congress at Mexico City.

He would become a leading Mexican participant on the side of Texas in the Texas Revolution, as well as in the subsequent development of the Republic and then the State of Texas.

Along with his uncle, José Francisco Ruiz, and Lorenzo de Zavala, Navarro was one of only three Mexican-Texans (Tejanos) that signed the Texas Declaration of Independence at the Convention of 1836. After independence was won, he was elected to the Congress of the Republic of Texas, where he sought to advance the rights of Tejanos.

A proponent of Texas statehood, Navarro represented San Antonio and Bexar County as the sole Hispanic member of the Convention of 1845. He was subsequently elected to the state legislature for two terms, but declined to run a third term in 1849.

2.3 Jose Antonio Navarro. Photo courtesy of Texas State Library & Archives Commission.

Always a strong advocate of states' rights, in 1861 he defended the right of Texas to secede from the Union. Although he was too advanced in years to participate in the Civil War, his four sons served in the Confederate military.

In 1825 Navarro married Margarita de la Garza; they had seven children. Navarro settled into a more private life before his death on January 13, 1871. Navarro County was established in his honor. Its county seat, Corsicana, was named for his father's birthplace of Corsica, Spain.

CALIFORNIA-MEXICAN FRONTIER (1840s)

One of California's most interesting Hispanic figures of this period in American history is Mariano Guadalupe Vallejo. Born to the upper class in 1808, Vallejo grew up during the turbulent years of the Mexican Revolution. An accomplished Mexican army officer by age 21, he gained the confidence of the Mexican governor and was named military commander of northern California. During the same period, he became a member of the territorial legislature and delegate to the Mexican Congress.

Despite these ties to his native Mexico, Vallejo believed it would be in the best interests of the California territories to yield their sovereignty to the U.S. He shifted loyalties and discretely helped Americans secure California. Later appointed as an agent for the U.S. government, he became one of eight Californians to write the state's first constitution and became one of the first members of the state senate in 1849. For his role in the westward expansion of America, Vallejo has been highly recognized.

The city of Vallejo, California was named in his honor, a vineyard produces wines with his name, and, in 1965, the U.S. Navy commissioned the nuclear-powered fleet ballistic missile submarine USS M.G. Vallejo, one of "the forty-one for freedom," in honor of this distinguished Hispanic hero.

THE CIVIL WAR (1861-1865)

During the U.S. Civil War approximately 10,000 Mexican Americans, mainly from California, Texas, Alabama, Missouri, and New Mexico, served in regular army or volunteer units.

The famous directive, "Damn the torpedoes! Full speed ahead," was issued by Admiral David

2.4 Admiral David Glasgow Farragut. Photo courtesy of www.WideOpenWest.com

Glasgow Farragut, commander of the Union forces at the Battle of Mobile Bay, in Alabama, on August 5, 1864. Farragut, perhaps the Civil War's best-known Hispanic, was the son of Jorge Farragut, a Spaniard born in Minorca who came to the U.S. to fight against the British in the American Revolution and later fought in the War of 1812 as part of the U.S. Navy.

In Texas, the Union raised 12 companies of Mexican-American cavalry, consolidated into the First Regiment of Texas Cavalry (Union). Most of the officers were non-Hispanic, although several

Mexican Texans (Tejanos) served as captains, such as George Trevino, Clemente Zapata, Cesario Falcon, and Jose Maria Martines and lieutenants, such as Ramon Garcia Falcon, Antonio Abad Dias, Santos Cadena and Cecilio Vela.

Colonel Santos Benavides, originally from Laredo, Texas, became the highest-ranking Mexican American in the Confederate Army. As the commander of the 33rd Cavalry, he drove Union forces back from Brownsville, Texas, in March 1864.

In 1863, the U.S. government established four military companies of Mexican American Californians (the first Battalion of Native Cavalry) to utilize their "extraordinary horsemanship." At least 469 Mexican Americans served under Major Salvador Vallejo, helping to defeat a Confederate invasion of New Mexico.

The first Hispanic to receive the Medal of Honor was a U.S. Navy sailor named John Ortega,

2.5 Loreta J. Velasquez. From *The Woman in Battle*. Photo courtesy of Univ. of North Carolina at Chapel Hill.

who was awarded the nation's highest award for valor during the Civil War. Two other Hispanics were also awarded the Medal of Honor during the Civil War.

Loreta Janeta Velázquez, born in Havana, Cuba, and raised in New Orleans, disguised herself as "Lieutenant Harry T. Buford" and fought for the Confederacy at Bull Run and other battles. A doctor treating her for a shrapnel wound in her arm discovered her true identity. Velázquez then became a Confederate spy in the North.

THE SPANISH AMERICAN WAR (1898)

Latino patriots sided with the U.S. to gain their independence from Spain in the island colonies of Puerto Rico and Cuba in the Spanish American War.

2.6 Spanish American War veterans. Photo courtesy of www.historyforkids.utah.gov.

Among the U.S. forces that landed in Cuba was the 1st U.S. Volunteer Cavalry under Colonel Leonard Wood and Lieutenant Colonel Theodore Roosevelt. The "Rough Riders" reflected American diversity with about five percent recent immigrants, and another 20 percent from Arizona, New Mexico, Oklahoma, and other states and U.S. territories.

There were several Hispanic members of Theodore Roosevelt's Rough Riders. Captain Maximiliano Luna was the most distinguished Hispanic "Rough Rider." A military camp in New Mexico was named after him. After the Spanish American War, George Armijo, another Hispanic "Rough Rider," became a member of the U.S. Congress.

WORLD WAR I (1914-1918)

The U. S. entered the war in 1917 and more than 4,000 Hispanics were trained for military service. However, non-English speaking Latino soldiers were often relegated to menial jobs and ridicule.

It was not until 1989 that the first Hispanic recipient of the Medal of Honor in WWI was recognized in a ceremony during Hispanic Heritage Week. David Barkley was awarded the Medal of Honor posthumously for bravery in action on the Meuse River, France, in November 1918. Barkley's

Hispanic background did not come to light until 71 years after he gave his life for his country. Barkley kept his Hispanic ancestry a secret to secure a combat assignment.

Army Private Marcelino Serna was a Latino who participated in World War I and fought gallantly and with distinction in the trenches of France. He was shot by a German soldier and seriously wounded. Private Serna was able to continue fighting and subsequently captured 24 German soldiers protecting them from execution by other U.S. soldiers. For his actions, he was awarded the Distinguished Service Cross and later was decorated with the French Croix de Guerre, the Victory Medal with three bars, and twice with the Purple Heart.

2.7 WWI Soldiers wait in a trench for an attack from the Germans. Photo courtesy of San Diego State Univ.

WORLD WAR II (1941-1945)

When the Japanese forces first attacked the U.S. at Pearl Harbor, Hawaii on December 7, 1941, two of the first U.S. casualties were Sgt. Felipe Trejo of Santa Fe, New Mexico and Epimenio Rubi of Winslow, Arizona.

Estimates range anywhere from 250,000 to 500,000 as to the number of Hispanics who served in the U.S. Armed Forces during WWII. Records are sketchy because, like the Census Bureau, the military did not closely track Hispanic members. Also, Puerto Ricans were not counted as Hispanic, but as Puerto Ricans. More than 53,000 Puerto Ricans served in the Armed Forces during WWII. Hispanics did not serve in segregated units like

Black soldiers did, with one exception–the Puerto Rican 65th Infantry Regiment.

However, Hispanic soldiers participated in all the major battles of WWII. The New Mexico National Guard, with its large representation of Hispanics, became the largest single American unit in the Philippines. Their knowledge of Spanish was a definite asset as Spanish was a principle language in the Philippines. Because of this presence, many Hispanic Americans were taken prisoner during the fall of the Philippines and participated in the– "Bataan Death March."

2.8 Marine Pfc Guy Gabaldon received the Silver Star for actions performed on Saipan in 1944 when he captured 1,500 Japanese soldiers and civilians. Photo courtesy of the U.S. Army.

Guy 'Gabby' Gabaldon was responsible for personally capturing more than 1,000 Japanese civilians and soldiers and forcing them to surrender to the U.S. military. He was able to do this despite immense pressure and with first hand knowledge of the Japanese "Bushido Code," whereby Japanese soldiers and civilians committed suicide rather than be captured by the Americans. As of August 2005, Gabaldon had not received a Medal of Honor for his valor, however, 13 other Hispanics were awarded the Congressional Medal of Honor during WWII.

Approximately 200 Puerto Rican women served in the Women's Army Corps. Carmen Contreras-Bozak became the first Hispanic woman to serve in the WAC as an interpreter and in numerous administrative capacities.

The 201st Mexican Fighter Squadron was an air force unit from Mexico attached to the U.S. 58th Fighter Group in the Philippines, where they began combat operation in June 1945. Carlos Foustinos, a former member of the squadron, flew approximately 25 missions, recording six Japanese

zero kills. For this feat he was awarded La Cruz de Honor (the Cross of Honor), equivalent to the U.S. Medal of Honor, by the Mexican government.

THE KOREAN WAR (1950 TO 1953)

During the Korean War, eight Hispanics received the Medal of Honor. The Puerto Rican 65th Infantry Division was the only all-Hispanic Division to serve during the Korean War. It earned four Distinguished Service Crosses and 124 Silver Stars.

The only Latino fighter pilot ace during the Korean War, Capt. Manuel J. Fernandez is credited with 14.5 kills during the Korean War and was also the third overall leading ace of the Korean War.

THE VIETNAM WAR (1959 TO 1975)

The Vietnam War was also the longest military conflict in U.S. history. The hostilities in Vietnam, Laos, and Cambodia claimed the lives of more than 58,000 Americans. Another 304,000 were wounded.

In 1965, the United States sent in troops to prevent the South Vietnamese government from collapsing. Ultimately, however, the United States failed to achieve its goal, and in 1975, Vietnam was reunified under Communist control.

More than 80,000 Hispanics served in the Armed Forces in Vietnam. While Hispanics made up only five percent of the U.S. population during the Vietnam era, they comprised 19 percent of the

2.9 U.S. Marine tending to his machine gun. He is dug in with the Marines in the trenches surrounding Con Thien, September 25, 1967. Photo courtesy of www.vietnampix.com.

2 ■ HISTORY OF HISPANICS IN THE U.S. MILITARY

casualties in the war. Tony Morales, of the American GI Forum, points out that more than one-fourth or about 15,660 of the names on the Vietnam Memorial are Hispanic.

There were 16 Latinos awarded the Congressional Medal of Honor during the Vietnam War.

In November 1963, a reinforced battalion of Viet Cong attacked the CIDG camp at Hiep Hoa,

2.10 SFC Isaac Camacho.
Photo courtesy of Valiant Press.

Long. The attack occurred at night and the defenders were taken completely by surprise as heavy machine gun and mortar fire bombarded the camp. Among the U.S. Special Forces personnel at Hiep Hoa was Sergeant First Class Isaac Camacho.

The camp defenders were pinned down by Viet Cong fire and Sergeant Camacho ran to a mortar position and began to return fire. Pressure from the attacking force soon opened the camp's defensive wall and the commanding officer ordered a withdrawal.

In the confusion of the battle and the darkness of the night, Sergeant Camacho became separated from his Special Forces comrades and was captured by the Viet Cong. He remained a prisoner for almost 20 months, until on July 9, 1965, when he was able to escape from his isolation and make his way to freedom crossing through miles of Viet Cong controlled areas.

Sgt. Camacho was the first POW in the Vietnam War and also the first POW to escape.

For his personal courage and action in defending Hiep Hoa and later escape, Sgt. Camacho was awarded the Silver Star and Bronze Star medals in September 1965. He was promoted to Master Sergeant and later given a battlefield commission to the rank of Captain. He retired from the Army to live in El Paso, Texas.

Navy Lieutenant Everett Alvarez, Jr. is another Latino patriot who distinguished himself in combat as a jet fighter pilot. He was one of the first Latinos to participate in the U.S. aerial campaign against Viet Cong forces. On Aug. 4, 1964, he was ordered to fly in and sink several North Vietnamese gunboats that had attacked two U.S. Navy destroyers.

Unfortunately, he and another Navy pilot were shot down by enemy fire in this attack. The other pilot died but North Vietnamese communists captured Lt. Alvarez. He was the first American pilot POW taken in the Vietnam War. He remained confined for more than eight years, making him the longest confirmed prisoner of war in American history. During this time, his family in the U.S. suffered greatly, but maintained contact with him by mail.

During his captivity, his sister became an anti-war activist, his wife divorced him, and relatives died. Yet, throughout his time as a prisoner of war, Alvarez remained duty-bound and held on to his strong religious faith and the values enshrined in the U.S. Constitution.

When release finally came in February 1973, Alvarez–a Salinas, California, native and the first college graduate in his family–used the determination that had seen him through his long years of imprisonment, to attend law school and become an attorney.

Alvarez wrote two books about his captivity, *Chained Eagle* and *Code of Conduct*. He is the recipient of numerous awards, including the Silver Star and the Distinguished Flying Cross, and was promoted to the rank of Lieutenant Commander.

2.11 Lt. Everett Alvarez, Jr., 2005.
Photo courtesy of
www.vietnamwar.com.

In March 1973, a city park in Santa Clara, California, was dedicated in his honor. He left the Navy soon thereafter, and later served as the Deputy Director for the U.S. Veterans Administration. He is currently employed as a private consultant.

Master Sergeant Roy P. Benavidez was awarded the Congressional Medal of Honor for his heroism on May 2, 1968 at a firefight west of Loc Ninh. Sgt. Benavidez joined a rescue helicopter team to rescue members of a 12 man Special Forces team that was overrun by a superior Viet Cong force. He was able to save the lives of eight Green Berets despite his 37 puncture wounds and heavy loss of blood.

Benavidez did not receive his medal until 1981 and the former army sergeant did not regard himself as a hero. He said of his actions:

"The real heroes are the ones who gave their lives for their country; I don't like to be called a hero. I just did what I was trained to do."

GULF WAR (DESERT SHIELD/ DESERT STORM) (1990-1991)

Approximately 20,000 Hispanic service members participated in Operation Desert Shield/Storm.

Brigadier General Michael J. Aguilar, currently Military Assistant to the Under Secretary of Defense for Policy is one Hispanic patriot who has risen to the top levels of the Marine Corps. Gen. Aguilar served as the Executive Officer of Marine Aircraft Group 16 that supported the air and ground initiatives that contributed to the coordinated effort to free Kuwait after its occupation by Iraqi forces.

Brigadier General Christopher Cortez, head of the Strategy and Plans Division at the Pentagon, across the Potomac River from Washington, D.C., also served with distinction during Operation Desert Shield/ Desert Storm. Brigadier General Cortez was only the second active-duty Hispanic general in the Marine Corps during this time period.

IRAQ WAR (2003-2004)

Three-star general Ricardo S. Sanchez was the highest-ranking U.S. military officer on the ground in Iraq and had what might have been the toughest job on the planet. He served as the military point man in U.S. led efforts to pacify and reconstruct this war-torn land. Just as importantly, he was charged with looking out for the welfare of 120,000 U.S. troops and 25,000 to 30,000 military personnel from 30 coalition countries under his command.

According to 2001 Department of Defense statistics, Latinos made up 18 percent of the infantry, gun crews, and seamanship occupations in all the service branches. Of those Latinos and Latinas in the Army, 25 percent occupy such jobs and in the Marine Corps, 20 percent. However, Latinos make up only 13 percent of the general population. Although women do not serve in the "Infantry," they can be found on gun crews and in other forms of hazardous duty. So it appears Latinos and Latinas may be over-represented in combat positions.

As of September 2004, 9 percent (100,281) of those serving on active duty were Hispanic. The

2.12 Gen. Ricardo Sanchez meeting a local leader in Iraq.
Photo courtesy of the U.S. Army.

highest representation was in the Marine Corps with 14 percent (24,246) being Hispanic, which was followed by the Army at 10 percent (50,879), the Navy at 8.6 percent (31,633), the Coast Guard at 8 percent (3,050), and the Air Force at 6 percent (20,473). Of these personnel, 11,198 or five percent were commissioned officers.

There were also 650 Hispanics serving in the highest noncommissioned officer rank (E-9). There were eleven Hispanic Generals or Admirals serving active duty as of September 2004.

Women comprised 19,885 or nine percent of female active duty personnel, and 1,789 or five percent of the total commissioned officers. These numbers should continue to increase as all three branches of the armed forces step up their recruitment of minorities and Latinos.

In 2005, the number of living Latino military veterans of the U.S. armed forces are estimated to be 1.1 million according to the 2004 Census Bureau.

Army   **Navy**   **Air Force**

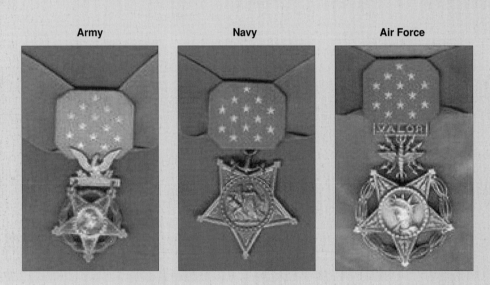

The three different Congressional Medals of Honor as awarded to the Army, Navy, and Air Force recipients.

42 HISPANIC MEDAL OF HONOR RECIPIENTS

■ ■ ■ ■ ■

3

42 Hispanic Medal of Honor Recipients

Note: The following stories are a compilation of articles written by various writers as noted. For details please see Bibliography.

Hispanic military heritage in the United States can be traced back to the Spanish conquistadores who explored the Southern and Southwestern parts of the United States, establishing permanent settlements long before the first English attempts at Jamestown and Plymouth.

However, some will argue the Aztec and Maya Indians from Mexico and Central and South America also contributed their warrior and survival skills the modern Mestizo men and women carry with them today.

Regardless, inevitable conflicts with the English colonies finally led to wars in which the Spanish lost the Carolinas and Georgia. Spanish conflicts with the French, who had established communities from Canada to Louisiana, were also hostile. However, when the French were defeated by the British in the French and Indian War, the French gave their former Louisiana territory to the Spanish rather than their hated English enemy.

Suddenly Spain found itself in possession of New Orleans, St. Louis, and all the land in between. Spanish colonists slowly moved into the area. They held the land for nearly 50 years, along with Alabama, Mississippi, and Florida. But more conflicts with the new United States of America slowly led to the loss of Alabama, Mississippi, and Florida and the Napoleonic Wars finally cost Spain their Louisiana Territory. In 1803, the United States purchased the area from France.

Spain continued to hold on to territory south and west of the Louisiana Purchase, but when

Mexico successfully revolted from Spain, all of the area in what was to later become the Southwestern United States became part of Mexico. The successful Texas revolt of 1836 and the Mexican War of 1848 slowly dissolved the Mexican empire.

In all of these conflicts Hispanics fought and died for their king, their president, and their honor. Since 1848, when all of the territory became part of the United States, Hispanics living in these areas have given their lives and have fought valiantly for causes in which they believed, from the Civil War through the current war in Iraq (2005).

The Medal of Honor is the highest U.S. military distinction awarded since the Civil War for "conspicuous gallantry and intrepidity at the risk of life above and beyond the call of duty."

Forty-two men of Hispanic origin have earned it, including 21 who sacrificed their lives, and whose citations proudly end: "*He gallantly gave his life for his country.*"

3.1 The Congressional Medal of Honor for the three different services. Photo courtesy of the U.S. Congressional Medal of Honor Society (CMOHS).

It is therefore no coincidence that Hispanics have received more Congressional Medals of Honor than other ethnic groups, in proportion to the number who served. Many fought discrimination to defend their country during World War II. In contrast to African Americans, who were segregated into units that were mono-racial, Hispanic Americans participated in many units over all theaters of war.

Their inclusion in the draft led to high numbers fighting in Korea and, more importantly, in Vietnam. Because of the long tradition of military service found in the Hispanic American community, many young men volunteered to serve during this conflict. Their large casualty rate was one of the reasons that led to the calls for a Chicano moratorium, the slow down of the recruitment of young Mexican Americans for this divisive war.

Recipients of the Medal of Honor receive $1,000 per month for life, a right to burial at Arlington National Cemetery, admission for them or their children to a service academy (if they qualify and quotas permit), and free travel on government aircraft to almost anywhere in the world, on a space-available basis.

MEMORIAL TO HISPANIC MEDAL OF HONOR RECIPIENTS APPROVED IN 2002

A $1 million war memorial saluting Hispanic recipients of the nation's highest military honor, the Medal of Honor, will be placed in Father Serra Park near Olvera Street in Los Angeles.

"We've been wanting for this for a long time," said Marine Corps veteran Bill Lansford, an East Los Angeles man who spearheaded the six-year effort was quoted by the Los Angeles Associated Press.

The nine-member governing board of the El Pueblo de Los Angeles Historical Monument, the site of the city's founding in 1781, approved the statue in 2002 to honor Hispanic Medal of Honor recipients.

The monument will be named after Eugene A. Obregón, an East Los Angeles Marine who was posthumously awarded the medal after saving the life of a fellow Marine during the Korean War.

The following are the 42 Hispanic American soldiers who have so far been awarded the United States Congressional Medal of Honor.

CIVIL WAR

1. Joseph H. De Castro

The first Hispanic soldier to receive the Congressional Medal of Honor.

Born: Nov. 14, 1844 in Boston, MA
Entered Service: 1863
Branch: U.S. Army
Rank: Corporal, Company I, 19th Massachusetts Infantry
Place and Date of Action: Gettysburg, PA, 3 July 1863
Medal Issue Date: December 1, 1864
Died: May 8, 1892

Note: Courtesy the U.S. Congressional Medal of Honor Society.

Citation:

Served in the Civil War as a corporal in Company I, 19th Massachusetts Volunteer Infantry. He was awarded the Medal of Honor for his bravery during his regiment's attack and repulse of elements of Pickett's Charge on the third day of the *Battle of Gettysburg*, Pennsylvania. He was one of seven 19th Massachusetts Infantry soldiers to be awarded the Medal of Honor for bravery during the War.

He was married to: Rosalia Rodriguez, her father was from the Canary Islands, Spain.

3.2 Battle of Gettysburg.
Image courtesy of Think Quest New York City.

2. John Ortega

Born: 1840 in Spain
Branch: U.S. Navy
Rank: Seaman
Place and Date of Action: On board the battleship
USS Saratoga
Medal Issue Date: December 31, 1864
Accredited to: Pennsylvania. G.O. No. 45

Note: Courtesy the U.S. Congressional Medal of Honor Society.

Citation:

Served as seaman on board the *U.S.S. Saratoga* during actions of that vessel on two occasions. Carrying out his duties courageously during these actions, Ortega conducted himself gallantly through both periods. Promoted to acting master's mate.

3.3 Reverse side of Ortega Medal. Photo courtesy of CMOHS.

3. Phillip Bazaar

Born: Chile, South America
Entered Service: June 1865
Branch: U.S. Navy
Rank: Ordinary Seaman
Place and Date of Action: On board the *USS Santiago de Cuba*, January 15, 1865

Note: Courtesy the U.S. Congressional Medal of Honor Society.

Citation:

On board the *U.S.S. Santiago de Cuba* during the assault on Fort Fisher on 15 January 1865. As one of a six-man boat crew detailed to one of the generals on shore, O.S. Bazaar bravely entered the fort in the assault and accompanied his party in carrying dispatches at the height of the battle. He was one of six men who courageously entered the fort and engaged in an assault on Fort Fisher.

3.4 Assault on Ft. Fisher.
Image courtesy of U.S. Dept. of Defense.

BOXER REBELLION (CHINA)

4. France Silva

Born: May 8, 1876 in Haywards, CA
Branch: U.S. Marine Corps.
Rank: Private
Date and Place of Action: June 28 to August 17, 1900 in Peking, China
Medal Issue Date: July 19, 1901
Died: April 10, 1951

Note: Courtesy the U.S. Congressional Medal of Honor Society.

Citation:

In Peking, China, Private Silva participated in the Boxer Rebellion. Throughout this period, Silva distinguished himself by meritorious conduct in the presence of the enemy during the action at Peking, China, 28 June to 17 August 1900. Silva was awarded

3.5 U.S. Marines fighting the Boxer rebels in 1900.
Image courtesy of www.historywiz.com.

the Congressional Medal of Honor for his bravery and heroic actions. Private Silva helped to protect the foreign legations against the fanatical followers of the "Boxers," societies that developed in China to protect its culture against foreign aggression, influence, and ideas. Private Silva was instrumental in securing order during events that would have jeopardized the safety of his fellow soldiers. He, along with his fellow marines and sailors, helped to preserve and maintain peace for weeks until the Allied Army relieved them in August 1900.

WORLD WAR I

5. David Cantu Barkley

Born: March 31, 1899 in Laredo, TX
Branch: U.S. Army
Rank: Private
Date and Place of Action: November 18, 1918 near Pouilly, France
Medal Issue Date: 1989
Killed in Action: Nov. 9, 1918

Note: James M. Myers wrote this article. For details please see Bibliography.

David Bennes Cantu Barkley was born in 1899, to Josef and Antonia Cantu Barkley in Laredo, Texas. When the United States entered World War I, Barkley enlisted as a private in the United States

3.6 PVT. David Cantu Barkley.
Photo courtesy of CMOHS.

Army. Family records indicate he did not want to be known as of Mexican descent, for fear he would not see action at the front.

He was assigned to Company A, 356th Infantry, Eighty-ninth Division. He volunteered to swim the icy Meuse River near Pouilly, France, in order to infiltrate German lines and gather information about

the strength and location of German artillery units and formations. Despite enemy resistance to any allied crossing of the Meuse, Barkley and another volunteer swam the cold river, crawled 400 yards behind enemy lines, and drew the required maps.

As Barkley was swimming back with the information, he was seized with cramps and drowned, on November 9, 1918. This was just two days before the armistice, which ended the war, went into effect. His partner returned safely and released the information and maps.

His sacrifice earned praise from Gen. John J. Pershing, the commander of the American Expeditionary Force. Barkley was one of three Texans awarded the nation's highest military honor, the Congressional Medal of Honor, for service in World War I. He was also awarded the Croix de Guerre (France) and the Croce Merito (Italy).

Barkley lay in state at the Alamo, the second person to be so honored. He was buried at the San Antonio National Cemetery. On January 10, 1941, the War Department named Camp Barkley for the Texas hero. In 1921 an elementary school in San Antonio was named for him.

WORLD WAR II

6. Joseph P. Martinez

Born: 1920 in Taos, NM
Entered Service: 1942 Ault, CO
Branch: U.S. Army
Rank: Private
Date and Place of Action: On Attu, Aleutians, May 26, 1943
Killed in Action: May 26, 1943

Note: This is a compilation of articles from the Aleutian's web site and Medal of Honor website. For details please see Bibliography.

Martinez was one of nine children. He moved with his family to Ault, Colorado in 1927 where his father found work as an agricultural laborer. He was drafted in August 1942 and took his basic training at Camp Roberts, California.

It was Wednesday, May 26, 1943. The weather was nice for a change…as nice as weather could get for Attu during this time of year. The battle for Attu was still raging…it would be three more days before major fighting for possession of Attu would end.

The bulk of the remaining Japanese defensive forces by now had retreated to Chichagof village, with pockets of Japanese defenders spread around the mountaintops and ridges protecting the village from U.S. Forces. Sixty-two Air Force planes in relays attacked Chichagof village this day until the Japanese camp was destroyed. The end of the Japanese occupation of Attu was near.

A battalion of the 4th Infantry reorganized into squads, elements, and individuals who inched up through the cold rocks in their attempt to drive the Japanese off the Ridge. Japanese soldiers, laying in trenches and concealed by snowdrifts and rocks along Fish Hook Ridge, held the Americans back by rolling hand grenades down into their positions.

Private Joe P. Martinez, born in Taos, New Mexico and having enlisted in the U.S. Army at Ault, Colorado, was an automatic rifleman in Company K of the 32nd Infantry. With his Company stalled by entrenched enemy soldiers, Martinez stood up and charged into the enemy's fire, and slaughtered five Japanese soldiers with grenades and his BAR (Browning Automatic Rifle). He reached the crest of the ridge before he collapsed with a mortal wound he had taken fifty yards down the hill.

The U.S. Northern Force followed him up the hill and took the northwestern razorback of the Fish Hook that Martinez had cleared. It was too late for Martinez to revel in their victory.

Joseph P. Martinez's posthumous reward was Attu's only Medal of Honor, and was awarded on October 27, 1943. He became an inspiration to many when the Army released his story.

A Disabled American Veterans chapter in Colorado and an American Legion post in California are named in his honor.

Citation:

For conspicuous gallantry and intrepidity above and beyond the call of duty in action with

the enemy. Over a period of several days, repeated efforts to drive the enemy from a key defensive position high in the snow-covered precipitous mountains between East Arm Holtz Bay and Chichagof Harbor had failed.

3.7 PVT Joseph P. Martinez.
Photo courtesy of CMOHS.

On 26 May 1943, troop dispositions were readjusted and a trial coordinated attack on this position by a reinforced battalion was launched. Initially successful, the attack hesitated. In the face of severe hostile machinegun, rifle, and mortar fire, Pvt. Martinez, an automatic rifleman, rose to his feet and resumed his advance.

Occasionally he stopped to urge his comrades on. His example inspired others to follow. After a most difficult climb, Pvt. Martinez eliminated resistance from part of the enemy position by BAR (Browning Automatic Rifle) fire and hand grenades, thus assisting the advance of other attacking elements.

This success only partially completed the action. The main Holtz-Chichagof Pass rose about 150 feet higher, flanked by steep rocky ridges and reached by a snow-filled defile. Passage was barred by enemy fire from either flank and from tiers of snow trenches in front. Despite these obstacles, and knowing of their existence, Pvt. Martinez again led the troops on and up, personally silencing several trenches with BAR fire and ultimately reaching the pass itself.

Here, just below the knifelike rim of the pass, Pvt. Martinez encountered a final enemy–occupied trench and as he was engaged in firing into it, he was mortally wounded. The pass, however, was taken, and its capture was an important preliminary to the end of organized hostile resistance on the island.

7. Rudolph Davila

Born: April 27, 1916 in El Paso, TX
Entered Service: Los Angeles, CA
Branch: U.S. Army
Rank: Staff Sergeant
Date and Place of Action: May 28, 1944, Artena, Italy
Medal Issue Date: May 2000
Died: Jan. 26, 2002

Note: The following is a compilation of information written by Michael J. Williams and the Medal of Honor web site. For details please see Bibliography.

In May 2000, a 56-year wait for Rudy Davila ended on the south lawn of the White House; when President Clinton awarded the Vista, California man the Medal of Honor.

"These American soldiers, with names we have at long last recognized as American names, made an impact that soars beyond the impact of any battle," Clinton said. "They left a lasting imprint on the meaning of America. They didn't give up on their country, even though too many of their countrymen had given up on them. They deserve, at least, the most we can give–the Medal of Honor."

For Davila, who is half-Filipino and half-Spanish, it was a proud but bittersweet moment. Proud because of the recognition he is finally receiving; bittersweet because his late wife, Harriet, was not there to share the moment with him.

3.8 President Clinton awards the Medal of Honor to SGT Rudolph Davila on May 2000 at the White House. Photo courtesy of *SSG David Bata*, U.S. Army.

Davila said his emotions nearly ran away with him after Clinton draped the award around his neck.

"I had a moment you know, in which I became like jelly," Davila said. "Right after I sat down and I saw the others going up there, and I said to myself, you know my wife would have just been in heaven out there in the audience watching me get the medal. She is in heaven, but you know what I mean."

While he was receiving the medal, Davila said Clinton privately told him: "Our nation is very proud of you, and I want to congratulate you."

While 19 of his relatives attended the ceremony, Davila said he met and married his wife while recuperating from his wounds in a Modesto Army hospital. Harriet Davila, his wife of 54 years, died Dec. 25, 1999. Davila said that right up until the time of her death, she never stopped believing that he deserved the Medal of Honor.

Davila said he was told he would be nominated for the Medal of Honor in 1944, after risking his life to save an exposed and vulnerable 130-man rifle company in Italy. But despite the fact he said he was told by a commanding officer that, he was given the Distinguished Service Cross instead, because too many minorities were winning the Medal of Honor.

Davila said he never believed he was slighted. "I don't think that way," he said.

Davila was awarded his Medal of Honor for single-handedly saving the lives of an estimated 125-man rifle company near Artena, Italy, on May 28, 1944. Then a 27-year-old staff sergeant, Davila was in charge of a 24-man heavy machine gun unit. The rifle company, traveling just ahead of Davila's unit as Allied forces pressed the retreating German army toward Rome, had just crested a small hill when it was caught, completely exposed, in an open field of tall grass by enemy machine guns entrenched behind distant railroad tracks.

Realizing the rifle company would be cut to ribbons, Davila said he tried to rouse his unit into action. But it too was pinned. So, Davila, sitting up on his knees, quickly set up one of his unit's water-cooled machine guns, and began firing on the enemy machine-gun nest, drawing its fire toward himself and away from the rifle company.

Davila says he remembers his men shouting to get down. "Sarge, (the bullets are) coming right at your head."

Even after Davila was wounded slightly in the leg by an enemy bullet, which ricocheted off the tripod of his machine gun, he did not falter. Davila said he got one of his men to take over his machine-gun position, then crawled toward the enemy to direct his unit's fire by hand signals.

Davila's men drove the enemy back about 200 yards. Davila, according to eyewitness accounts that day, then dashed forward and straddled the turret of a burning U.S. tank—an act Davila said he does not remember to this day—and began firing at the enemy with the tank's machine gun.

Finally, after spotting a gun barrel firing from the upstairs window of a nearby house, he dropped down from the tank, took a rifle and two hand grenades from a wounded soldier and started crawling toward the house. Reaching the house, Davila began firing into it through a large shell-hole in one of the walls. Finally, he said, he threw the hand grenades into the open window, killing the remaining five enemy soldiers.

Sitting in his comfortable Vista, CA home last week, the soft-spoken retired schoolteacher downplayed his actions, saying he believes that everyone has the capacity for heroism inside himself or herself.

"I don't remember being afraid or timid," he said.

"It just happened. I wasn't that kind of person. I wasn't violent. In fact, I was kind of a passive kind of guy. I just wanted to be a good soldier."

Ironically, the war for Davila ended just a few short weeks later in France, when shrapnel from a German tank ripped apart his right shoulder, just moments after Davila had dragged a young wounded German soldier to safety after the tank began firing on surrendering troops.

Davila was awarded the Distinguished Service Cross in 1944 while at the Modesto hospital. Davila spent six years recuperating from his wounds, eventually losing all use of his right arm.

He retired to Vista after teaching history for 26 years in the Los Angeles Unified School District.

After retiring from teaching in Los Angeles, Davila moved to Vista, CA in 1977 with his wife, Harriet Davila. Davila was born in El Paso to a Filipino mother and Spanish father, and raised in Watts.

3.9 Painting titled, "Relentless Leadership," by artist Matt Hall depicts SGT Rudolph Davila taking control of a machinegun from atop a burned out tank. Work commissioned by the CMOHS.

His son, Roland Davila said that while growing up, the children were unaware of their father's heroic feats. Later, his wife lobbied army officials to award the Medal of Honor to her husband.

An officer in the rifle company said he would recommend Davila for the Medal of Honor, the highest honor for battlefield valor. While Davila received the Distinguished Service Cross, the second highest military honor, he was not awarded the medal.

Though Davila said he did not believe discrimination was involved, many Asian-American veterans as well as Black veterans alleged their battlefield deeds were not properly recognized. As a result of legislation waiving time limits for granting medals, Davila was among 21 Asian-American World War II veterans who received the Medal of Honor at a White House ceremony in May 2000, several months after his wife had died.

"It was quite an experience for us to realize his name was basically going to be immortalized," Roland Davila said. Subsequently, Davila was honored by the city. He served as the guest speaker at the Veterans of Foreign Wars' Memorial Day ceremony in 2001.

"He was a proud warrior," said Ralph Gibbs, the quartermaster of VFW Post 7041. "He's one of the chosen few. Not too many have received the first and second highest awards for heroism."

Davila died January 26, 2002 of natural causes after a long illness. He was 85.

_____

8. Lucian Adams

Born: 1923 in Port Arthur, TX
Entered Service: Houston, TX
Branch: U.S. Army
Rank: Sergeant
Date and Place of Action: 1944, the Vosges Mountains in eastern France
Medal Issue Date: April 22, 1945
Died: March 31, 2003

Note: Carmina Danini wrote the following. For details please see Bibliography.

Lucian Adams was awarded the medal for his actions in the autumn of 1944, when the Third Infantry Division was fighting in the Vosges Mountains of eastern France, having come ashore on the Riviera on Aug. 15 in Operation Anvil, the invasion of southern France.

On Oct. 28, 1944, Sergeant Adams's company in the division's 30th Infantry was blocked by German troops in a forest near Saint-Dié while trying to reinforce troops that had been cut off.

The company had advanced less than 10 yards, suffering three dead and six wounded, when Sergeant Adams charged forward in the face of German machine-gun fire, dodging from tree to tree while firing a BAR.

While machine-gun bullets flew and rifle grenades struck the trees over his head, showering him with broken branches, Sergeant Adams pressed forward. He came within 10 yards of the closest machine gun and killed the gunner with a hand grenade. Next, he used his rifle to kill a German soldier who was throwing grenades at him from 10 yards away.

3.10 SGT Lucian Adams. Photo courtesy of www.homeofheroes.com.

Sergeant Adams then killed a machine-gunner 15 yards away with a hand grenade and forced the surrender of two German infantrymen. The remainder of the German force continued to direct machine-gun fire at him, but he made

3.11 SGT Lucian Adams. Photo courtesy of the CMOHS.

his way through the wooded area and killed five more Germans. He then killed another German machine-gunner.

When Sergeant Adams's one-man attack ended, he had killed nine Germans, eliminated three machine guns, cleared the woods and re-opened the severed supply lines.

"I'd seen all my buddies go down and calling for medics, and I didn't want to go down with any ammunition still on me, so I just kept firing, and lucky for me that I got them before they got me," he told *The Dallas Morning News* in 1993.

"In combat, I had no fear," he said in an interview with *The San Antonio Express-News* in 2002. "None, until the events were over, and then I began to realize how serious and how dangerous the situations were."

Mr. Adams received the Medal of Honor, the nation's highest military honor, on April 22, 1945, at Nuremberg, Germany. The medal was presented to five members of the Third Division by Lt. Gen. Alexander M. Patch, commander of the Seventh Army, in a ceremony at Zeppelin Field, once the site of Hitler's huge Nazi rallies.

Mr. Adams, a native of Port Arthur, TX, who also won the Bronze Star and the Purple Heart for gallantry in action during the Casino campaign in Italy. Adams left military service in 1945. He then worked for 40 years as a benefits counselor for the Veterans Administration in San Antonio.

"I never brought up the fact that I'd been in combat myself and been awarded the Medal of Honor," Mr. Adams told *The San Antonio Express-News* in recalling his years as a veterans' counselor. "Because I'm no hero. I'm just an ex-soldier."

To honor Adams for his achievements, Aurora Park in Port Arthur, TX was renamed Lucian Adams Field, and a monument was erected in 1974. In 1986 a section of 61st Street in Port Arthur was renamed in his honor. Adams was also honored on Veterans Day in 1988 with the dedication of a bust to be displayed in the Museum of the Gulf Coast.

Adams graduated from Franklin Jr. High and Port Arthur High School. He enlisted right out of high school. He retired from the VA in 1986 and died March 31, 2003 in San Antonio. He was 80.

---

9. Macario Garcia

Born: January 2, 1920 in Villa de Castaño, Mexico
Entered Service: November 11, 1942
Branch: U.S. Army
Rank: Sergeant
Date and Place of Action: November 27, 1944, near Grosshau, Germany
Medal Issue Date: August 23, 1945
Died: December 24, 1972

Note: María-Cristina Garcia wrote the following. For details please see Bibliography.

Macario Garcia was born on January 2, 1920, in Villa de Castaño, Mexico, to Luciano and Josefa Garcia, farm workers who raised ten children.

In 1923 the family moved to Texas and eventually settled in Sugar Land. Like the rest of his

3.12 SGT Macario Garcia.
Photo courtesy of the CMOHS.

brothers and sisters, he contributed to the family's support by picking crops. He was working on the Paul Schumann Ranch near Sugar Land when he was drafted into the army on November 11, 1942.

Garcia was wounded in action at Normandy in June 1944, but after his recovery he rejoined

his unit, Company B, First Battalion, Twenty-second Infantry Regiment, Fourth Infantry Division. On November 27, 1944, near Grosshau, Germany, he single-handedly assaulted two German machine-gun emplacements that were blocking his company's advance.

Wounded in the shoulder and foot, he crawled forward alone toward the machine-gun nests, killed

3.13 SGT Macario Garcia being presented the Medal of Honor by President Harry S. Truman. Photo courtesy of the U.S. Army.

six enemy soldiers, captured four, and destroyed the German nests with grenades. Only after the company had secured its position did Garcia allow himself to be evacuated for medical treatment.

He was awarded the Congressional Medal of Honor with twenty-seven other soldiers at a White House ceremony on August 23, 1945, by President Harry S. Truman. Garcia also received the Purple Heart, the Bronze Star, and the Combat Infantryman's Badge, as well as the medal of Merito Militar, the Mexican equivalent to the Medal of Honor, during a ceremony in Mexico City on January 8, 1946. After three years of active service, one of which was overseas, Garcia received an honorable discharge from the Army with the rank of sergeant.

He returned to Sugar Land, TX and found that he had become a celebrity around the state.

Newspapers published accounts of his heroism, and he was asked to appear at meetings and banquets.

The League of United Latin American Citizens (LULAC) Council No. 60 in Houston honored him at a special ceremony at the courthouse.

In September 1945, shortly after his return to Texas, Garcia again attracted media attention when he was denied service at a restaurant in Richmond, a few miles south of Houston, because he was *Mexican*. Outraged that he was treated like a second-class citizen after having risked his life for his country, Garcia fought with the owner until police were called in. He was arrested and charged in the incident.

His case immediately became a cause célebre, symbolizing not only the plight of Hispanic soldiers who returned from the war, but also the plight of the Hispanic community as a whole. Numerous groups and private citizens rallied to his aid.

LULAC Council No. 60 and the Comité Patriótico Mexicano sponsored benefits in his honor to raise money to pay for his defense. After a trial in which he was defended by Gustavo (Gus) Garcia and John J. Herrera, Garcia was acquitted.

On June 25, 1947, he became an American citizen. Garcia earned a high school diploma in 1951, and married Alicia Reyes on May 18, 1952. They raised three children. Like other GIs who returned from the war, Garcia encountered many difficulties in finding employment. He eventually found a job as a counselor in the Veterans' Administration, and remained with the VA for the next twenty-five years.

In 1970 Garcia and his family moved to Alief, Texas, not far from Houston.

He died on December 24, 1972, in a car crash and was buried in the National Cemetery in Houston. In 1981 the Houston City Council officially changed the name of Sixty-ninth Street to Macario Garcia Drive. This one-mile thoroughfare runs through the heart of the city's east side Mexican-American community.

In 1983 Vice President George Bush dedicated Houston's new Macario Garcia Army Reserve Center, and in 1994 a Sugar Land middle school was named in Garcia's honor.

10. Jose Mendoza Lopez

Born: June 1, 1912 in Santiago Huitlan, Mexico
Entered Service: Brownsville, TX
Branch: U.S. Army
Rank: Sergeant
Date and Place of Action: December 17, 1944 near Krinkelt, Belgium
Medal Issue Date: June 19, 1945
Died: May 16, 2005

Note: The following reporters contributed to this article; Kevin Garcia, Carmina Danini and Scott Huddleston. For details please see Bibliography.

Brownsville, Texas native Jose Mendoza Lopez, the oldest living Hispanic recipient of the Medal of Honor, was buried with full military honors May 22, 2005 in San Antonio.

Lopez, 94, is well known throughout South Texas as a World War II hero who single-handedly repelled German infantry forces advancing on his U.S. Army unit near the start of the Battle of the Bulge. About 80,000 U.S. troops were killed in this battle.

"He was a great hero, a super guy and a super dad," said his son John Lopez.

3.14 SGT Jose M. Lopez, shown in January 2005, fought at Normandy and in the Battle of the Bulge. Photo courtesy www.medalofhonor.com.

Jose Lopez died a few weeks after returning from the hospital where he had been undergoing treatment for cancer that spread from his kidneys.

His burial was a mark of closure for some, but his memory will live on for generations in Brownsville, where a statue is modeled after him at the Veterans International Bridge.

The statue, unveiled in January 2003, depicts a grizzled, battle-worn soldier standing proudly above a plaque relating his heroic tale.

"I like it," the former sergeant told The Brownsville Herald during the unveiling ceremony at the bridge. "It is very good, but the gun is not the right one. I had the one you'd put in a tripod, a 30-caliber machine gun."

On Dec. 17, 1944, Lopez, with the 23rd Infantry, 2nd Infantry Division, fended off dozens of German troops and tanks trying to overrun his Company K near Krinkelt, Belgium. He lugged his .30-caliber weapon, jumped into a shallow hole and killed several German soldiers.

"I was doing my duty to stop the enemy," Lopez recalled at the ceremony. "They gave me credit for killing 100 enemies and somebody recommended me for the Medal of Honor."

His Medal of Honor citation states:

Sgt. Lopez's gallantry and intrepidity, on seemingly suicidal missions in which he killed at least 100 of the enemy, were almost solely responsible for allowing Company K to avoid being enveloped, to withdraw successfully and to give other forces coming up in support time to build a line which repelled the enemy drive.

Nearly 50 years after the battle, he returned to the site in Belgium with journalist Bill Moyers and a PBS documentary film crew. Questioned by Moyers about his bravery, the man who had prayed to the Virgin of Guadalupe as he fired at Germans replied, "I believe any man would do the same thing."

Though his medal citation and most biographies list his birthplace as Mission, Jose Lopez was born in Santiago Huitlan, Mexico. To join the Merchant Marine, he bought a false birth certificate in 1935.

Returning to the United States from Hawaii after the Dec. 7, 1941, Japanese attack on Pearl Harbor, he almost was arrested. Authorities thought he was Japanese.

"I let them see my papers, that I was Mexican, and they let me go. They were going to put me in the prison," he told an interviewer for the U.S. Latinos and Latinas & World War II oral history project.

In 1942, Lopez enlisted in the Army. He received a minor wound but rejoined his unit after being treated.

3.15 SGT Jose Mendoza Lopez. Photo courtesy of the CMOHS.

Lopez also was awarded the Bronze Star and the Purple Heart. But his Medal of Honor was what he cherished most among his many mementos.

After his World War II service, he fought in Korea until a ranking officer heard that a Medal of Honor recipient was in battle. He was ordered to the rear and spent months picking up bodies and registering them for burial.

He later was a recruiter, mowed lawns and plowed snow. He was placed in charge of a motor pool and oversaw large crews of maintenance personnel. He retired in 1973.

To maintain his physique, Sgt. Lopez jogged until age 88. He also saw a trainer three times a week, a regimen that ended in March 2005, as his illness worsened.

His son reflected Monday on a man who lived a humble life.

"He was a hero, without being a hero around his family," John Lopez said.

"Last Sunday, Jose Lopez had enough strength to squeeze relatives' hands as they spoke to him," said June Pedraza, a granddaughter. "Monday, he was unresponsive," she said.

"I told him, you're really sick, grandpa. It's OK if you go today," said Pedraza, 25.

A short time later, after family members dispersed for lunch, the sergeant died with only a nurse in the room, she said.

Pedraza said she doubted Lopez had any fear of dying because he'd always told her, "Fear is the one thing that will hold you back in life."

11. Jose F. Valdez

Born: January 20, 1925 in Gobernador, New Mexico
Entered Service: Pleasant Grove, UT
Branch: U.S. Army
Rank: Private First Class
Date and Place of Action: January 25, 1945 near
  Rosenkrantz, France
Medal Issue Date: Posthumously in 1946
Killed in Action: January 25, 1945

Note: Carol Cohea wrote this article. For details please see
Bibliography.

For more than 55 years the man who was critically wounded during a hail of German gunfire and whose life was saved by a young private from Gobernador, had wanted to tell the boy's mother her son had died a hero.

Saturday (August 3, 2002) at the commemoration of a memorial for Congressional Medal of Honor recipient Jose F. Valdez, Willis Daniel, 77, of Roanoke Rapids, N.C., was finally able to tell the Valdez family the poignant story behind the medal.

3.16 PFC Jose F. Valdez.
Photo courtesy of the CMOHS.

Only 3,458 members of the armed services have received the Congressional Medal of Honor. It is the highest award for valor in action against an enemy force that can be given to an individual serving in the armed services. Jose F. Valdez received the honor posthumously in 1946.

"I would have liked his mother to be here today. I would have hugged her neck and cried with her," Daniel said.

Later in an interview with *The Daily Times*, he began telling the story of a group of young infantry riflemen, most in their early 20s, who were just fighting to stay alive that cold, winter day so far from home. "I was with him when he got shot,

though I had never met him before that day," Daniel began. "He had turned 20 five days before the day he got shot…he was 20 when he died.

"We had crossed the Fecht River. The bridge was under heavy shellfire. We swung to the right. Snow was on the ground," Daniel recalled of that January day in 1945.

"We had one bank of the river; the Germans had the other. We came from the rear into the town the Germans were holding. Valdez was with us all this time," Daniel said.

Then because words alone couldn't describe the scene, he borrowed a reporter's notebook and began sketching a crude map of the battle scene.

He told of the five Americans on outpost duty dressed in camouflage white. On one side were the woods about 500 yards away. On the other side was a railroad track with a bomb crater in the center. Between the two, stood the town's railroad station. Two piles of railroad ties stood at the farthest end of the platform.

Daniel said they'd made their way to the railroad station. Some had taken cover in it. He was behind the nearest pile of ties, just off the platform end. Valdez had made his way to a second pile of ties, separated by a short distance from the first. As the five waited and listened, a deer broke from the woods, then a rabbit.

Then came the opening barrage of enemy fire. The men were blasted with bullets. Valdez volunteered to cover his companions as they began to withdraw, one by one, to the American lines, first to the shelter of the railroad station and then to the depression of the bomb crater in the railroad track.

Three were wounded in the withdrawal and Valdez was struck in the abdomen by a bullet that came out his back. Despite his wound and what must have been agonizing pain, he continued to fire until all were safe.

By field telephone he called for artillery and mortar fire against the Germans, correcting the range until he had shells falling within 50 yards of his position, repulsing the attack. It also enabled his own rescue.

"It was after the war I found out he had died," said Daniel. "I was trying to locate a member of his

3.17 USNS PFC Jose F. Valdez. Photo courtesy of the U.S. Navy.

Saturday's ceremony was not the first time Valdez had been recognized for his heroic actions near Rosenkrantz, France, on January 25, 1945. A U.S. Navy Vessel, the *USNS PFC Jose F. Valdez* TAG-169, was named in his honor, as are schools, streets, training centers and armories in Utah, Colorado and Georgia. But this is New Mexico's first memorial to him in the community that gave him the strength and character to be called a hero. He is buried in the National Cemetery in Santa Fe.

Driven by the desire to bring the honor and the man home to his boyhood community, the PFC Jose F. Valdez Memorial Committee was formed by Valdez' relatives and friends. They worked for more than two years to raise funds to erect the permanent manorial and make it a reality.

Meanwhile, retired U.S. Army Reserve Lt. Col. Juan C. Gomez, of Center, Colo., began his efforts to organize the ceremony which included the three men who served with Valdez and two additional Medal of Honor recipients, Capt. Raymond G. Murphy of Albuquerque and Cpl. Hiroshi Miyarmura of Gallup.

"It was important to bring closure to the Valdez family and to the men who served with him. It was important to bring Jose home," Gomez said.

family. At one point I heard his mom was living in Durango. I called every Valdez in the book, trying to find her," he added.

Steve Kovatch, 78, of Boseman, Montana, was about 21 at the time.

"I was one of the last to see Valdez alive. He'd been hit and paralyzed from the waist down. Four of us went out to get him and carried him back to the railroad station," Kovatch said. "He was in bad shape then. I knew he wasn't going to live."

Abundio Castro, 81, of Holtville, CA, was with Co. D, 7th Infantry Regiment, 3rd Infantry Division. He was a machine gunner. He recalled, "Valdez was a quiet individual. He was a soldier you would want to be in your outfit. They sent him to the outposts. He was the type of fellow to stay awake all night, guarding and guarding. He was always alert and quiet. That keeps up the morale of the rest of the troops in the front line. Your life is at stake," Castro said.

"Now that I see where he came from, I realize his senses were sharpened by this country," Castro said.

Though Valdez was born in the Gobernador area in 1925 and raised doing day work at nearby ranches, he enlisted at Pleasant Grove, Utah: therefore, he is officially listed as a Utah Congressional Medal of Honor recipient.

The citation of his Medal of Honor citation reads in part:

…He was struck by a bullet that entered his stomach, and, passing through his body, emerged from the back. Overcoming agonizing pain, he regained control of himself and resumed his firing position, delivering a protection screen of bullets until all others of the patrol were safe. By field telephone, he called for artillery and mortar fire on the Germans and corrected the range until he had shells falling within fifty yards of his position.

For fifteen minutes he refused to be dislodged by more than two hundred of the enemy, then seeing that the barrage had broken the counterattack, he dragged himself back to his own lines. He later died as a result of his wounds.

Through his valiant, intrepid stand and at the cost of his own life, Pfc. Valdez made it possible for his comrades to escape, and was directly responsible for repulsing an attack by vastly superior enemy forces.

The 2nd and 3rd Battalions did final mopping-up of Houssen the same day. The following day Audie Murphy earned his Medal of Honor.

---

12. Cleto Rodriguez

Born: April 26, 1923 in San Marcos, TX
Entered Service: 1944, San Antonio, TX
Branch: U.S. Army
Rank: Technical Sergeant
Date and Place of Action: February 9, 1945 Paco Railroad Station, Manila, Philippine Islands
Medal Issue Date: October 12, 1945 by Pres. Harry S. Truman,
Died: December 7, 1990

Note: Cynthia E. Orozco wrote this article. For details please see Bibliography.

Cleto L. Rodriguez was born on April 26, 1923, and raised in San Marcos and San Antonio. After his parents died when he was nine, he moved to San Antonio with relatives. He worked at the Gunter Hotel and as a newsboy. He attended Washington, Irving, and Ivanhoe schools.

Rodriguez married Flora Muñiz on November 11, 1945, and they had four children. Rodriguez entered the United States Army in early 1944 and served as a technical sergeant.

He was an automatic rifleman with Company B, 148th Infantry, when his unit attacked the strongly defended Paco Railroad Station during the battle for Manila in the Philippine Islands. He and his partner, John M. Reece of Oklahoma, killed

eighty-two enemy soldiers and disorganized their defense, thus facilitating the defeat of the Japanese at their strong point.

Two days later, Rodriguez single-handedly killed six enemy soldiers and destroyed a twenty-millimeter gun. Thus on two occasions he "materially aided the advance of U.S. troops in Manila." Later, he was promoted to staff sergeant.

3.18 This rendition of SGT Rodriguez in the Philippine Islands (1945) was done by Henry Lozano. The painting is part of the Army's American War Life Collection.

Rodriguez was the seventh person of Mexican descent to win the Medal of Honor in WWII. Fourteen Texans received the award for service in World War II, six of whom were of Mexican descent. Rodriguez was also the first Mexican American GI to win the highest award in the South Pacific.

Upon his return to San Antonio, city officials and the public greeted him and gave him a key to the city. Rodriguez joined LULAC Council 2, in 1946. In 1947 he began work as a veterans representative for the Veterans Administration. He served in the United States Air Force from 1952 to 1954 and again in the Army from 1955 to 1970.

Ivanhoe Elementary School in San Antonio was renamed Cleto Rodriguez Elementary School in 1975.

Rodriguez died on December 7, 1990, and is buried at Fort Sam Houston National Cemetery.

13. Manuel Perez, Jr.

Born: March 3, 1923 in Oklahoma City, OK
Entered Service: Chicago, IL
Branch: U.S. Army
Rank: Private First Class
Date and Place of Action: February 13, 1945 at
    Fort William McKinley, Luzon, Philippine Islands
Medal Issue Date: 1945
Killed in Action: February 13, 1945

Note: Courtesy the U.S. Congressional Medal of Honor Society.

Citation:

He was lead scout for Company A, which had destroyed 11 of 12 pillboxes in a strongly fortified sector defending the approach to enemy-held Fort William McKinley on Luzon, Philippine Islands. In the reduction of these pillboxes, he killed five Japanese in the open and blasted others in pillboxes with grenades.

3.19 PFC Manuel Perez, Jr.
Photo courtesy of the CMOHS.

Realizing the urgent need for taking the last emplacement, which contained two twin-mount .50-caliber dual-purpose machineguns, he took a circuitous route to within 20 yards of the position, killing four of the enemy in his advance. He threw a grenade into the pillbox, and, as the crew started withdrawing through a tunnel just to the rear of the emplacement, shot and killed four before exhausting his clip.

He had reloaded and killed four more when an escaping Japanese threw his rifle with fixed bayonet at him. In warding off this thrust, his own rifle was knocked to the ground. Seizing the Japanese rifle, he continued firing, killing two more of the enemy.

He rushed the remaining Japanese, killed three of them with the butt of the rifle and entered the pillbox, where he bayoneted the one surviving hostile soldier. Single-handedly, he killed 18 of the enemy in neutralizing the position that had held up the advance of his entire company. Through his courageous determination and heroic disregard of grave danger, PFC Perez made possible the successful advance of his unit toward a valuable objective and provided a lasting inspiration for his comrades.

PFC Manuel Perez, Jr., was killed in action a week later.

14. Silvestre Herrera

Born: 1917 in Camargo, Chihuahua, Mexico
Entered Service: Phoenix, AZ
Branch: U.S. Army
Rank: Private First Class
Date and Place of Action: March 15, 1945 near
    Mertzwiller, France
Medal Issue Date: August 23, 1945

Note: The Pueblo Chieftan newspaper reported the following. For details please see Bibliography.

Silvestre leaned forward in his chair, trying to comprehend with all his might what his father was telling him. For the young 27-year-old Arizonan it had been a day of surprises, not all of them happy ones. It had begun with a letter in the mail, written notice that the father of three young children was being drafted to military service. The year was 1944 and the United States Army was engaged in a massive world war. Now they needed young Silvestre's service.

Silvestre wasn't opposed to serving his country, but felt he needed to let his family know what was happening. His wife was expecting their fourth child and if Silvestre had to be gone, it would be important for his parents to be there for him. The quick visit to his father had brought a stunning revelation...

"Son, you don't have to go, they can't draft you."

"What do you mean, they can't draft me?" Silvestre asked.

Then came the stunning news, "Silvestre, you aren't an American citizen."

In the moment of silence that followed young Silvestre's mind reeled with the shocking statement. Then came more.

"Silvestre," his father continued, "you know that I have raised you all your life as if you were my own...but YOU ARE NOT! I am not your real father."

Slowly the story unfolded, a story that Silvestre learned for the first time that day. The young man had been born in Camargo, Chihuahua, Mexico. His parents died when Silvestre was only a year old, and the man he had always thought was his father was really an uncle who had brought the 18-month old Silvestre to El Paso to provide him a better life in the United States.

Legally, Silvestre was a Mexican National and didn't owe service to the United States. But as Silvestre later said, "I thought, I'm going anyway. I didn't want anybody to die in my place... I felt that I had my adopted country that had been so nice to me. I thought to myself; I have an American wife and kids, and one more on the way."

And, so it was, that Silvestre Herrera joined the men of the Texas National Guard, the 36th Infantry Division, to train for combat in Europe. It was a unit Silvestre was proud to be a member of, the first American unit to have landed in Europe during World War II.

Months later as young Private First Class, Silvestre Herrera was fighting for survival in France; he was also studying to become a United States Citizen. Survival took precedence over study, and he still had a long way to go before taking his citizenship test.

Silvestre's unit was operating in the vicinity of Mertzwiller, France when on March 15, 1945 events occurred that changed Silvestre's life forever. As his platoon was moving down a road, they came under heavy enemy fire from the woods, forcing most of the men to seek cover. Not Silvestre.

His one-man charge on the enemy stronghold ended their threat and resulted in his single-handed capture of eight enemy soldiers. But Silvestre's day was just beginning.

The immediate threat ended, the platoon continued down the road. Suddenly, they came under fire again, from a second enemy stronghold. This time a minefield stood between the soldiers and the enemy gun emplacement. The pinned down platoon was at the mercy of the enemy guns...Silvestre's fellow soldiers were helpless before inevitable disaster.

With incredible courage the young PFC stood to his feet and entered the minefield to attack the enemy. Mines exploded around him but he continued on, attempting to not only attack the enemy but to draw their fire away from his comrades. Suddenly a mine exploded beneath him, severing his leg below the knee. Enemy fire continued to rake the field as Silvestre collapsed to the ground, then struggled back up on his one good leg and the shattered remains of the other, to continue the attack.

Private Herrera couldn't be stopped. He was determined to attack the enemy that threatened to destroy his platoon. Then, another mine exploded, this one hitting his remaining good leg, severing it below the knee.

Unable to continue his advance, despite intense pain and the unchecked bleeding of the stumps below his knees, Silvestre lay in the minefield to pin down the enemy while others of his platoon skirted the minefield to flank and capture the enemy.

Later Silvestre said, "I was protecting my squad with a machinegun. I was trying to draw their fire. I stepped on one land mine and it blew me straight up. I lost one foot. Then I stepped on another one and I lost my other foot. I was fighting them on my knees."

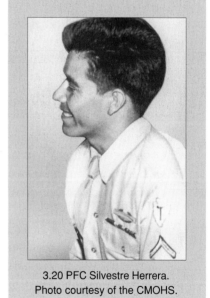

3.20 PFC Silvestre Herrera. Photo courtesy of the CMOHS.

Silvestre's courage and fighting spirit became legendary, but it also presented the United States with a problem. The young hero STILL was not an American citizen. As he recovered from the loss of both feet, an intense program began to grant Silvestre Herrera United States citizenship.

Then too, there were concerns about his health. President Truman wasn't sure the young hero was well enough for a formal presentation of the award for which he had been submitted. After all, the young man had lost both legs.

While recovering from wounds at an army hospital, it was suggested that Silvestre call home to let his family know he had survived and would be coming home. Sheepishly, Silvestre admitted that the family was so poor they didn't even have a telephone. Finally, a call was placed to a third party to get the message to his family.

But before Silvestre went home a special event awaited him. To the President's surprise, Silvestre WAS well enough. Five months earlier the loss of two legs couldn't stop the fearless soldier from fighting to protect his platoon, and it wouldn't stand in his way now.

On August 23, 1945 Silvestre wheeled his wheel chair across the White House lawn so the President could present him with the Medal of Honor.

Silvestre became the first soldier from Arizona to receive the Medal of Honor during World War II, and returned to a hero's welcome. The citizens of his home state raised $14,000 to provide him and his growing family with a new home. Eventually he had three more children, and today is the grandfather of 11 and great-grandfather of two.

A year after Silvestre received his adopted Nation's highest award, the Medal of Honor, the Nation of his birth took the unprecedented step of awarding him its highest award for valor, the "Premier Merito Militar."

Today, Silvestre wears both with pride; he is the only living person in the world authorized to wear the Medal of Honor and Mexico's equivalent. Silvestre is proud of his Mexican birth and heritage, and equally proud to be a citizen of the United States of America.

His hometown has named an elementary school for him. His service both during World War II as a soldier, and as a patriot since that fateful period of

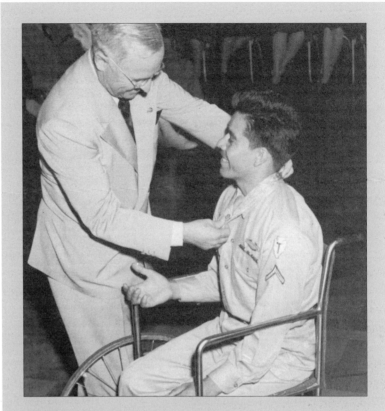

3.21 PFC Silvestre Herrera being presented the Medal of Honor by President Harry S. Truman August 23, 1945. Photo courtesy of the U.S. Army.

his life, has brought him continued honors and distinction. Still he remains a humble man, proud not so much of his own achievements, but proud of both his heritage and his citizenship.

Silvestre now calls himself a "retired leather worker and silversmith." The many neighborhood children he invites to see his work in his garage at home are sure to doubt the "retired" part; Silvestre is a man who never stops.

Despite the prosthesis that replaced the legs he lost in World War II, he goes dancing every week. He is a frequent guest at service clubs and speaks passionately about the privileges of United States citizenship to students at schools wherever he finds the opportunity. He is a dedicated American and a true hero. He seldom speaks of his own hardships.

Regarding the loss of both legs he says, "I coped with my disability very well. I wasn't sorry for it. I felt that I didn't want anybody to be sorry for me. I have lived a very happy life."

15. Ysmeal R. Villegas

Born: March 19, 1924 in Casa Blanca, CA
Entered Service: Casa Blanca, CA
Branch: U.S. Army
Rank: Staff Sergeant
Date and Place of Action: March 20, 1945 at Villa Verde Trail, Luzon, Philippine Islands
Medal Issue Date: Oct. 19, 1945
Killed in Action: March 20, 1945

Note: The Riverside, CA Press-Enterprise reported the following. For details please see Bibliography.

Villegas, a staff sergeant in the U.S. Army during World War II, served in Luzon, an island of the Philippines. After about eight months in the infantry, and a day before his 21st birthday, he was fatally shot by enemy Japanese soldiers.

He successfully had charged five rifle pits but didn't make it to the sixth one. His leadership galvanized his men into action, and they pressed forward to sweep the Japanese from the field.

Ysmael Villegas was the first-born of 13 children and the one who felt most obligated to shoulder family responsibilities. That's why he deferred his draft three times, or nine months, the maximum allowed, to stay and look after his family a little longer, said Dario Villegas, the second-born brother.

Both brothers served in the Philippines and saw each other during basic training. Ysmael was just starting at Camp Roberts in Paso Robles near Sacramento, while Dario was finishing and ready to ship out.

Dario Villegas, 14 months younger than Ysmael, said they were very close and enjoyed similar activities. They both worked in the orange groves and liked to dance. But Dario was the more active one, playing on baseball teams.

"Ysmael liked to smile a lot, earning him the nickname 'Smiley.' He easily attracted the attentions of many young women," Dario said.

3.22 SSG Ysmeal R. Villegas.
Photo courtesy of the CMOHS.

"Smiley always pinned a carnation on his left lapel," he said. "He would put on a lot of perfume for the ladies."

Dario's war

Dario served in the army as a paratrooper for about 2 1/2 years. He also served in Japan after the war ended, playing a safeguarding role. It was in Japan, a year after Ysmael had died, that Dario learned the awful news. A friend from Casa Blanca ran into him in the mess hall and offered his condolence.

"I was shocked," he said. "I couldn't believe it."

Dario's mother had purposely prevented the Army from contacting Dario. She wanted him to return home, he said. Dario clearly remembers how he confronted his mother the morning he returned home. The first words out of his mouth were: "Why didn't you tell me about what happened to Smiley?"

His mom fainted. The family revived her. He apologized. "My mother did the right thing," he said. "I would have sought revenge and would probably have died, too."

It took him a long time to grieve and to put the war behind him, and even today, Dario does not want to reminisce about his battle days. He returned with yellow jaundice as a result of contracting malaria. He lost too many friends.

"I don't want to remember nothing," he said. "Let it slide."

The Villegas family in Riverside spans four generations and about 300 live in the city. Charlie, Ysmael's son who was born 12 days after his father was killed in action, works at Lowe's Hardware in Perris.

Most of Dario's siblings still live in Riverside, but one sister now lives in Utah and a brother resides in Vacaville.

Citation:

He was a squad leader when his unit, in a forward position, clashed with an enemy strongly entrenched in connected caves and foxholes on commanding ground. He moved boldly from man to man, in the face of bursting grenades and demolition charges, through heavy machinegun and rifle fire, to bolster the spirit of his comrades.

Inspired by his gallantry, his men pressed forward to the crest of the hill. Numerous enemy riflemen, refusing to flee, continued firing from their foxholes. SSG Villegas, with complete disregard for his own safety and the bullets that kicked up the dirt at his feet, charged an enemy position, and, firing at point-blank range killed the Japanese in a foxhole.

He rushed a second foxhole while bullets missed him by inches, and killed one more of the enemy. In rapid succession he charged a third, a fourth, a fifth foxhole, each time destroying the enemy within. The fire against him increased in intensity, but he pressed onward to attack a sixth position.

As he neared his goal, he was hit and killed by enemy fire. Through his heroism and indomitable fighting spirit, SSG Villegas, at the cost of his life, inspired his men to a determined attack in which they swept the enemy from the field.

16. Harold Gonsalves

Born: January 28, 1926 in Alameda, CA
Entered Service: May 27, 1943
Branch: U.S. Marine Corps
Rank: Private First Class
Date and Place of Action: April 15, 1945 Okinawa
Medal Issue Date: June 19, 1946
Killed in Action: April 15, 1945

Note: The United States Marine Corps History and Museums Division reports the following on its website. For details please see Bibliography.

Private First Class Harold Gonsalves threw himself on a grenade at the age of 19 on Okinawa, saving the lives of two comrades, to become another of his country's heroes who gave his life that others might live.

Harold Gonsalves was the son of John and Annie Gonsalves. His father was a native of Massachusetts, while his mother was born in Honolulu, Hawaii. Harold attended school at Alameda and after two and one half years of high school, quit to take a job as a stock clerk with Montgomery Ward's in Oakland. In high school he had taken part in football, baseball, track, and swimming, besides singing tenor in the school glee club.

He enlisted in the Marine Corps Reserve on May 27, 1943 and was called to active duty on June 17. He went through boot camp at San Diego and then, at his own request, was sent to the Raiders at Camp Pendleton, CA. After three weeks with them, he was transferred to the artillery at the same camp. He was

3.23 PFC Harold Gonsalves.
Photo courtesy of the CMOHS.

classified as a cannoneer on 75 and 105-millimeter guns before he joined the 30th Replacement Battalion in the fall of 1943.

Gonsalves left the United States on November 8 and at the end of that month was assigned to the 2nd Pack Howitzer Battalion, which was then in Hawaii. He was promoted to Private First Class in March 1944, and with his battalion became part of the 22nd Marines two months later. With the 22nd Marines, he participated in the assault, capture, and occupation of Engebi and Parry Islands, in the Marshalls. At Engebi, the Marines took the island in six hours, killing more than one thousand of the enemy.

Major General T.E. Watson, commanding general of Tactical Group I, cited the regiment for their part in the Marshalls' campaign. From Eniwetok, Gonsalves accompanied the 22nd Marines to Kwajelein, to Guadalcanal, back to Kwajelein and Eniwetok, then up to Guam in July where he took part in the liberation of that pre-war American island. After Guam, the regiment went back to the 'Canal, where in November they were detached from the 22nd Marines and joined the 15th Marines of the 6th Marine Division.

It was with that outfit that Gonsalves landed on Okinawa on April 1, 1945. Two weeks later, on April 15, the young Marine was a member of an eight-man forward observer team, which was engaged in directing artillery fire in support of an attack by the infantry on Japanese positions on Motobu Peninsula.

When it finally became necessary for the team to advance to the actual front lines, the officer in charge took Gonsalves and one other man with him. Gonsalves was acting scout sergeant of the team. He and the other Marine were to lay telephone lines for communication with the artillery battalion. As the team advanced to the front, they came under heavy enemy rifle, grenade and mortar fire. Just as the three had reached the front lines, a Japanese grenade landed among them.

It was less than one foot from the lieutenant and the other PFC. Without a moment's hesitation, Gonsalves flung himself on the deadly missile, taking the full explosion into his own body. He gallantly gave his life for his fellow Marines and his country.

The other two were not even touched by grenade fragments and they successfully completed their mission. The Medal of Honor, with citation signed by President Harry S. Truman, was presented to Private First Class Gonsalves' sister in the presence of his parents at ceremonies in the office of the commanding general of the Department of the Pacific at San Francisco, on June 19, 1946, by Major General Henry L. Larsen, USMC.

The hero's parents, Mr. and Mrs. John Gonsalves, and sister, Marie, lived in Alameda, California. Following the war, PFC Gonsalves' remains were returned to the United States for reinterment. He was buried with full military honors at the Golden Gate National Cemetery in San Bruno, California, March 20, 1949.

---

17. David H. Gonzales

Born: June 9, 1923 in Pacoima, CA
Entered Service: Pacoima, CA
Branch: U.S. Army
Rank: Private First Class
Date and Place of Action: April 25, 1945, Villa Verde Trail, Luzon, Philippine Islands
Killed in Action: April 25, 1945

Note: Los Angeles Mission College provided a News Release with the following information. For details please see Bibliography.

Private First Class David H. Gonzales was the first Los Angeles County resident to receive a Congressional Medal of Honor during World War II, for heroic actions that saved the lives of five companions in the Philippines. Gonzales, a Pacoima resident, was fatally wounded while digging out his comrades, who had been buried alive when a bomb struck their camp. Gonzales was posthumously awarded the Medal of Honor by President Harry S. Truman in 1945.

California Congressman Howard Berman presented the family with various military decorations earned by Gonzales but never given to his relatives.

3.24 PFC David H. Gonzales. Photo courtesy of the CMOHS.

Congressman Berman discovered the omission of the medals while helping the family in their efforts to right *another* error. For years, a photo of a soldier, who is not Gonzales, but identified as that of the medal winner, was erroneously displayed in the Pentagon's Hall of Heroes. Consequently, this mistake has been replicated over the years in other shrines, publications and websites.

Thanks to the efforts of Berman and his staff, the Department of the Army has told the family that the correct photo will be displayed when the renovation of the Pentagon–made necessary by the 9/11 attack–is completed.

Los Angeles Mission College holds a Veterans Day Ceremony annually to mark its close ties with veterans in the northeast San Fernando Valley. Each year, Mission College serves more than 400 veterans who come to the campus with questions about their benefits and about educational and career opportunities available to them.

Citation:

He was pinned down with his company. As enemy fire swept the area, making any movement extremely hazardous, a 500-pound bomb smashed into the company's perimeter, burying five men with its explosion. PFC Gonzales, without hesitation, seized an entrenching tool and under a hail of fire crawled 15 yards to his entombed comrades, where his commanding officer, who had also rushed forward, was beginning to dig the men out. Nearing his goal, he saw the officer struck and instantly killed by machinegun fire.

Undismayed, he set to work swiftly and surely with his hands and the entrenching tool while enemy sniper and machinegun bullets struck all about him. He succeeded in digging one of the men out of the pile of rock and sand. To dig faster he stood up regardless of the greater danger from so exposing himself. He extricated a second man, and then another.

As he completed the liberation of the third, he was hit and mortally wounded, but the comrades for whom he so gallantly gave his life were safely evacuated. PFC Gonzales' valiant and intrepid conduct exemplifies the highest tradition of the military service.

18. Alejandro Renteria Ruiz

Born: June 26, 1924 in Loving, NM
Entered Service: Carlsbad, NM
Branch: U.S. Army
Rank: Private First Class
Place of Action: April 28, 1945 Okinawa, Ryukyu Islands

Note: The Times Union newspaper published the following story. For details please see Bibliography.

History came alive December 21, 2002, as some Warsaw Community High School students got an education in the realities of war and an appreciation of the men who have fought in war.

As a Veterans Day project, David Hoffert's Indiana high school world history students wrote letters of appreciation to recipients of the Congressional Medal of Honor. Of the 140 living MOH recipients, the students wrote to about 90 men, and, Hoffert said, "70 have written back so far.

"This is the last generation of students to have contact with these men," said Hoffert, a WCHS graduate who is in his first year of teaching. "The response has been incredible–they're so grateful that somebody would notice."

To honor the veterans, Hoffert created a Heroes Wall of Fame, where the students post pictures

of the veterans they wrote to, along with copies of the Medal of Honor recipients' letters. The students took the project seriously, he said, and wrote respectful letters asking questions about how the war changed the veterans' lives. "You can't help but be in awe of what these people did," he said.

Hoffert said the students in his classes read through the veterans' letters while they were learning about such events as D-Day and the Battle of the Bulge, and the experience had a definite effect on the students.

"It's something that they'll walk away from and never forget," he said.

Excerpt from Alejandro R. Ruiz letter:

"…I never questioned my duty since I believe that as Americans we have a responsibility to serve our country and preserve our way of life and freedoms. Too many people take our freedom for granted and expect the benefits without giving back in service. But no community or country can survive or become great if our citizens take that attitude.

"…All I can say is that I did what I had to do. Someone had to take this action or the lives of my men and my own would have been sacrificed. When you are in battle, you have to rely on your men. You have to count on one another. So my only thought was to save my men.

"…During the White House ceremony, President Truman awarded me the medal and as Commander in Chief saluted me and told me that he would rather have the medal than be president. "

"But upon my return to El Paso, Texas, where I was stationed at Fort Bliss, I was not

3.25 PFC Alejandro Renteria Ruiz. Photo courtesy of the CMOHS.

allowed to eat in the restaurant when I took my wife out to eat to celebrate. They had segregation at the time and there was a sign that said, "No Mexicans or Dogs Allowed.

3.26 PFC Alejandro R. Ruiz being congratulated by President Truman upon receiving the Medal of Honor. Photo courtesy of the U.S. Army.

"I had to eat in the kitchen since my parents were of Mexican descent. I did not let this experience bother me since I believe in the values of this country and that if we insist that all American's live up to these values, that this country will live up to its wonderful dream."

Mr. Ruiz now lives in Mt. Pleasant, SC.

Citation:

When a skillfully camouflaged enemy pillbox stopped his unit, he displayed conspicuous gallantry and intrepidity above and beyond the call of duty. His squad, suddenly brought under a hail of machinegun fire and a vicious grenade attack, was pinned down. Jumping to his feet, Pfc. Ruiz seized an automatic rifle and lunged through the flying grenades and rifle and automatic fire for the top of the emplacement.

When an enemy soldier charged him, his rifle jammed. Undaunted, Pfc. Ruiz whirled on his assailant and clubbed him down. Then he ran back through bullets and grenades, seized more ammunition and another automatic rifle, and again made for the pillbox.

Enemy fire now was concentrated on him, but he charged on, miraculously reaching the position, and in plain view he climbed to the top. Leaping

from one opening to another, he sent burst after burst into the pillbox, killing 12 of the enemy and completely destroying the position. Pfc. Ruiz's heroic conduct, in the face of overwhelming odds, saved the lives of many comrades and eliminated an obstacle that long would have checked his unit's advance.

KOREAN WAR

19. Baldomero Lopez

Born: August 23, 1925 in Tampa, FL
Entered Service: Tampa, FL
Branch: U.S. Marine Corps
Rank: First Lieutenant
Place of Action: September 15, 1950 during Inchon invasion in Korea
Medal Issue Date: August 30, 1951
Killed in Action: September 15, 1950

Note: The USMC History and Museums Division reports the following on its website. For details please see Bibliography.

Marine First Lieutenant Baldomero Lopez earned the Medal of Honor in Korea for sacrificing his life to protect his men.

Lieutenant Lopez, 25, was posthumously awarded the Nation's top military decoration for smothering a hand grenade with his own body during the Inchon landing on September 15, 1950.

Lieutenant Lopez was born August 23, 1925, at Tampa, Florida, and went to high school in that city, where he starred as a basketball player. On July 8, 1943, he enlisted in the United States Navy, and served until June 11, 1944. After his discharge Lieutenant Lopez was appointed to the U.S. Naval Academy, and on graduating June 6, 1947, was commissioned a second lieutenant in the Marine Corps.

He took basic officer instructions at Quantico, Virginia, after which he became a platoon commander in the

3.27 1st Lt. Baldomero Lopez. Photo courtesy of the CMOHS.

Platoon Leaders Class Training Regiment. In 1948, Lieutenant Lopez went to China, where he served as a mortar section commander and later as a rifle platoon commander at Tsingtao and Shanghai. On his return from China he was assigned to Camp Pendleton, Oceanside, California.

He was serving there when, shortly after the outbreak of the Korean War, he volunteered for duty as an infantry officer in Korea.

3.28 1st Lt. Baldomero Lopez, United States Marine Corps, scales the sea wall at Red Beach during the Inchon Landing, Sept. 15, 1950. Minutes after this photo was taken, Lopez sacrificed his life to save his own men and earned the Medal of Honor. Photo courtesy of the U.S. Dept. of Defense.

News of his heroic death spread quickly among fellow Marines on the battlefronts. On September 25, 1950, a Scripps-Howard war correspondent, Jerry Thorp, said in a news story on Lieutenant Lopez's deed that he "died with the courage that makes men great."

In addition to the Medal of Honor, Lieutenant Lopez's decorations include the Purple Heart Medal, Presidential Unit Citation with one bronze star, China Service Medal, and Korean Service Medal with two bronze stars.

Citation:

For conspicuous gallantry and intrepidity at the risk of his life above and beyond the call of duty as a marine platoon commander of Company A, in action against enemy aggressor forces.

With his platoon, 1st Lt. Lopez was engaged in the reduction of immediate enemy beach defenses after landing with the assault waves. Exposing himself to hostile fire, he moved forward alongside a

bunker and prepared to throw a hand grenade into the next pillbox whose fire was pinning down that sector of the beach.

Taken under fire by an enemy automatic weapon and hit in the right shoulder and chest as he lifted his arm to throw, he fell backward and dropped the deadly missile. After a moment, he turned and dragged his body forward in an effort to retrieve the grenade and throw it.

In critical condition from pain and loss of blood, and unable to grasp the hand grenade firmly enough to hurl it, he chose to sacrifice himself rather than endanger the lives of his men and, with a sweeping motion of his wounded right arm, cradled the grenade under him and absorbed the full impact of the explosion.

His exceptional courage, fortitude, and devotion to duty reflect the highest credit upon 1st Lt. Lopez and the U.S. Naval Service. He gallantly gave his life for his country.

---

20. Eugene Arnold Obregon

Born: November 12, 1930 in Los Angeles, CA
Entered Service: June 7, 1948 Los Angeles, CA
Branch: U.S. Marine Corps
Rank: Private First Class
Place of Action: September 26, 1950 Seoul, Korea
Medal Issue Date: August 30, 1951
Killed in Action: September 26, 1950

Note: The Medal of Honor website tells this story. For details please see Bibliography.

Private First Class Obregon attended elementary school and Roosevelt High School in Los Angeles before enlisting in the Marine Corps on June 7, 1948, at the age of seventeen.

Following recruit training at San Diego, California, he was assigned to the Marine Corps Supply Depot, Barstow, California, where he served as a fireman until the outbreak of the war in Korea. He was transferred to the 1st Marine Provisional Brigade and served as a machine gun ammunition carrier. His unit departed the United States on July 14, 1950 and arrived at Pusan, Korea on August 3, 1950.

He was in action by August 8, 1950, along the Naktong River, and participated in the Inchon landing. Then, on September 26, during the assault on the city of Seoul, came the act in which he gave his life.

PFC Eugene Obregon was 19, a small, quick kid from East L.A. PFC Bert Johnson, also 19, was a tall, rangy boy from Grand Prairie, Texas. Texans and Chicanos weren't supposed to get along, but "Obie" Obregon and "Bobo" Johnson had made it together from boot camp to the same machinegun squad in Korea. They were like brothers, as other Marines would later recall.

3.29 PFC Eugene Arnold Obregon.
Photo Courtesy of the CMOHS.

That afternoon of September 26, 1950, as the leading elements of the First Marine Division fought their way down a wide, war-torn boulevard toward Changkok Palace, in the South Korean capital of Seoul, these two young Leathernecks were about to lend a new meaning to their Corps' motto: **Semper Fidelis–Always Faithful**.

"Suddenly the silence was shattered by fire from a camouflaged North Korean machinegun," Fred Davidson, a fellow Marine, later wrote.

"Bert went down."

Young Johnson had taken hits in his side, both legs and the right elbow. A fifth bullet hitting his helmet fractured his skull.

Seeing his buddy fall, Obregon shouted. "Stay put, Bobo. I'm coming for you!" Johnson yelled back: "Don't try it Obie! Keep your cover!" But Obregon was already on his way.

Armed only with a pistol, firing as he ran, Obregon reached Johnson and dragged him to a curb, where he began bandaging his wounds. And at that moment a platoon-sized force of North Koreans attacked.

Quickly grabbing Johnson's carbine, Obregon placed himself as a shield in front of his buddy and continued firing until the enemy fell back, leaving 22 dead behind. This time, the determined North Koreans brought up a machinegun to support their attack. But refusing to give way, Obregon continued firing, protecting his friend, until two machinegun bullets struck him in the face.

Obie's death had not been in vain. With time to reorganize, the Marines attacked, killing the remaining North Koreans. Despite his wounds, Bert Johnson survived, rotated home, and lived for 44 more years. "And never did a day go by," recalled Johnson's friends, "when Bobo didn't think of Gene Obregon, and the price he'd paid to give Bert back his life…"

In addition to the Medal of Honor, Private First Class Obregon was posthumously awarded the Purple Heart Medal, Presidential Unit Citation, and Korean Service Medal with three Bronze Stars.

But Eugene Obregon's story tells us something else about these Americans. It tells us that the divisions of race, religion or color have no place in an America in which a Latino from East Los Angeles can give his life for his friend–an Anglo from Texas. Truly, this is the brotherhood America is all about.

The Medal was presented to his parents, Mr. and Mrs. Peter R. Obregon of Los Angeles by Secretary of the Navy Kimball on August 30, 1951.

21. Joseph C. Rodriguez

Born: November 14, 1928 in San Bernardino, CA
Entered Service: October 1950, CA
Branch: U.S. Army
Rank: Sergeant
Place of Action: May 21, 1951 near Munye-ri, Korea
Medal Issue Date: January 21, 1952

Note: The following text is from the U.S. Army European Command. For details please see Bibliography.

Joseph C. Rodriguez graduated from San Bernardino Valley College and soon after entered the Army in October 1950. Less than seven months later, he was engaged with the enemy in combat in Korea. One week after the event for which he was recognized, he was wounded in a combat action. He was evacuated to a hospital in Japan for three months.

Having recuperated from his wounds, he requested to be returned to his unit in Korea. He served in Korea until late November 1951, when he was flown back to the United States because the recommendation to be awarded the Nation's highest military award had been approved. President Harry S. Truman presented the Congressional Medal of Honor to him on January 21, 1952.

He served as an enlisted man in the Infantry and served every rank except Master Sergeant. In June 1952, he was commissioned a Second Lieutenant in the Corps of Engineers. He was assigned to the Far East, to include two tours in Korea and one in Vietnam. Also stationed in Latin America, Bolivia, Argentina, Puerto Rico, and twice in the Panama Canal Zone.

He served twelve consecutive years overseas. His last assignment was at Fort Bliss, Texas, as the Facilities Engineer of the Installation. During his military career, he attended various military schools and universities. He retired as a Colonel after serving thirty years in the Army.

After retiring from the Army, he went to work at the University of Texas, El Paso as the Director of the Physical Plant, responsible for all new construction and maintenance of all facilities. He retired again after ten years of employment with the university.

He married the former Miss Rose Aranda of Colton, California in November 1952. They have three children and eleven grandchildren.

3.30 SGT Joseph C. Rodriguez. Photo courtesy of the CMOHS.

Citation:

Sgt. Rodriguez distinguished himself by conspicuous gallantry and intrepidity at the risk of his life above and beyond the call of duty in action against an armed enemy of the United Nations.

Sgt. Rodriguez, an assistant squad leader of the 2nd Platoon, was participating in an attack against a fanatical hostile force occupying well-fortified positions on rugged commanding terrain, when his squad's advance was halted within approximately 60 yards by a withering barrage of automatic weapons and small-arms fire from five emplacements directly to the front and right and left flanks, together with grenades which the enemy rolled down the hill toward the advancing troops.

Fully aware of the odds against him, Sgt. Rodriguez leaped to his feet, dashed 60 yards up the fire-swept slope, and, after lobbing grenades into the first foxhole with deadly accuracy, ran around the left flank, silenced an automatic weapon with two grenades and continued his whirlwind assault to the top of the peak, wiping out two more foxholes and then, reaching the right flank, he tossed grenades into the remaining emplacement, destroying the gun and annihilating its crew.

Sgt. Rodriguez' intrepid actions exacted a toll of 15 enemy dead and, as a result of his incredible display of valor, the defense of the opposition was broken, and the enemy routed, and the strategic strongpoint secured. His unflinching courage under fire and inspirational devotion to duty reflect highest credit on himself and uphold the honored traditions of the military service.

---

22. Rodolfo P. Hernandez

Born: April 14, 1931 in Colton, CA
Entered Service: Fowler, CA
Branch: U.S. Army
Rank: Corporal
Date and Place of Action: May 31, 1951 near Wontong-ni, Korea

Note: Courtesy of the U.S. Congressional Medal of Honor Society.

Citation:

Cpl. Hernandez, a member of Company G, distinguished himself by conspicuous gallantry and intrepidity above and beyond the call of duty in action against the enemy. His platoon, in defensive positions on Hill 420, came under ruthless attack by a numerically superior and fanatical hostile force, accompanied by heavy artillery, mortar, and machinegun fire, which inflicted numerous casualties on the platoon.

His comrades were forced to withdraw due to lack of ammunition but Cpl. Hernandez, although wounded in an exchange of grenades, continued to deliver deadly fire into the ranks of the onrushing assailants until a ruptured cartridge rendered his rifle inoperative. Immediately leaving his position, Cpl. Hernandez rushed the enemy armed only with rifle and bayonet.

3.31 CPL Rodolfo P. Hernandez. Photo courtesy of the CMOHS.

Fearlessly engaging the foe, he killed six of the enemy before falling unconscious from grenade, bayonet, and bullet wounds but his heroic action momentarily halted the enemy advance and enabled his unit to counterattack and retake the lost ground. The indomitable fighting spirit, outstanding courage, and tenacious devotion to duty clearing demonstrated by Cpl. Hernandez reflect the highest credit upon himself, the infantry, and the U.S. Army.

23. Edward Gomez

Born: August 10, 1932 in Omaha, NE
Branch: U.S. Marine Corps
Rank: Private First Class
Date and Place of Action: September 14, 1951, at Kajon-ni, Korea
Killed In Action: September 14, 1951

Note: The USMC History and Museums Division provided the following text. For details please see Bibliography.

Marine Private First Class Edward Gomez, 19, of Omaha, Nebraska, earned the Medal of Honor in Korea for sacrificing his life to save the lives of four comrades in his machine gun team.

The nation's highest decoration for valor was awarded to the young Marine for extraordinary heroism September 14, 1951, at Kajon-ni, when he smothered a hand grenade with his own body to prevent destruction of his Marine machine gun team.

PFC Gomez was the 18th Marine to receive the Medal of Honor in the Korean fighting. Born

August 10, 1932, at Omaha, he attended Omaha High School before enlisting in the Marine Corps Reserve August 11, 1949, at the age of seventeen.

After recruit training at San Diego, California, he trained at Camp Pendleton, California, and went to Korea with the 7th Replacement Draft. His parents are Mr. and Mrs. Modesto Gomez of Omaha, Nebraska. In addition to the Medal of Honor, PFC Gomez was awarded a Gold Star in lieu of a second Purple Heart Medal, the Korean Service Medal with Bronze Star, and the United Nations Service Medal.

Citation:

For conspicuous gallantry and intrepidity at the risk of his life above and beyond the call of duty while serving as an Ammunition Bearer in Company E, Second Battalion, First Marines, First Marine Division (Reinforced), in action against enemy aggressor forces in Korea on 14 September 1951.

Boldly advancing with his squad in support of a group of riflemen assaulting a series of strongly fortified and bitterly defended hostile positions on Hill 749, Private First Class Gomez consistently exposed himself to the withering barrage to keep his machine gun supplied with ammunition during the drive forward to seize the objective.

As his squad deployed to meet an imminent counterattack, he voluntarily moved down an abandoned trench to search for a new location for the gun and, when a hostile grenade landed between himself and his weapon, shouted a warning to those around him as he grasped the activated charge in his hand.

3.32 PFC Edward Gomez. Photo courtesy of the CMOHS.

Determined to save his comrades, he unhesitatingly chose to sacrifice himself and, diving into the ditch with the deadly missile, absorbed the shattering violence of the explosion in his own body.

By his stouthearted courage, incomparable valor, and decisive spirit of self-sacrifice, Private First Class Gomez inspired the others to heroic efforts in subsequently repelling the outnumbering foe, and his valiant conduct throughout sustained and enhanced the finest traditions of the United States Naval Service. He gallantly gave his life for his country.

---

24. Fernando Luis Garcia

Born: October 14, 1929 in Utuado, Puerto Rico
Entered Service: Sept. 19, 1951
Branch: U.S. Marine Corps
Rank: Private First Class
Date and Place of Action: September 5, 1952, at Outpost Bruce-Korea
Medal Issue Date: October 25, 1953
Killed in Action: September 5, 1952

Note: The Medal of Honor website reports the following information. For details please see Bibliography.

Private Garcia went to both grade and high school at Utuado, Puerto Rico. He was working as a file clerk for the Texas Company in San Juan, Puerto Rico, when he was inducted into the Marine Corps on September 19, 1951.

On completing "boot" training at Parris Island, South Carolina, he was promoted to private first class in December 1951. The following month he was transferred to Camp Pendleton, California, for further training. In March 1952, he embarked for Korea where he joined the 3rd Battalion, 5th Marines.

Private Garcia was a member of Company I, 3rd Battalion, 5th Marines, 1st Marine Division, in Korea, when he sacrificed his life by throwing himself on an enemy grenade to save a comrade, September 5, 1952, at Outpost Bruce in the "Bunker Hill" area.

The outpost had been under a pre-dawn enemy attack for almost an hour. Garcia, already suffering painful wounds, was getting hand grenades from Staff Sergeant Floyd V. Wiley, the acting platoon sergeant when an enemy grenade landed nearby. "I'll get it," shouted Garcia and he threw himself upon the missile just as it exploded. The sergeant was wounded and knocked unconscious by the explosion.

When he recovered he found Garcia dead. Later the enemy completely overran the position and Garcia's body was not recovered.

In addition to the Medal of Honor, Private Garcia's medals and decorations include: the Purple Heart, the Navy Unit Commendation, the National Defense Service Medal, the Korean Service Medal with two bronze stars, the United Nations Service Medal and the Korean Presidential Unit Citation.

3.33 PFC Fernando Luis Garcia. Photo courtesy of the CMOHS.

Private Garcia was survived by his parents, Mr. and Mrs. German Garcia-Toledo of Utuado, Puerto Rico; two sisters, Daisy and Carmen; and a brother Hector. On October 25, 1953, at a ceremony held in the City Hall at Utuado, Private Garcia's parents were presented his Congressional Medal of Honor.

On February 5, 1959, Camp Fernando Luis Garcia was dedicated at Vieques, Puerto Rico, in honor of the deceased Marine hero.

Citation:

For conspicuous gallantry and intrepidity at the risk of his life above and beyond the call of duty while serving as a member of Company I, Third Battalion, Fifth Marines, First Marine Division (Reinforced), in action against enemy aggressor forces in Korea on September 5, 1952.

While participating in the defense of a combat outpost located more than one mile forward of the main line of resistance during a savage night attack by a fanatical enemy force employing grenades, mortars and artillery, Private First Class Garcia, although suffering painful wounds, moved through the intense hall of hostile fire to a supply point to secure more hand grenades.

Quick to act when a hostile grenade landed nearby, endangering the life of another Marine, as well as his own, he unhesitatingly chose to sacrifice himself and immediately threw his body upon the deadly missile, receiving the full impact of the explosion. His great personal valor and cool decision in the face of almost certain death sustain and enhance the finest traditions of the United States Naval Service. He gallantly gave his life for his country.

25. Benito Martinez

Born: March 21, 1931 in Fort Hancock, TX
Entered Service: Fort Hancock, TX
Branch: U. S. Army
Rank: Corporal
Place of Action: September 6, 1952 at Satae-ri, Korea
Killed in Action: September 6, 1952

Note: The following is from George W. Langdale's book, *Wolfhounds of Sandbag Castle: A 96 Day Defense-Korea.* For details please see Bibliography.

Benito Martinez and Outpost Agnes

Corporal Benito Martinez brushed the dust from his face and out of his eyes while privately thanking those who had built the outpost well enough to withstand the Russian made 120mm mortar rounds that exploded all around his position. Outpost Agnes, as it had become called, was an outpost built on the front edge of the Main Line of Resistance (MLR) along a finger ridge hat led directly to the North Korean line.

Corporal Martinez's unit, 2nd Platoon, Able Company of the Twenty Seventh Infantry "Wolfhounds," had inherited the position along with the

3.35 CPL Benito Martinez.
Photo courtesy of the U.S. Army.

positions on the MLR known as Sandbag Castle from Charlie Company, who had inherited it from the Turkish Brigade.

Corporal Martinez could hear the North Koreans moving around outside of his position. Glad that the outpost had survived the shelling, he began to assess the situation and developed a plan. When the shelling stopped, the Wolfhounds in the castle would start firing at the North Koreans. The North Koreans would take cover in shell holes and call for mortar fire again.

3.34 CPL Benito Martinez.
Photo courtesy of the CMOHS.

This was a dangerous tactic but the North Korean's faith in their mortar crew's skill was paying off and they were closing in on Agnes. Martinez realized this and ordered the three other Wolfhounds with him to fall back to their units. He would stay behind and cover their withdrawal with machine-gun fire. Two of the three soldiers made it back to their platoon alive.

Martinez's lieutenant called him on the sound power telephone and ordered him to get out. Martinez, knowing the situation better than anyone, replied that he would have to stay on and delay the North Koreans as long as possible. He requested that no one try to attempt a rescue since the enemy was all around him.

The North Koreans then began their assault on Agnes with satchel charges. Martinez left his machine gun to take up the lighter, more maneuverable BAR. He made his way through the trench to one of the flanking bunkers, which had been partially destroyed in the shelling. From here he could see the North Korean soldiers in the dim light of the early morning. He took up a good firing position and opened up with a deadly hail of fire on enemy. The North Koreans were surprised at first by this unexpected volley of fire but soon recovered and began to maneuver on the partially destroyed bunker.

Shortly before dawn a call came in over the telephone in the Second Platoon command post. It was Martinez reporting that the enemy was converging on his position. Those words were the last spoken to any American from the lone survivor in Outpost Agnes.

Later the North Korean attack tapered off as reinforcements from Love Company arrived. Lieutenant McLean was awarded the Silver Star for his valiant actions in leading the counter attacks and Corporal Benito Martinez was posthumously awarded the Medal of Honor for his heroic stand at Outpost Agnes. The number of lives saved by his actions is difficult to estimate.

Citation:

Corporal Benito Martinez, machine-gunner with Company A, 27th Infantry Regiment, 25th Infantry Division, distinguished himself by conspicuous gallantry and outstanding courage above and beyond the call of duty in action against the enemy near Satae-ri, Korea, on September 6, 1952.

While manning a forward listening post forward of the manning line of resistance, his position was attacked by a hostile force of reinforced company strength. In the bitter fighting which ensued, the enemy infiltrated the defense perimeter and realizing that encirclement was imminent, Corporal Martinez elected to remain at his post in an attempt to stem the onslaught.

In a daring defense, he raked the attacking troops with crippling fire, inflicting numerous casualties.

Although contacted by sound power phone several times, he insisted that no attempt be made to rescue him because of the danger involved. Soon thereafter, the hostile forces rushed the emplacement, forcing him to make a limited withdrawal with only an automatic rifle and pistol to defend himself. After a courageous 6-hour stand and shortly before dawn, he called for the last time, stating that the enemy was converging on his position.

His magnificent stand enabled friendly elements to reorganize, attack, and regain the key terrain. Corporal Martinez's incredible valor and supreme sacrifice reflect lasting glory upon himself and are in keeping with the honored traditions of the military service.

Inspired by the actions of Corporal Martinez and other Wolfhounds, Private First Class Joseph H. Young (BAR man, Company C, 27th Infantry), wrote the following poem:

When the Wolfhounds Perform in Sandbag Castle

Gung-ho, gung-ho
When the Wolfhounds perform,
When we go into action,
We're busier than bees that swarm

Gung-ho, gung-ho
When the Wolfhounds perform,
Then very soon the fighting,
Will really be getting warm.

At 0-300 the action will start!
By the "L.P." on "Sandbag Castle"
When the word is given "Over the Top!"
We will charge "In front"

In "Torrid Beaten Ground!"
"Never Fear on Earth" is our "Martyrdom"
Rockets will blast, Shrapnel will fly,
But the Devil "Hell's Angels can't stop us"

We will leap out of the trenches,
With grenades in our hands,
We will fight along braver-ally,
Out into "No Man's Land"

Gung-ho, gung-ho,
When the Wolfhounds perform
We'll rally up one hellible storm;
A Gutting, Shooting, Burning,
Shrapnel Storm

26. Ambrosio Guillen

Born: December 7, 1929 in La Juanta, CO
Entered Service: El Paso, TX
Branch: U.S. Marine Corps
Rank: Staff Sergeant
Place of Action: July 25, 1953 Songuch-on, Korea
Killed in Action: July 25, 1953

Note: Art Leatherwood wrote the following article. For details please see Bibliography.

Staff Sergeant Ambrosio Guillen was a member of Company F, Second Battalion, Seventh Marines, First Marine Division near Songuch-on, Korea, on July 25, 1953, when he and his platoon were participating in the defense of an outpost forward of the main line of resistance.

This action was only two days before the official cease-fire of the war was declared.

At night, over unfamiliar terrain and in the face of hostile fire, he maneuvered the platoon into fighting positions. When pinned down by an estimated enemy force of two battalions, he exposed himself to heavy mortar and artillery fire to direct his men and supervise the care and evacuation of the wounded.

Guillen was critically wounded during the battle but refused medical treatment and continued to direct his men until the enemy was defeated. He succumbed to his wounds a few hours later. His outstanding valor was directly responsible for his platoon's repelling a numerically superior enemy force. Guillen is buried in Fort Bliss National Cemetery at El Paso, Texas.

Citation:

For conspicuous gallantry and intrepidity at the risk of his life above and beyond the call of duty while serving as a platoon sergeant of Company F in action against enemy aggressor forces.

Participating in the defense of an outpost forward of the main line of resistance, SSG Guillen maneuvered his platoon over unfamiliar terrain in the face of hostile fire and placed his men in fighting positions. With his unit pinned down when the outpost was attacked under cover of darkness by an estimated force of two enemy battalions supported by mortar and artillery fire, he deliberately exposed himself to the heavy barrage and attacks to direct his men in defending their positions and personally supervise the treatment and evacuation of the wounded.

Inspired by his leadership, the platoon quickly rallied and engaged the enemy in fierce hand-to-hand combat. Although critically wounded during the course of the battle, SSG Guillen refused medical aid and continued to direct his men throughout the remainder of the engagement until the enemy was defeated and thrown into disorderly retreat.

3.36 SSgt Ambrosio Guillen. Photo courtesy of the CMOHS.

Succumbing to his wounds within a few hours, SSG Guillen, by his outstanding courage and indomitable fighting spirit, was directly responsible for the success of his platoon in repelling a numerically superior enemy force.

His personal valor reflects the highest credit upon himself and enhances the finest traditions of the U.S. Naval Service.

He gallantly gave his life for his country.

VIETNAM WAR

27. Humbert Roque "Rocky" Versace

Born: July 2, 1937 in Albuquerque, NM
Entered Service: 1959 Norfolk, VA
Branch: U.S. Army
Rank: Captain
Date and Place of Action: September 26, 1965
Medal Issue Date: July 2002
Killed as a Prisoner of War (POW): September 26, 1965

Note: The Medal of Honor website compiled the following information from numerous sources, including writer Steve Vogel. For details, please see Bibliography.

Humbert Roque Versace is listed as Missing in Action. His remains have never been recovered.

Versace's stone at Arlington National Cemetery stands above an empty grave. His father, Humbert Joseph Versace, United States Military Academy Class of 1933, is buried in Arlington National Cemetery.

In 1963, while stationed in Vietnam, Green Beret Army Captain Humbert Roque 'Rocky' Versace wanted to become a priest and work with Vietnamese orphans. He had already been accepted into a seminary, but his dream was not to be fulfilled.

Two weeks before he was due to return home, Versace, 27, was captured on October 29, 1963, by Viet Cong guerrillas who spent the next two years torturing and trying to brainwash him. In return, he mounted four escape attempts, ridiculed his interrogators, swore at them in three languages and confounded them as best he could, according to two U.S. soldiers captured with him, Lieutenant Nick Rowe and Sergeant Dan Pitzer.

For much of the next two years, their home would be bamboo cages, six feet long, two feet wide, and three feet high. They were given little to eat, and little protection against the elements. On nights when their netting was taken away, so many mosquitoes would swarm their shackled feet it looked like they were wearing black socks.

3.37 CPT Humbert Roque "Rocky" Versace receives his 90-day combat infantry badge from his father, Col. Humbert Joseph Versace. Photo courtesy of the U.S. Army.

The point was not merely to physically torture the prisoners, but also to persuade them to confess to phony crimes and use their confessions for propaganda. But Rocky's captors clearly had no idea who they were dealing with. Four times he tried to escape, the first time crawling on his stomach because his leg injuries prevented him from walking. He insisted on giving no more information than required by the Geneva Convention; and cited the treaty, chapter and verse, over and over again.

The witnesses said the unbroken Versace sang "God Bless America" at the top of his lungs the night before he was executed on September 26, 1965. His remains have never been recovered.

Nominations starting in 1969 to award Versace the Medal of Honor failed; he received the Silver Star posthumously instead. Language added by Congress in the 2002 Defense Authorization Act ended the standoff and authorized the award of the nation's highest military decoration for combat valor.

On July 8, 2002, President Bush and the nation recognized Versace for his courage and defiance. Bush said the Army captain was "a soldier's soldier, a West Point graduate, a Green Beret who lived and breathed the code of duty, and honor and country."

"Last Tuesday would have been Rocky's 65th birthday," the president said. "So today, we award Rocky the first Medal of Honor given to an Army POW for actions taken during captivity in Southeast Asia.

"In his defiance and later his death," Bush said, "he set an example of extraordinary dedication that changed the lives of his fellow soldiers who saw it firsthand. His story echoes across the years, reminding us of liberty's high price and of the noble passion that caused one good man to pay that price in full."

Versace's brother Steve accepted the award during a White House ceremony witnessed by family members and many of the friends and supporters who had worked for years to have Versace's Silver Star upgraded.

Versace grew up in Norfolk and Alexandria, Virginia, and attended Gonzaga College High School. He graduated from West Point in 1959 and became a member of the Ranger Hall of Fame at Fort Benning, Georgia, and a member of Army Special Forces.

3.38 CPT Humbert Roque 'Rocky' Versace with orphan kids in Vietnam. Photo courtesy of www.washingtonian.com.

Bush said a fellow soldier recalled that Versace "was the kind of person you only had to know a few weeks before you felt like you'd known him for years. As an intelligence adviser in the Mekong Delta, he befriended many local citizens. He had that kind of personality," the president said.

"One of Rocky's superiors said that the term 'gung-ho' fit him perfectly," he noted. Others remember his strong sense of moral purpose and unbending belief in his principles. As his brother Steve once jokingly recalled, if he thought he was right, he was a pain in the neck. If he knew he was right, he was absolutely atrocious."

The Vietnamese tortured prisoners to persuade them to confess to phony crimes. Versace gave only his name, rank, and serial number as required by the Geneva Convention. "He cited the treaty chapter and verse over and over again," the president said. "He was fluent in English, French and Vietnamese and would tell his guards to go to hell in all three."

Versace knew what he was doing, Bush said. "By focusing his captors' anger on him, he made life a measure more tolerable for his fellow prisoners, who looked to him as a role model of principled resistance."

Unlike the Air Force, Navy and Marines, the Army had never awarded the Medal of Honor to a POW from Vietnam for actions during captivity. Pentagon officials said this would be the first time in the modern era that the medal has gone to an Army POW for heroism during captivity in any war.

Another prisoner held with Versace, James "Nick" Rowe, escaped in 1968 after five years of captivity. Rowe made an impassioned plea to President Richard M. Nixon that Versace receive the Medal of Honor, describing how his resistance deflected punishment from other captives and stiffened their will to resist.

The Army downgraded the award to a Silver Star. Rowe, embittered, kept talking about Versace until the day he died, assassinated by communist rebels in 1989 while serving as a U.S. military adviser to the Philippine armed forces.

This honor will focus attention on a group of POWs who have received little recognition. While the ordeals suffered by downed aviators who were imprisoned in North Vietnam, such as Sen. John McCain (R-AZ), are well documented, less has been said about the more than 200 prisoners, mostly infantry soldiers, held in horrendous jungle camps in South Vietnam.

Versace is "a perfect symbol for a lot of the guys in the South who were overlooked," said Stuart Rochester, a Department of Defense historian and co-author of a history on Vietnam POWs. "The guys in the South really took tougher punishment than the guys in the North."

The medal will come too late for Versace's mother, who died in 1999, never fully accepting that her son was gone.

"My mother, she never gave up," said one of Rocky's brothers, Dick Versace, president of the National Basketball Association's Vancouver Grizzlies. "Until she died, she thought he'd come walking out of those jungles any day."

Captain Versace's mother, Marie Teresa Rios Versace (Pen Name: Tere Rios) died on October 17, 1999 and was laid to rest in Arlington National Cemetery. Tere Rios was the author of the *Fifteenth Pelican* from which the TV Show, *The Flying Nun*, was based on.

Brother Steve Versace credits the Special Operations Command, Rocky's classmates from the West Point Class of 1959 and a group of Alexandrians called Friends of Rocky Versace for influencing the Medal of Honor decision.

The award ceremony was "the culmination of three years of intense work on their part," Steve Versace said. "These people have put their lives on hold to help with this."

28. Daniel Fernandez

Born: June 30, 1944 in Albuquerque, NM
Entered Service: Albuquerque, NM
Branch: U.S. Army
Rank: Specialist Fourth Class
Date and Place of Action: February 18, 1966 Cu Chi,
    Hau Nghia Province, Vietnam
Killed In Action: February 18, 1966

Note: The following is a reprint from the Tropic Lightning News. For details please see Bibliography.

Sp4c Daniel Fernandez was a rare young soldier who was both admired and respected by his contemporaries. He was quiet, competent, unselfish, cheerful, the type they choose as president of the senior class. When he died on February 18, 1966, he was a rifleman for Co. C, 1st Bn (mech), 5th infantry, and everyone who had known him mourned him.

He was not a career soldier. He used to joke with his friends that he was in the Army for three years because he had flipped a coin with his draft board, and lost. Actually he had enlisted for three years. While he was in the Army he wanted to be a good Soldier.

However, he spent hours at Scholfield Barrack in Hawaii pouring over infantry handbooks. His platoon leader, Lt. Joseph V. Dorso of Norwalk Connecticut called him the type of guy he could always count on no matter the situation. SSG David M. Thompson of Belair, New York, who used to go ski diving with him in Hawaii, said simply, "Danny was my best man."

The members of his squad, a tight little group of 15 men, one subsection of a huge division, looked upon him as a father confessor. Even those who were older called him "Uncle Dan," and went to him with their troubles and their complaints.

3.39 SPC Daniel Fernandez. Photo courtesy of the CMOHS.

Specialist Fernandez had been in Vietnam once before as a volunteer machine gunner on an Army helicopter. So it was it was not surprising that he was one of 16 men who volunteered for an Ambush patrol that was sent out of Cu Chi just after midnight on February 18, 1966.

About 7:00 a.m. as the patrol lay in wait in a jungle clearing for the Viet Cong. Specialist Joseph T. Benton of Hetford, N.C. spotted seven VC in the woods behind a burned out hut. He began firing his machine gun, then reached for a hand grenade. Before he could pull the pin out a Communist sniper killed him. Specialist Fernandez crawled to one side of the hut to cover the right flank, and Sp4 James P. McKeown of Willingsboro, N.J. moved into place on the other side.

Behind the hut PFC David R. Masingale of Fresno Calif., the platoons 18-year-old medic, bent over Specialist Benton. A moment later the Viet Cong opened up with machine guns, and a bullet smashed into the leg of Sgt. Ray E. Sue, knocking him to the ground.

Sp4 George E. Snodgrass of Pomton Lakes, N.J., who had come up with Sgt. Sue to get Specialist Benton out, hit the dirt. Now all five men were pinned down in an area no bigger than a living room. PFC Masingale treated Sgt. Sue, two flank men riddled the bushes and Specialist Snodgrass fired behind Specialist Benton's body.

At that instant, a grenade fired from a rifle by one of the guerrillas landed by Specialist Fernandez' leg. Without hesitation, so quickly that PFC Masingale is sure he didn't have time to consider the consequences of his action, Specialist Fernandez shouted, "move out" and threw himself onto the grenade.

When the others reached him after the explosion he was still conscious. Specialist Snodgrass helped make a litter from three shirts and bamboo poles and dragged Specialist Fernandez to an open area where a helicopter could land.

"It hurts," Fernandez said, "I can't breathe," Specialist Snodgrass a devoted Roman Catholic who often went to mass with Specialist Fernandez, told him to "make a good act of contrition," because no priest was present. "I will," Specialist Fernandez said, and shortly after died.

Citation:

For conspicuous gallantry and intrepidity at the risk of his life above and beyond the call of duty. Sp4c. Fernandez demonstrated indomitable courage when the patrol was ambushed by a Viet Cong rifle company and driven back by the intense enemy automatic weapons fire before it could evacuate an American soldier who had been wounded in the Viet Cong attack.

Sp4c. Fernandez, a sergeant and two other volunteers immediately fought their way through devastating fire and exploding grenades to reach the fallen soldier. Upon reaching their fallen comrade the sergeant was struck in the knee by machinegun fire and immobilized.

Sp4c. Fernandez took charge, rallied the left flank of his patrol and began to assist in the recovery of the wounded sergeant. While first aid was being administered to the wounded man, a sudden increase in the accuracy and intensity of enemy fire forced the volunteer group to take cover. As they did, an enemy grenade landed in the midst of the group, although some men did not see it.

Realizing there was no time for the wounded sergeant or the other men to protect themselves from the grenade blast, Sp4c. Fernandez vaulted over the wounded sergeant and threw himself on the grenade as it exploded, saving the lives of his four comrades at the sacrifice of his life.

Sp4c. Fernandez profound concern for his fellow soldiers, at the risk of his life above and beyond the call of duty are in the highest traditions of the U.S. Army and reflect great credit upon himself and the armed forces of his country.

---

29. Alfred Rascon

Born: 1945 in Chihuahua, Mexico
Branch: U.S. Army
Rank: Specialist Fourth Class
Date and Place of Action: March 16, 1966, Vietnam
Medal Issue Date: 1990

Note: The following was compiled from articles written by Sonya Ross and CNN. For details please see Bibliography.

His Army uniform aglow with ribbons and his eyes trained on the floor, Alfred Rascon seemed embarrassed to be at the White House in Feb. 2000, receiving lavish praise—much less America's highest military honor.

Rascon was a 21-year-old battalion medic with the U.S. Army's 173rd Airborne Brigade on March 16, 1966, when his unit was attacked by North Vietnamese troops. In the fighting that ensued, Rascon repeatedly ran into the line of fire—treating three men, saving two of them—despite being wounded himself.

Only after President Clinton draped the Medal of Honor around his neck did a smile play across Rascon's face. He had glanced at the men he covered with his body in a Vietnamese jungle 34 years ago to absorb grenade blasts and shrapnel that would have killed them and almost killed him.

"The honor is not really mine," Rascon said. "It ends up being those who were with me that day."

He asked the guys from his platoon to stand up, and they did, tears welling in their eyes. The former Army medic accepted his medal and saluted the commander in chief that presented it.

It was a glorious moment long denied to Rascon, 54, the son of Mexican immigrants, who joined the U.S. Army out of love for his adopted homeland. He was not yet a U.S. citizen when he went to Vietnam. But when, recovered from his wounds, he returned to Vietnam later in the war, it was as an American.

"This man gave everything he had, utterly and selflessly, to protect his platoon mates and the nation he was still not yet a citizen of," Clinton said. "You have honored us by your choice to become an American. Thank you for

3.40 SPC Alfred Rascon. Photo courtesy of the U.S. Army.

reminding us that being an American has nothing to do with the place of your birth, the color of your skin, the language of your parents or the way you worship God."

Rascon is not the first immigrant to receive the Medal of Honor. Immigrants received one in five of the 3,427 medals authorized since the honor was created in 1861. There were 166 living Medal of Honor recipients in 2000.

"I happened to have gotten shot, happened to have gotten hit by a hand grenade," Rascon said.

Pvt. Neil Haffey was one of those who credit the self-effacing Rascon with saving their lives. Already wounded, Rascon dove on Haffey as a grenade exploded just five feet away.

"I didn't even know he was gonna do it, and I just turned my head away because I didn't want to see death coming," Haffey said. "I thought I was dead, you know?"

Rascon's heroism turned the tide, rallying his battalion and saving his men, who were carried out of the field by helicopter. Rascon spent six months in Japan recovering from his wounds. Within days of his battlefield bravery, the men he saved recommended him for the Medal of Honor. The paperwork was lost, as Clinton said, "in a thicket of red tape," and Rascon received the Silver Star instead.

"But it wasn't what we had written up," one of the men, Ray Compton, told reporters Tuesday. "Neither one of us would be here today if it hadn't been for Al. Maybe not in his own eyes, but in our eyes, he's a hero. No doubt about it."

Compton said he wasn't aware that Rascon never received the honor until, in 1993, he asked Rascon what it was like to have the Medal of Honor. Rascon replied that he didn't know. Compton, fellow platoon members Neil Haffey and Larry Gibson and other veterans sought to correct the oversight.'

They received a pivotal assist from Rep. Lane Evans, D-Ill., an advocate for Vietnam veterans. The Pentagon would not reconsider Rascon's case because so much time had elapsed, so Evans gave a packet of information about it to President Clinton in 1987.

The Pentagon relented in May 1989, and Defense Secretary William Cohen approved the honor in November.

Clinton praised Rascon for his "long, patient wait for recognition" and the continual commitment to

3.41 SPC Alfred Rascon being presented the Medal of Honor by President Clinton in 1990. Photo courtesy of www.1stcavmedic.com.

serving his country that he has displayed since March 16, 1966.

That day, Rascon's platoon came under attack in a Vietnamese jungle. The young medic ignored orders to stay down and ran past flying bullets to get to Haffey, who was wounded. Rascon was shot in the hip and suffered several shrapnel wounds. A grenade exploded in his face.

Still, Rascon dragged Haffey to safety. Despite his wounds, he went out again to deliver ammunition to a machine gunner. He then covered Compton and Gibson with his body to protect them from harm as he treated their wounds.

"Through this extraordinary succession of courageous acts, he never gave a single thought to himself," Clinton said. "Except," he admits, "for the instant when the grenade exploded near his face," and he thought, "Oh God, my good looks are gone."

Rascon was so badly wounded that last rites were administered. He nevertheless recuperated at a U.S. Army hospital in Japan and was discharged in May 1966.

Rascon went on to be graduated from college and the U.S. Army's Infantry Officer Candidate School. A native of Chihuahua, Mexico, Rascon was naturalized an American in 1967 and returned to Vietnam for a second tour in the 1970s, this time as a military adviser.

Rascon, a civil servant since 1983, is inspector general of the Selective Service System in Arlington, Virginia. He lives in Laurel, Maryland, with his wife and two children.

"I have four daughters, and four beautiful grandchildren. I have a wonderful wife," Haffey said. "Those are all gifts from Doc."

30. Euripides Rubio

Born: March 1, 1938 in Ponce, Puerto Rico
Entered Service: Fort Buchanan, Puerto Rico
Branch: U.S. Army
Rank: Captain
Place of Action: November 8, 1966, Tay Ninh Province, Vietnam
Killed in Action: November 8, 1966

Note: The Puerto Rico Herald wrote this profile. For details please see Bibliography.

"Rubio's inspiration got us into the thickest fighting and most of us paid the price for it, willingly, just as he did," Enrique V. Pujals said. "None of us begrudged him anything and least of all the recognition for his example."

3.42 CPT Euripides Rubio. Photo courtesy of the CMOHS.

He was the second Puerto Rican to receive the Congressional Medal of Honor and one of 1,225 Puerto Ricans to have sacrificed their lives in the service of their country, up to that time.

Rubio enlisted in the U.S. Army at Fort Buchanan, Puerto Rico, and rose to the rank of captain in the 1st Battalion, of the 28th Infantry. Rubio's efforts during the Vietnam War reflect not only his dedication to his country, but his commitment to the men he commanded.

Captain Rubio was well liked by the men who served with him and [was] quite an inspiring leader.

Pujals remembers CPT Rubio as his company commander when he entered active duty in September of 1964. Pujals was one of the thirteen platoon leaders in Rubio's company when they volunteered for Vietnam in late July of 1965. Many of the company were ordered to Vietnam to fill the ranks of the first and second Battalions of the 7th U.S. Cavalry Regiment. Many were from Puerto Rico and of these "most ended up as casualties" in the Ia Drang Valley battles of November 1965, either killed or wounded.

"I felt very sad when I heard the news that [Rubio] had been killed," Pujals, one of the wounded from the battle, said. At the time of Rubio's death in Tay Ninh Province November 8, 1966, Pujals was stationed at Fort Buchanan, Puerto Rico, recovering after seven months in a hospital bed.

Citation:

For conspicuous gallantry and intrepidity in action at the risk of his life above and beyond the call of duty.

CPT Rubio, Infantry, was serving as communications officer, 1st Battalion, when a numerically superior enemy force launched a massive attack against the battalion defense position. Intense enemy machinegun fire raked the area while mortar rounds and rifle grenades exploded within the perimeter. Leaving the relative safety of his post, CPT Rubio received two serious wounds as he braved the withering fire to go to the area of most intense action where he distributed ammunition, re-established positions and rendered aid to the wounded.

Disregarding the painful wounds, he unhesitatingly assumed command when a rifle company commander was medically evacuated.

CPT Rubio was wounded a third time as he selflessly exposed himself to the devastating enemy fire to move among his men to encourage them to fight with renewed effort. While aiding the evacuation of wounded personnel, he noted that a smoke grenade, which was intended to mark the Viet Cong position for air strikes, had fallen dangerously close to the friendly lines.

CPT Rubio ran to reposition the grenade but was immediately struck to his knees by enemy fire. Despite his several wounds, CPT Rubio scooped up the grenade, ran through the deadly hail of fire to within 20 meters of the enemy position and hurled the already smoking grenade into the midst of the enemy before he fell for the final time.

Using the repositioned grenade as a marker, friendly air strikes were directed to destroy the hostile positions. CPT Rubio's singularly heroic act turned the tide of battle, and his extraordinary leadership and valor were a magnificent inspiration to his men. His remarkable bravery and selfless concern for his men are in keeping with the highest traditions of the military service and reflect great credit on CPT Rubio and the U.S. Army.

His death made a difference. The hostile position was destroyed because the friendly air strikes were able to use the repositioned grenade as a marker.

31. Maximo Yabes

Born: January 29, 1932 in Lodi, CA
Entered Service: Eugene, OR
Branch: U.S. Army
Rank: First Sergeant
Place of Action: February 26, 1967 near Phu Hoa Dong, Republic of Vietnam
Killed in Action: February 26, 1967

Note: Courtesy of the U.S. Congressional Medal of Honor Society.

Citation:

For conspicuous gallantry and intrepidity at the risk of his life above and beyond the call of duty.

1st Sgt. Yabes distinguished himself with Company A, which was providing security for a land clearing operation. Early in the morning the company suddenly came under intense automatic weapons and mortar fire followed by a battalion sized assault from three sides.

Penetrating the defensive perimeter the enemy advanced on the company command post bunker. The command post received increasingly heavy fire and was in danger of being overwhelmed. When several enemy grenades landed within the command post, 1st Sgt. Yabes shouted a warning and used his body as a shield to protect others in the bunker.

Although painfully wounded by numerous grenade fragments, and despite the vicious enemy fire on the bunker, he remained there to provide covering fire and enable the others in the command group to relocate. When the command group had reached a new position, 1st Sgt. Yabes moved

3.43 1SG Maximo Yabes.
Photo courtesy of the U.S. Army.

through a withering hail of enemy fire to another bunker 50 meters away.

There he secured a grenade launcher from a fallen comrade and fired point blank into the attacking Viet Cong stopping further penetration of the perimeter. Noting two wounded men helpless in the fire swept area, he moved them to a safer position where they could be given medical treatment.

He resumed his accurate and effective fire killing several enemy soldiers and forcing others to withdraw from the vicinity of the command post. As the battle continued, he observed an enemy machinegun within the perimeter, which threatened the whole position. On his own, he dashed across the exposed area, assaulted the machinegun, killed the crew, destroyed the weapon, and fell mortally wounded.

First Sgt. Yabes' valiant and selfless actions saved the lives of many of his fellow soldiers and inspired his comrades to effectively repel the enemy assault. His indomitable fighting spirit, extraordinary courage and intrepidity at the cost of his life are in the highest military traditions and reflect great credit upon himself and the armed forces of his country.

32. Carlos James Lozada

Born: September 6, 1946 in Caguas, Puerto Rico
Entered Service: New York, N.Y.
Branch: U.S. Army
Rank: Private First Class
Date and Place of Action: November 20, 1967 Dak To, Republic of Vietnam
Killed in Action: November 20, 1967

Note: Courtesy of the U.S. Congressional Medal of Honor Society.

Citation:

For conspicuous gallantry and intrepidity in action at the risk of his life above and beyond the call of duty.

Pfc Lozada, U.S. Army, distinguished himself at the risk of his life above and beyond the call of duty in the battle of Dak To. While serving as a machine gunner with 1st platoon, Company A, Pfc. Lozada was part of a 4-man early warning outpost, located 35 meters from his company's lines.

At 1400 hours, a North Vietnamese Army company rapidly approached the outpost along a well-defined trail. Pfc. Lozada alerted his comrades and commenced firing at the enemy who were within 10 meters of the outpost. His heavy and accurate machinegun fire killed at least 20 North Vietnamese soldiers and completely disrupted their initial attack.

Pfc Lozada remained in an exposed position and continued to pour deadly fire upon the enemy despite the urgent pleas of his comrades to withdraw. The enemy continued their assault, attempting to envelop the outpost. At the same time, enemy forces launched a heavy attack on the forward west flank of Company A with the intent to cut them off from their battalion. Company A was given the order to withdraw.

Pfc Lozada apparently realized that if he abandoned his position there would be nothing to hold back the surging North Vietnamese soldiers and that the entire company withdrawal would be jeopardized. He called for his comrades to move back and that he would stay and provide cover for them. He made this decision realizing that the enemy was converging on three sides of his position and only meters away, and a delay in withdrawal meant almost certain death.

Pfc Lozada continued to deliver a heavy, accurate volume of suppressive fire against the enemy until he was mortally wounded and had to be carried during the withdrawal. His heroic deed served as an example and an inspiration to his comrades throughout the ensuing four-day battle.

3.44 PFC Carlos James Lozada. Photo courtesy of the U.S. Army.

Pfc Lozada's actions are in the highest traditions of the U.S. Army and reflect great credit upon himself, his unit, and the U.S. Army.

A park at Fort Campbell is named for this division hero.

---

33. Alfredo (Freddy) Cantu Gonzalez

Born: May 23, 1946 in Edinburg, TX
Entered Service: San Antonio on June 3, 1965
Branch: U.S. Marine Corps
Rank: Sergeant
Date and Place of Action: February 4, 1968 near the village of Lang Van Lrong
Killed in Action: February 4, 1968

Note: The following text is from John Flores and the Handbook of Texas Online. For details please see Bibliography.

Alfredo (Freddy) Cantu Gonzalez was the son of Andres Cantu and Dolia Gonzalez. He graduated in 1965 from Edinburg High School, where he played football.

He enlisted in the United States Marine Corps Reserve at San Antonio on June 3, 1965, under his mother's name, Gonzalez. He enlisted in the regular Marines on July 6, 1965.

Nearly three decades after his death in Hue City, Vietnam, Marine Sergeant Alfredo "Freddy" Gonzalez resumed his battle watch October 12, 1996 at Naval Station Ingleside, near Corpus Christi, Texas. On that day, the Navy commissioned the *U.S.S. Gonzalez*, a guided-missile destroyer. It is the Navy's most advanced warship and the first modern destroyer named for a Mexican American.

3.45 USS Gonzalez DDG-66. Photo courtesy of the U.S. Navy.

Born May 23, 1946, in Edinburg, Texas, Freddy enlisted in the Marine Corps soon after his graduation from high school. He was killed February 4, 1968, at the St. Joan of Arc Catholic Church in Hue City, Vietnam, while serving his second tour of duty. The next year, Vice President Spiro T. Agnew awarded the Medal of Honor to Sergeant Gonzalez for the actions in Hue City that saved many of his fellow Marines. Dolia, his mom, was there to receive the medal for her son, who was buried in Edinburg's Hillcrest Memorial Cemetery the day after the Hue City fighting ended in a Marine victory. He was the only Marine in the Tet Offensive combat to receive the award.

Dolia still works as a waitress and is now employed at the old Echo Hotel in Edinburg. It was where Freddy and his friends had their high school proms and other parties. Today it is the central meeting place for city and county officials and the many Winter Texans who live in the Rio Grande Valley during the cold months.

"I never had any problems with him when he was growing up," Dolia says fondly. "I'd even tell him to go out with his friends when he was in high school, but a lot of times he'd say no…that he wanted to spend time with me. You know, looking back, I think Freddy knew he wouldn't live a long time, so he wanted to spend time with me while he could."

She recounts stories of Freddy when he was a boy, working in the South Texas fields with her during the summertime. "One time, we were all working in a cotton field…me and my sister Jo, and Freddy. He would always carry a hoe and use it to kill snakes. He found a rattlesnake up ahead of Jo, and after he killed it he coiled it up again like it was alive," she says, laughing. "And when Jo saw it, she screamed and jumped up about two feet in the air and tried to run off. We all had a good laugh about that."

Anybody who knew Freddy remembers him, whether it was a classmate, friend, football coach, or commanding officer, and most of them attended the commissioning of the U.S.S. Gonzalez.

Torn between his conscience and his country, Freddy had to make a battlefield decision on the morning of February 4, 1968, at the St. Joan of Arc Catholic Church in Hue City, Vietnam. Few

American troops were in the city–the old imperial and cultural capitol of Vietnam–when the communists broke a cease-fire during Tet, the Vietnamese New Year. North Vietnamese troops, many dressed as civilians, infiltrated the city.

Freddy was serving as platoon sergeant with Company A, 1st Battalion, 1st Marines. His platoon was ambushed on its way into Hue in the Van Lrong Village. He maneuvered the platoon to safety, and then knocked out enemy bunkers with hand grenades. He then

3.46 Sgt Alfredo 'Freddy' Cantu Gonzalez. Photo courtesy of SSG David Baca.

took cover behind a nearby American armored vehicle and spotted a wounded Marine lying in the road ahead.

Colonel Marcus Gravel, commanding officer of the Marine division, detailed Freddy's actions in the 1975 dedication of an Edinburg elementary school named for him: "Without hesitation, he leaped from the tank and dashed into the street and returned with his injured comrade. Then, as the column moved against the enemy force, we were met by withering machine gun fire…again Freddy left his place of safety and assaulted the bunker, silencing it with hand grenades… Disregarding his own wounds, he told the corpsman who attempted to treat him to take care of the others."

Larry Lewis, from Chattanooga, Tennessee, was a rifleman in the platoon. He had come to Vietnam for the first time in September 1967 and had been under Freddy's command since that time. He was only a few feet away from Freddy when he was killed. "Our battalion had gotten split up. The resistance was just tremendous…demolition crews, mortar fire, rocket fire, machine guns, snipers," says Lewis. "By the time we got to Hue, Sergeant G at that time was probably one of the highest ranking [Marines]. Most of the officers were either killed or wounded."

Lewis was only a few feet away from Freddy in the schoolyard of the church. The platoon of about

35 men was pinned down, and Freddy told them to keep down out of the line of fire while he went on ahead to try to find a way to move the men. Lewis followed him, against orders, to give him cover. He watched Freddy grab an armload of small anti-tank rockets and enter the area of the church where the North Vietnamese Army were most heavily entrenched. Freddy began firing the rockets at the enemy troops. After hitting all the visible positions and silencing fire, Lewis says he thought Freddy had neutralized all the enemy positions. One last rocket came out of the rubble, Lewis says.

"I was on the second floor of the building. He was directly below me. I saw the rocket hit him. He took a direct hit. It was hard to believe that he was hit. I went down there and laid him on a door. His heart was still beating when I got him, but he died pretty soon after that," Lewis says."

Freddy died beside the bullet-riddled statue of Saint Joan of Arc.

"Prior to that, he was almost like Houdini. It seemed like he was everywhere all at the same time. I remember that he carried a twelve-gauge shotgun, a big bag of grenades, and a forty-five pistol… He was always there in the front, never in the back, waiting. He was always there for us," Lewis says.

Because he took out so many enemy positions with the hand grenades and rockets, Freddy saved the lives of the men in his platoon. What he did that day is indelibly etched in each man's mind.

---

34. Jay R. Vargas

Born: July 29, 1940 in Winslow, AZ
Entered Service: Winslow, AZ
Branch: U.S. Marine Corps
Rank: Captain
Date and Place of Action: April 30 to May 2, 1968
　　Dai Do, Republic of Vietnam
Medal Issue Date: May 1970

The actual recorded recipient is Vargas, M. Sando. Before Jay Vargas could receive his honor, his mother passed away. At his request, her name was engraved on the medal and added to the rolls instead of his.

Note: The following information is from the official biography provided by the California Department of Veterans Affairs. For details please see Bibliography.

On June 1, 1993, California Governor Pete Wilson named fellow Marine, Colonel Jay Vargas, Secretary of the California Department of Veterans Affairs. Shortly after assuming his position he directed that a new motto, "PUTTING VETERANS FIRST," be adopted by the Department, which reflects the character of his leadership. By an Executive Order signed September 23, 1994, Governor Pete Wilson made the California Department of Veterans Affairs a Cabinet level department.

3.47 CPT Jay R. Vargas.
Photo courtesy of the USMC.

Jay Vargas is the son of immigrants, an Italian mother and Hispanic father, who came to the United States in 1917. His family taught him that the price of success is hard work and the cost of freedom is personal sacrifice. Each of the four sons wore the uniform of their country in time of war; brothers Angelo at Iwo Jima and Frank at Okinawa in World War II, brother Joseph in Korea and Jay in Vietnam.

Before joining the Marines, Vargas attended Arizona State University on an academic and athletic scholarship, and graduated with the degree of Bachelor of Science in Education. He continued his education while on active duty, and received a Master of Arts in Education degree with honors from the United States International University at San Diego. He is also a graduate of the Amphibious Warfare School, The Marine Corps Command and Staff College, and the National War College.

Secretary Vargas brings to his position a "get it done–but do it together" style that has been honed by his Marine Corps experience. He commanded and led Marines at every level, from a rifle platoon to an infantry regiment.

His final tour of duty as a Marine officer found him on the staff of the Commander, U.S. Forces,

Pacific, where he served as Force Marine. From staff boardrooms to the battlefield, in peacetime and in combat, Vargas has demonstrated his ability to lead through the use of sound judgment and a steady hand.

Of his many accomplishments as a Marine officer, the most widely publicized was achieved in combat. In the spring of 1968, while serving in the Republic of Vietnam, Vargas' unit engaged in fierce combat with the enemy at the village of Dai Do.

During the battle, he was able to free one of his platoons, pinned down by heavy fire, by personally destroying three enemy machine gun positions. Vargas was then able to carry to safety his seriously wounded battalion commander and save seven other Marines. His actions left 15 of the enemy dead and caused him to sustain wounds at three different times. He refused to leave the field of battle until the severity of his injuries compelled him to do so. It was for his actions at Dai Do that, in a May 1970 ceremony at The White House, President Richard M. Nixon presented Colonel Vargas with our nation's highest decoration for military valor, The Congressional Medal of Honor.

In addition to the Medal of Honor, Jay Vargas' personal decorations include: the Silver Star; the Purple Heart with four Gold Stars: the Combat Action Ribbon; the Meritorious Service Medal; and the Vietnamese Gallantry Cross with Silver Star and Palm.

Secretary Vargas has received the National Collegiate Athletic Association's (NCAA) Commemorative Plaque for excelling in collegiate athletics and having made a significant contribution to his country. He has also been awarded The American Academy of Achievement's "Gold Plate Award." This prestigious award is given to national leaders, drawn from all professional fields, which have made significant contributions to their country.

Secretary Vargas and his wife of more than thirty years, Dottie, are the proud parents of three grown daughters, Kris, Julie, and Gina.

Colonel Jay R. Vargas retired in July 1992 after more than 30 years service in the Marine Corps.

35. Roy Benavidez

Born: April 24, 1946 in Palestine, TX
Entered Service: June 1955 Houston, TX
Branch: U.S. Army
Rank: Master Sergeant
Date and Place of Action: May 2, 1968 West of Loc Ninh, Viet Vam
Medal Issue Date: February 24, 1981
Died: November 29, 1998

Note: The following is a compilation of articles written by Barry Halvorson, Richard Goldstein, Sig Christenson, and the Psychological Operations website. For details please see Bibliography.

Born in south Texas, the son of a sharecropper, Benavidez was orphaned as a youngster. He went to live with an uncle, but dropped out of middle school because he was needed to pick sugar beets and cotton. He joined the Army at 19, went to airborne school, and then was injured by a land mine in South Vietnam in 1964. Doctors feared he would never walk again, but he recovered and became a Green Beret. He was on his second Vietnam tour when he carried out his rescue mission.

Loyalty and a strong sense of duty drove Roy P. Benavidez to save a Special Forces unit cut down in a vicious firefight, even after he was clubbed, stabbed, and shot more times than he could recall.

As the medevac chopper landed the wounded were examined one by one. Staff Sergeant Benavidez could only hear what was going on around him. He had more than thirty-seven puncture wounds. His intestines were exposed. He could not see, his eyes

3.48 MSG Roy Benavidez.
Photo courtesy of the U.S. Army.

were caked in blood and he was unable to open them. Neither could he speak, his jaw broken,

3.49 MSG Roy Benavidez having just been presented the Medal of Honor by President Ronald Reagan on Feb. 24, 1981. Photo courtesy of the U.S. Dept. of Defense.

clubbed by a North Vietnamese rifle. But he knew what was happening, and it was the scariest moment of his life, even more so than the earlier events of the day.

He lay in a body bag, bathed in his own blood. Jerry Cottingham, a friend screamed "That's Benavidez! Get a doc." When the doctor arrived he placed his hand on Roy's chest to feel for a heartbeat. He pronounced him dead. The physician shook his head. "There's nothing I can do for him." As the doctor bent over to zip up the body bag, Benavidez did the only thing he could think of to let the doctor know that he was alive. He spit in the doctor's face. The surprised doctor reversed Roy's condition from dead to, "He won't make it, but we'll try."

The 32-year-old son of a Texas sharecropper had just performed for six hours one of the most remarkable feats of the Vietnam War. Benavidez, part Yaqui Indian and part Mexican, was a seventh-grade dropout and an orphan who grew up taunted by the term 'dumb Mexican,' in southeast Texas. But, as Ronald Reagan noted, "if the story of what he accomplished was made into a movie, no one would believe it really happened."

Roy Benavidez' ordeal began at Loc Ninh, a Green Beret outpost near the Cambodian border. It

was 1:30 p.m., May 2, 1968. A chaplain was holding a prayer service around a jeep for the sergeant and several other soldiers. Suddenly, shouts rang out from a nearby short-wave radio. "Get us out of here!" someone screamed. "For God's sake, get us out!"

A 12-man team consisting of Sergeant First Class Leroy Wright, Staff Sergeant Lloyd "Frenchie" Mousseau, Specialist Four Brian O'Connor and nine Nung tribesmen monitoring enemy troop movements in the jungle had found itself surrounded by a North Vietnamese army battalion. Without orders, Benavidez volunteered so quickly that he didn't even bring his M-16 when he dashed for the helicopter preparing for a rescue attempt. The sole weapon he carried was a bowie knife on his belt. "I'm coming with you," he told the three crewmembers.

Airborne, they spotted the soldiers in a tight circle. A few hundred enemy troops surrounded them in the jungle, some within 25 yards of the Americans' position. The chopper dropped low, ran into withering fire and quickly retreated. Spotting a small clearing 75 yards away, Benavidez told the pilot, "Over there, over there."

The helicopter reached the clearing and hovered 10 feet off the ground. Benavidez made the sign of the cross, jumped out carrying a medic bag and began running the 75 yards towards the trapped men. Almost immediately, an AK-47 slug hit Benavidez in his right leg. He stumbled and fell, but got back up convincing himself that he'd only snagged a thorn bush and kept running to the brush pile where Wright's men lay. An exploding hand grenade knocked Roy down and ripped his face with shrapnel. He shouted prayers, got up again and staggered to the men.

Four of the soldiers were dead, the other eight wounded and pinned down in two groups. Benavidez bound their wounds, injected morphine and, ignoring NVA bullets and grenades, passed around ammunition that he had taken from several bodies and armed himself with an AK.

Then Benavidez directed air strikes and called for the Huey helicopter to a landing near one group. While calling in support he was shot again in the right thigh, his second gunshot wound.

He dragged the dead and wounded aboard. The chopper lifted a few feet off the ground and moved toward the second group, with Benavidez running beneath it, firing a rifle he had picked up. He spotted the body of the team leader Sergeant First Class Wright. Ordering the other soldiers to crawl toward the chopper, he retrieved a pouch dangling from the dead man's neck; in the pouch were classified papers with radio codes and call signs. As he shoved the papers into his shirt, a bullet struck his stomach and a grenade shattered his back. The helicopter, barely off the ground, suddenly crashed, its pilot shot dead.

Coughing blood, Benavidez made his way to the Huey and pulled the wounded from the wreckage, forming a small perimeter. As he passed out ammunition taken from the dead, the air support he had earlier radioed for arrived. Jets and helicopter gunships strafed threatening enemy soldiers while Benavidez tended the wounded. "Are you hurt bad, Sarge?" one soldier asked. "Hell, no,"

said Benavidez, about to collapse from blood loss. "I've been hit so many times I don't give a damn no more."

While mortar shells burst everywhere, Benavidez called in Phantoms "danger close." Enemy fire raked the perimeter. Several of the wounded were hit again, including Benavidez. By this time he had blood streaming down his face, blinding him. Still he called in air strikes, adjusting their targets by sound. Several times, pilots thought he was dead, but then his voice would come back on the radio, calling for closer strikes. Throughout the fighting, Benavidez, a devout Catholic, made the sign of the cross so many times; his arms "were going like an airplane prop." But he never gave into fear.

Finally, a helicopter landed. "Pray and move out," Benavidez told the men as he helped each one aboard. As he carried a seriously wounded Frenchie Mousseau over his shoulder a fallen NVA soldier stood up, swung his rifle and clubbed Benavidez in the head. Benavidez fell, rolled over

3.50 Soldiers preparing to be evacuated by helicopter. U.S. 1st Cavalrymen wounded in the battle for control of the vital A Shau Valley. Similar situation as happened to MSG Benavidez. Photo courtesy of www.corbis.com.

and got up just as the soldier lunged forward with his bayonet. Benavidez grabbed it, slashing his right hand, and pulled his attacker toward him. With his left hand, he drew his own bowie knife and stabbed the NVA but not before the bayonet poked completely through his left forearm.

As Benavidez dragged Mousseau to the chopper, he saw two more NVA materialize out of the jungle. He snatched a fallen AK-47 rifle and shot both. Benavidez made one more trip to the clearing and came back with a Vietnamese interpreter. Only then did the sergeant let the others pull him aboard the helicopter.

Blood dripped from the door as the chopper lumbered into the air. Benavidez was holding in his intestines with his hand. Bleeding almost into unconsciousness, Benavidez lay against the badly wounded Mousseau and held his hand. Just before they landed at the Medevac hospital, "I felt his fingers dig into my palm," Benavidez recalled, "his arm twitching and jumping as if electric current was pouring through his body into mine."

At Loc Ninh, Benavidez was so immobile they placed him with the dead. Even after he spit in the

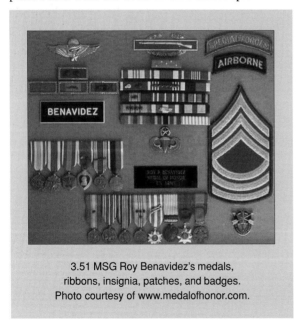

3.51 MSG Roy Benavidez's medals, ribbons, insignia, patches, and badges. Photo courtesy of www.medalofhonor.com.

doctor's face and was taken from the body bag, Benavidez was considered a goner.

Benavidez spent almost a year in hospitals to recover from his injuries. He had seven major gunshot wounds; a bayonet had slashed holes and both arms. Benavidez had shrapnel in his head, scalp, shoulder, buttocks, feet, and legs. His right lung was destroyed. He had injuries to his mouth and back of his head from being clubbed with a rifle butt. One of the AK-47 bullets had entered his back exiting just beneath his heart. He had won the battle and lived. When told his one man battle was awesome and extraordinary, Benavidez replied: *"No, that's duty."*

Wright and Mousseau were each awarded the Distinguish Service Cross posthumously. Although Master Sergeant Benavidez' commander felt that he deserved the Congressional Medal of Honor for his valor in saving eight lives, he put Roy in for the Distinguished Service Cross. The process for awarding a Medal of Honor would have taken much longer, and he was sure Benavidez would die before he got it.

The recommendation for the Distinguish Service Cross was rushed through approval channels and Master Sergeant Benavidez was presented the award by General William C. Westmoreland while he was recovering from his wounds at Fort Sam Houston Hospital in San Antonio.

Years later, his former commander learned that Benavidez had survived the war. The officer also learned more details of the sergeant's mission and concluded that Benavidez merited a higher honor. Years of red tape followed until finally on February 24, 1981, President Reagan told White House reporters, "You are going to hear something you would not believe if it were a script." Reagan then read Roy Benavidez' Citation for the Congressional Medal of Honor.

Benavidez however, did not regard himself as a hero. He said of his actions. *"The real heroes are the ones who gave their lives for their country, I don't like to be called a hero. I just did what I was trained to do."*

Upon retirement in 1976 Master Sergeant Benavidez lived in El Campo, Texas, with his wife, Lala, and three children, Noël, Yvette and Denise.

Shortly before Memorial Day 1983, Benavidez came forward to say that the Social Security Administration planned to cut off disability payments he had been receiving since he retired from the Army as a master sergeant. He still had two pieces

3.52 MSG Roy Benavidez.
Photo courtesy of the U.S. Army.

of shrapnel in his heart and a punctured lung and was in constant pain from his wounds.

The government, as part of a cost-cutting review that had led to the termination of disability assistance to 350,000 people over the preceding two years, had decided that Benavidez could find employment.

"It seems like they want to open up your wounds and pour a little salt in," Benavidez said. "I don't like to use my Medal of Honor for political purposes or personal gain, but if they can do this to me, what will they do to all the others?"

A White House spokesman said that Reagan was "personally concerned" about Benavidez' situation, and 10 days later Health and Human Services Secretary Margaret Heckler said the disability reviews would become more "humane and compassionate."

Soon afterward, wearing his Medal of Honor, Benavidez told the House Select Committee on Aging that "the administration that put this medal around my neck is curtailing my benefits."

Benavidez appealed the termination of assistance to an administrative law judge, who ruled in July 1983 that he should continue receiving payments.

Fifteen years later, the proud and feisty Benavidez couldn't fend off a plethora of health problems that had hobbled him in recent months.

Master Sergeant Roy Benavidez died on November 29, 1998. More than 1,500 people attended his funeral in San Antonio to say goodbye. He is buried in the shade of a live oak tree at the Fort Sam Houston National Cemetery, a fitting final resting place for someone who gave so much of himself to this great nation.

"He went as a soldier," said retired Army Master Sgt. Ben Guerrero, who was with family members at Benavidez' side when he died. "He went the way the good Lord wanted to take him."

In addition to his heroic actions in combat, he will also be remembered for his work with youths. He spoke at schools and colleges and even runaway shelters. He promoted patriotism, staying-in school, encouraged continuing education, and drug free programs for students.

Saying, "quitters never win and winners never quit," Benavidez said in his last interview that he "wanted to recover so he could continue working as a motivational speaker."

Vision Quest, an organization known for working with problem youths, named a youth boot camp 'Fort Roy P. Benavidez' in Uvalde, Texas after him. The naming of the Roy P. Benavidez Elementary School in Houston, Texas further recognized Master Sergeant Benavidez.

In August 1999, the U.S. Army dedicated the $14 million Master Sergeant Roy P. Benavidez Special Operations Logistics Complex at Fort Bragg, NC.

On September 14, 2000, U.S. Navy Secretary Richard Danzig announced that the U.S. Navy planned to name a new ship after Master Sergeant Roy P. Benavidez. The ship was christened in 2001, as the *USNS Benavidez*. It is the seventh in a class of large, medium speed roll-on/roll-off sealift ships.

Of all the honors bestowed upon Medal of Honor recipient Master Sgt. Roy Benavidez, his children said the naming of a U.S. Navy supply ship after him is by far the most appropriate and the one that would have given their father the most satisfaction.

"It is ironic, I guess, that the U.S. Navy would be honoring a career Army veteran," said his daughter, Yvette Garcia. "But when you see the grand vessel it is and the name 'Benavidez' on it, things come full circle. We are very proud of our father and this is just one more of those honors. And because it will be shipping goods that are

3.53 USNS Benavidez. Photo courtesy of the U.S. Navy.

needed by soldiers, I think this is the one honor that he would have been truly pleased with."

And while they take the loading of each ship seriously, John Roby, the Director of logistics for the Port of Beaumont, said there was a special feeling about preparing the Benavidez for its first trip.

"We were aware of the fact that Sgt. Benavidez was from Texas, and we know his story here," he said.

"It is something we don't encounter very often. We're loading ships all the time and know that the names on the ships are important, but don't really recognize them. So when we have one we do recognize and it has a Texas connection, we take extra pride in the work being done."

There are also elementary schools named after Sgt. Benavidez in San Antonio and Houston, a city park in Colorado Springs, Colo., and even a GI Joe action figure named after him. The action figure has since become a serious collectable.

"When I was growing up, I had Star Wars figures instead of GI Joe's," son Noel said. "But it was exciting to have one named for Dad. It was the only one that has been done for a Hispanic, which we take great pride in."

Yvette added, "Having a Navy vessel named for him was an amazing thing. It fits the kind of person he was. He would have probably laughed at the GI Joe."

Benavidez' children said he tended to downplay his role in the incident during his life. "Father never wanted to take the credit," Yvette said. "He wanted the others to be recognized, in particular those that didn't make it back."

In addition to those other reminders, Benavidez' immediate family has also established a foundation named for their father. The foundation presents two graduating seniors from El Campo High School with a $250 scholarship each year. But the eventual goal of the foundation is much more.

"We would like to be able to sponsor after-school programs across the country that will focus on good academics, staying away from drugs and alcohol and avoiding gangs," son Noel said. "He always emphasized education. He didn't have the opportunity to go to college as a young man and so he went into the military. But he knew that education was going to be the key to success for the future."

His daughter Yvette added, "the idea for the foundation came from her father and the attention it brought him.

"Immediately after he received the medal, every time he turned around someone was asking for him as a speaker," she said.

"President Reagan wanted him to help spread the message for students to stay off drugs and stay in school. He said that after a year people would begin to forget and things would go back to normal."

Ever since then he's not been forgotten and will never be forgotten. He has become an American icon. Each of the scholarship recipients are given a copy of his Medal of Honor citation and a photo of him, so they know the legacy they have to live up to, and will pass that along. No, he is never going to be forgotten.

36. Hector Santiago-Colon

Born: December 20, 1942 in Salinas, Puerto Rico
Entered Service: New York, NY
Branch: U.S. Army
Rank: Specialist 4th Class
Date and Place of Action: June 28, 1968 Quang Tri Province, Republic of Vietnam
Killed in Action: June 28, 1968

Note: Courtesy of the U.S. Congressional Medal of Honor Society.

Citation:

For conspicuous gallantry and intrepidity in action at the risk of his life above and beyond the call of duty. Sp4c Santiago-Colon distinguished at the cost of his life while serving as a gunner in the mortar platoon of Company B.

While serving as a perimeter sentry, Sp4c Santiago Colon heard distinct movement in the heavily wooded area to his front and flanks. Immediately he alerted his fellow sentries in the area to move to their foxholes and remain alert for any enemy probing forces.

From the wooded area around his position heavy enemy automatic weapons and small-arms

fire suddenly broke out, but extreme darkness rendered difficult the precise location and identification of the hostile force. Only the muzzle flashes from enemy weapons indicated their position.

Sp4c Santiago-Colon and the other members of his position immediately began to repel the attackers, utilizing hand grenades, antipersonnel mines, and small-arms fire. Due to the heavy volume of enemy fire and exploding grenades around them, a North Vietnamese soldier was able to crawl, undetected, to their position.

Suddenly, the enemy soldier lobbed a hand grenade into Sp4c. Santiago-Colon's foxhole. Realizing that there was no time to throw the grenade out of his position, Santiago-Colon retrieved the grenade, tucked it in to his stomach and, turning away from his comrades, absorbed the full impact of the blast.

His heroic self-sacrifice saved the lives of those who occupied the foxhole with him, and provided them with the inspiration to continue fighting until they had forced the enemy to retreat from the perimeter. By his gallantry at the cost of his life and in the highest traditions of the military service, Sp4c Santiago-colon has reflected great credit upon himself, his unit, and the U.S. Army.

3.54 SPC Hector Santiago-Colon.
Photo courtesy of the U.S. Army.

37. Jose Francisco Jimenez

Born: March 20, 1946 in Mexico City, Mexico
Entered Service: Phoenix, AZ
Branch: U.S. Marine Corps
Rank: Lance Corporal
Date and Place of Action: August 28, 1969 Quang Nam Province, Republic of Vietnam
Killed in Action: August 28, 1969

Note: The USMC History and Museums Division provided the following information. For details please see Bibliography.

Jose Francisco Jimenez attended Bonito Juarez School and Jose Maria Morelos School in Morelia, Mexico. He graduated from Santa Cruz Valley Union High School, Eloy, Arizona, in June 1968. Enlisting in the U.S. Marine Corps Reserve at Phoenix, Arizona, on June 7, 1968, he was discharged to enlist in the regular Marine Corps, August 12, 1968.

Private Jimenez completed recruit training with the 1st Recruit Training Battalion at the Marine Corps Recruit Depot, San Diego, California, in October 1968. He was promoted to private first class, October 1, 1968.

3.55 LCpl Jose Francisco Jimenez.
Photo courtesy of the USMC.

His medals and decorations include: the Medal of Honor, the Purple Heart, the National Defense Service Medal, the Vietnam Service Medal with two bronze stars, the Republic of Vietnam Cross of Gallantry with Palm, and the Republic of Vietnam Campaign Medal.

Lance Corporal Jimenez was survived by his mother, Mrs. Basilia J. Chagoll of Eloy, Arizona, and one sister.

Citation:

For conspicuous gallantry and intrepidity at the risk of his life above and beyond the call of duty while serving as a fire team leader with Company K, in operations against the enemy.

LCpl Jimenez' unit came under heavy attack by North Vietnamese soldiers concealed in well-camouflaged emplacements. LCpl Jimenez reacted by seizing the initiative and plunging forward toward the enemy positions.

He personally destroyed several enemy personnel and silenced an antiaircraft weapon. Shouting encouragement to his companions, LCpl Jimenez continued his aggressive forward movement. He slowly maneuvered to within 10 feet of hostile soldiers who were firing automatic weapons from a trench and, in the face of vicious enemy fire, destroyed the position.

Although he was by now the target of concentrated fire from hostile gunners intent upon halting his assault, LCpl. Jimenez continued to press forward. As he moved to attack another enemy soldier, he was mortally wounded.

LCpl Jimenez' indomitable courage, aggressive fighting spirit, and unfaltering devotion to duty upheld the highest traditions of the Marine Corps and of the U.S. Naval Service.

38. Ralph E. Dias

Born: July 15, 1950 in Indiana, PA
Entered Service: October 9, 1967, in Pittsburgh, PA
Branch: U.S. Marine Corps
Rank: Private First Class
Date and Place of Action: November 12, 1969 Quang Nam Province
Killed in Action: November 12, 1969

Note: The USMC History and Museums Division provided the following information. For details please see Bibliography.

Ralph Ellis Dias graduated from elementary school in 1965, and then attended Elderton Joint High School in Shelocta, Pennsylvania, for two years.

He enlisted in the U.S. Marine Corps, October 9, 1967, at Pittsburgh, Pennsylvania, and underwent recruit training with the 2nd Recruit Training Battalion, Marine Corps Recruit Depot, Parris Island, South Carolina. Upon completion of recruit training in December, he was transferred to the 2nd Infantry Training Battalion, 1st Infantry Training Regiment, Camp Lejeune, North Carolina, for special infantry training.

3.56 PFC Ralph E. Dias.
Photo courtesy of the USMC.

In February 1968, he was ordered to the Marine Corps Base, Camp Pendleton, California, for duty with Company B, 1st Battalion, 28th Marines, 5th Marine Division. In April 1969, he was ordered to the Republic of Vietnam for duty as a rifleman with Company D, 1st Battalion, 7th Marines, 1st Marine Division, Fleet Marine Force.

His medals and decorations include: the Medal of Honor, the Purple Heart, the Combat Action Ribbon, the Meritorious Unit Commendation with one bronze star, the National Defense Service Medal, the Vietnam Service Medal with three bronze stars, the Republic of Vietnam Meritorious Unit Commendation (Gallantry Cross Color) with palm and frame, the Republic of Vietnam Meritorious Unit Commendation (Civil Action Medal, First Class Color) with palm and frame, and the Republic of Vietnam Campaign Medal with device.

Citation:

For conspicuous gallantry and intrepidity at the risk of his life above and beyond the call of duty, while serving as a Rifleman with Company D, First Battalion, Seventh Marines, First Marine Division in the Republic of Vietnam on 12 November 1969.

As a member of a reaction force which was pinned down by enemy fire while assisting a platoon in the same circumstance, Private First Class Dias, observing that both units were sustaining casualties, initiated an aggressive assault against an enemy machine gun bunker which was the principal source of hostile fire.

Severely wounded by enemy snipers while charging across the open area, he pulled himself to the shelter of a nearby rock. Braving enemy fire for a second time, PFC Dias was again wounded. Unable to walk, he crawled fifteen meters to the protection of a rock located near his objective and, repeatedly exposing himself to intense hostile fire, unsuccessfully threw several hand grenades at the machine gun emplacement.

Still determined to destroy the emplacement, PFC Dias again moved into the open and was wounded a third time by sniper fire. As he threw a last grenade, which destroyed the enemy position, he was mortally wounded by another enemy round.

PFC Dias' indomitable courage, dynamic initiative, and selfless devotion to duty upheld the highest traditions of the Marine Corps and the United States Naval Service. He gallantly gave his life in service to his country.

Private Dias was survived by his parents, Mrs. Anna M. Dias of Spotswood, New Jersey and Mr. Melvin Dias of Salem, Ohio, along with four sisters and three brothers.

---

39. John P. Baca

Born: January 10, 1949 in Providence, RI
Entered Service: Fort Ord, CA
Branch: U.S. Army
Rank: Specialist Fourth Class
Place of Action: February 10, 1970 Phuoc Long Province, Republic of Vietnam

Note: Courtesy of the U.S. Congressional Medal of Honor Society.

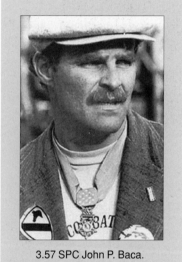

3.57 SPC John P. Baca.
Photo courtesy of www.neta.com.

Citation:

For conspicuous gallantry and intrepidity in action at the risk of his life above and beyond the call of duty. Sp4c Baca distinguished himself while serving on a recoilless rifle team during a night ambush mission.

A platoon from his company was sent to investigate the detonation of an automatic ambush device forward of his unit's main position and soon came under intense enemy fire from concealed positions along the trail. Hearing the heavy firing from the platoon position and realizing that his recoilless rifle team could assist the members of the besieged patrol, Spc4 Baca led his team through the hail of enemy fire to a firing position within the patrol's defensive perimeter.

As they prepared to engage the enemy, a fragmentation grenade was thrown into the midst of the patrol. Fully aware of the danger to his comrades, Sp4c Baca unhesitatingly, and with complete disregard for his own safety, covered the grenade with his steel helmet and fell on it as the grenade exploded, thereby absorbing the lethal fragments and concussion with his body.

His gallant action and total disregard for his personal well being directly saved eight men from certain serious injury or death. The extraordinary courage and selflessness displayed by Sp4c Baca, at the risk of his life, are in the highest traditions of the military service and reflect great credit on him, his unit, and the U.S. Army.

The John P. Baca Park was dedicated to the former Huntington Beach, CA resident.

---

40. Emilio De La Garza, Jr.

Born: June 23, 1949 in East Chicago, IN
Entered Service: February 4, 1969, in Chicago, IL
Branch: U.S. Marine Corps
Rank: Lance Corporal
Date and Place of Action: April 11, 1970 about four miles south of Da Nang
Killed in Action: April 11, 1970

Note: the USMC History and Museums Division provided the following information. For details please see Bibliography.

Emilio Albert De La Garza, Jr., graduated from Washington High School in East Chicago, Indiana in 1968.

He was employed by Inland Steel in East Chicago for a year. He enlisted in the U.S. Marine Corps February 4, 1969, in Chicago, Illinois. Transferred to the Marine Corps Recruit Depot, San Diego, California, he received recruit training with the 2nd Recruit Training Battalion, Recruit Training Regiment.

Upon completion of recruit training, he was ordered to the Marine Corps Base, Camp Pendleton, California, where he joined the 2nd Infantry Training Regiment and underwent individual combat training with the 1st and 2nd Battalions, and weapons training with the Basic Infantry Training Battalion. Promoted to private first class, July 1, 1969, he arrived in the Republic of Vietnam on the 25th of July for duty as ammo carrier, Company H, 2nd Battalion, 3rd Marines, 3rd Marine Division.

On September 29, 1969, he was reassigned to the 1st Marine Division and served as a Marine Corps exchange man with Headquarters and Service Company, 2nd Battalion, 1st Marines, until the following December. He was promoted to lance corporal on February 1, 1970.

Corporal De La Garza then joined Company E, 2nd Battalion, 1st Marines, 1st Marine Division. While serving as a machine gunner on a squad size patrol with the 3d Platoon of Company E, about four miles south of Da Nang on April 11, 1970, he was mortally wounded.

3.58 LCpl Emilio De La Garza.
Photo courtesy of the USMC.

His medals and decorations include: the Medal of Honor, the Purple Heart, the Combat Action Ribbon, the National Defense Service Medal, the Vietnam Service Medal with one bronze star, and the Republic of Vietnam Campaign Medal. His wife, Mrs. Rosemary De La Garza and daughter, Renee, of East Chicago, Indiana, his parents, Mr. and Mrs. Emilio De La Garza, Sr., East Chicago, and one brother survived Corporal De La Garza.

Citation:

For conspicuous gallantry and intrepidity at the risk of his life above and beyond the call of duty while serving as a machine gunner with Company E, Second Battalion, First Marines, First Marine Division, in the Republic of Vietnam on April 11, 1970.

Returning with his squad from a night ambush operation, Lance Corporal De La Garza joined his Platoon commander and another Marine in searching for two enemy soldiers who had been observed fleeing for cover toward a small pond.

Moments later, he located one of the enemy soldiers hiding among the reeds and brush. As the three Marines attempted to remove the resisting soldier from the pond, Lance Corporal De La Garza observed him pull the pin on a grenade. Shouting a warning, Lance Corporal De La Garza placed himself between the other two Marines and the ensuing blast from the grenade, thereby saving the lives of his comrades at the sacrifice of his own.

By his prompt and decisive action, and his great personal valor in the face of almost certain death, Lance Corporal De La Garza upheld and further enhanced the finest traditions of the Marine Corps and the United States Naval Service.

41. Miguel Hernandez Keith

Born: June 2, 1951 in San Antonio, TX
Entered Service: Omaha, NE
Branch: U.S. Marine Corps
Rank: Lance Corporal
Place of Action: May 8, 1970 Quang Ngai Province, Republic of Vietnam
Killed in Action: May 8, 1970

Note: Art Leatherwood wrote the following. For details please see Bibliography.

Lance Corporal Keith, United States Marine Corps, was a member of the Third Marine Amphibious Force at Quang Ngai Province, Vietnam, on May 8, 1970. In the early morning he was seriously wounded during a ground attack by a large enemy force.

In spite of his wounds, he ran across fire-swept terrain to check the security of vital defense positions. Completely exposed, he proceeded to deliver a hail of machine-gun fire against the enemy.

As five of the enemy approached the command post he rushed forward and disposed of three of the attackers and dispersed the others. A grenade exploded near Keith, knocking him to the ground, and inflicted further severe wounds.

3.59 LCpl Miguel Hernandez Keith. Photo courtesy USMC.

He again braved concentrated hostile fire and charged an estimated twenty-five enemy soldiers. His assault and well-placed fire eliminated four of the enemy and scattered the remainder.

During this valiant effort he was mortally wounded. Keith's heroic effort contributed to the success of his platoon in routing the enemy force. He is buried in Forest Lawn Cemetery at Omaha, Nebraska.

His medals and decorations include: the Medal of Honor, the Purple Heart, the Combat Action Ribbon, the National Defense Service Medal, the Vietnam Service Medal with one bronze star, and the Republic of Vietnam Campaign Medal.

Corporal Keith was survived by his mother and stepfather, Mr. and Mrs. Bobbie G. Keith of Abilene, Texas, his father, Mr. Miguel Hernandez of San Antonio, Texas, three brothers, and one sister.

42. Louis R. Rocco

Born: November 19, 1938 in Albuquerque, NM
Entered Service: Los Angeles, CA
Branch: U.S. Army
Rank: Warrant Officer (Sergeant First Class at time of action)
Place of Action: May 24, 1970 Northeast of Katum, Republic of Vietnam
Died: October 31, 2002

Note: The following is a compilation of articles written by Carmin Danini, Lisa Harrison Rivas, Scott Huddleston, Dennis McCllellan, and Kate Nelson. For details please see Bibliography.

For 28 years, Louis Richard Rocco, a poor kid from the South Valley near Albuquerque, New Mexico, opened the medal's navy blue case. For 28 years, he tied a sky-blue ribbon around his neck. For 28 years, he turned a violent memory of Vietnam into a mighty lever, a formidable honor, and an endless duty.

After saving three men from a burning helicopter and countless more from their coming-home miseries, Rocco faced his most brazen foe.

"It's scary," he says of the cancer that infected his lungs and spine. His voice is a whisper, wrenched slowly, reluctantly, from a body hunched in pain.

"I was always hoping that the medal would open doors for Vietnam vets," he says. "There were a lot of programs that needed to be done; drug and alcohol treatment, employment, housing."

In 1974, he became the only New Mexican to receive the Medal of Honor for Vietnam service while still alive. The medal, our nation's highest military honor, requires even generals to salute its recipients.

Sgt. 1st Class Rocco, a medic, was on his second tour of duty in Vietnam on May 24, 1970, when he volunteered to accompany a medical evacuation team on an urgent mission to pick up eight critically wounded South Vietnamese soldiers near the village of Katum.

As the helicopter Rocco was riding in neared the landing zone, it came under heavy enemy fire. The pilot was shot in the leg; the helicopter crashed into a field. Rocco suffered a fractured wrist and hip, and a severely bruised back.

But he ignored his injuries and the intense enemy fire to pull three unconscious crewmembers from the burning chopper. Suffering burns to his hands in the process, he carried each man across about 20 yards of exposed terrain. He then helped administer first aid to them before he lost consciousness.

Rocco and the other crewmen were rescued the next day. Lt. Lee Caubareaux, the helicopter's co-pilot whose shattered arm was saved by doctors, later lobbied for Rocco to receive the Medal of Honor. "If not for Rocco," Caubareaux later said, "he and the other crewmen would have burned to death."

On Dec. 12, 1974, President Ford presented the Medal of Honor to Rocco, the only resident of

3.60 WO1 Louis R. Rocco.
Photo courtesy of the CMOHS.

the State of New Mexico to receive the nation's highest award for valor during the Vietnam War.

"Nobody-nobody-would have faulted him when he got out to safety if he had stayed there," retired Army Lt. Gen. Ed Baca said at a ceremony in Albuquerque honoring Rocco. "But, instead, he charged into that helicopter."

"You really don't get a chance to think about what you are doing," Rocco said at that ceremony. "You want to save lives and live too. I was lucky; I was able to do that. God looked after me."

Rocco retired from the U.S. Army as a chief warrant officer in 1978 after 22 years of military service. He re-enlisted in 1991, in the Persian Gulf War, and spent six months at Fort Sam Houston, Texas, recruiting medical personnel.

Among veterans, the Medal of Honor carries a mythic status. Around Rocco's neck, it became a tool for creating a host of programs and services that eased the coming-home agonies of Vietnam veterans.

"I've known Richard since '78 when he started the Vet Center on Fourth Street," said Pete Stines, a Marine Corps veteran and one of Rocco's best friends. "I went there because I needed help.

"He understood where I was coming from with my problems of post-traumatic stress disorder. He was that way with everyone-trying to help them with their fears and anxieties," Stines added.

Besides the Vet Center, Rocco started a shelter for homeless veterans, a nursing home in Truth or Consequences and tuition waivers for veterans attending state-run colleges. He served as director of the state's Veterans Service Commission and later counseled veterans leaving the service of New Mexico military bases.

In recent years, even as his health failed, Rocco worked on programs to keep children away from drugs and violence.

"Richard was a hero while serving in Vietnam," U.S. Rep. Heather Wilson said in a prepared statement. "He was even more of a hero to our veterans after he came home." Wilson, an Albuquerque Republican, met Rocco during a ceremony at the Albuquerque International Balloon Fiesta. Local veterans announced during the event that they were

3.61 Three Medal of Honor recipients in San Antonio at a Spurs basketball game in 2000. Left-to-right; SGT Jose M. Lopez, SSG Lucian Adams and WO1 Louis Rocco. Photo by Linda D. Kozaryn. Photo courtesy of medalofhonor.com.

naming a park next to the Westside Community Center after him: the Richard Rocco Medal of Honor Park.

Rocco called the ceremony, "an honor that I hold above presidents and legislators, because these are my people. For them to honor me, it makes me feel so good."

Rocco was born in the South Valley and spent much of his youth there, mired in poverty. He fell into trouble with the law as a teenager and, in 1956, was one step short of a jail term when an Army recruiter saved him.

"That was the first time an adult in my life didn't judge me," Rocco says. "Sgt. Martinez didn't try to change my mind. He just listened, actively listened. And it was the first time that I spilled my guts. All the pain and anger inside me came out."

Sgt. Martinez offered to talk to the judge. They agreed that Rocco would spend a year in a delinquency home and, at 17; his parents would sign a waiver giving him over to the Army. It was his last, best chance. It changed everything.

"The Army was what I needed," Rocco says. "I didn't have structure. I didn't have discipline. I needed that desperately. I needed what the Army had."

A few years after joining the Army, Rocco was serving as a medic at Fort MacArthur in San Pedro, California He looked across the room and saw a familiar face: Sgt. Martinez, lying on a litter and badly wounded.

"I went up and said, do you remember me?" Rocco says. "He didn't. He had taken care of so many kids that he couldn't recognize me. I told him, you're going to walk out of here."

He made sure the sergeant got special attention and round-the-clock care. You could say that was when Rocco saved his first life. Rocco would say he was only returning the favor. He still remembers the heat of Vietnam, and the humidity, the stench, and the danger.

"As we pulled in the first time," Rocco says, "they were loading caskets into a plane." If he remembers much more, he'd rather not say. The hallmark of heroism, after all, is humility.

"Just doing my job. Doing what anyone would do."

Lee Caubarreaux disagrees.

"Had it not been for him," the Louisiana retiree says of Rocco, "three of us would have burned up in the ship." The former injured pilot added, "I can't screw in a light bulb with my arm, but I can still hug my wife."

Al Valdez, an Army veteran and Rocco's longtime friend said, "a medic's primary duty is to save and protect, and Richard spent his whole life healing." As a former Bernalillo County commissioner, Valdez is accustomed to the rough-and-tumble world of politics. But when discussing Rocco, his composure crumbled.

"My favorite memory of him is his hug," Valdez said, his voice catching on each word. "His hug, his handshake and, when you looked in his eye, the commitment-that sense of security you had when Richard said he was going to do something. "He's probably the best example to me of an officer and a gentleman."

Many of his friends noted Rocco's humility and his reluctance to even mention the Medal of Honor. Stines had known him for months before he learned of it.

"He was the kind of person you looked up to as a mentor, a friend and a buddy-someone who would do anything for you," Stines said. "And you knew that he would because he'd already done it."

Rocco was an avid cook and once won the New Mexico Chile Cook-Off-an award that he bragged about to his future wife before letting on about the Medal of Honor.

"We'll go to the White House two or three times a year, and he'll talk to the president of the United States, the same as the guy who delivered dirt to us in Mexico," Maria Rocco said of her husband. She smiles at her husband's humility, but isn't about to ignore his heroism.

When they moved to San Antonio in 1998, she opened the boxes that Rocco had stashed away. The contents are now on display across the walls and shelves of his home office. Plaque upon plaque. Picture upon picture; Rocco with President Reagan, Rocco with President Clinton, Rocco with Carlos Santana, Rocco with the San Antonio Spurs.

He also adored hot rods and, upon his cancer diagnosis, lamented that he would never get to realize his lifelong dream of owning a souped-up '34 Ford coupe. But while he recovered from lung surgery, Gordon Chisenhall, a San Antonio friend, managed to snag the perfect car. He doctored it up in secret and surprised Rocco upon his release from the hospital.

"He was always doing things for other people," Chisenhall said. "This was exactly what he wanted, an ultimate little toy."

In an interview with *The Tribune*, Rocco said he had put aside his anger at the Vietnam War and at how its veterans were treated upon coming home.

He suspected that his cancer was linked to exposure to Agent Orange in Vietnam, but he told an interviewer, as he was dying, that he was forgiving. "It doesn't bother me anymore," he said. "I'm at peace. I'm going to die. I don't want to die angry."

Just before 6 a.m. October 31, 2002, in his San Antonio, Texas, home, he rested in the arms of his wife, Maria. He had said he felt cold; she was trying to keep him warm. Rocco, 63, had battled cancer in his lungs and spine for 10 months–two months more than doctors predicted he would live.

Even so, he seemed to be doing well.

"We thought we would have another Christmas with him," said Linda Hastings, Maria's daughter, who lives in Albuquerque.

Quietly, gently and finally at peace with the demons of the Vietnam War, Rocco died in his wife's arms.

"This is such a huge loss, for everyone," Hastings said.

3.62 CWO Louis Rocco at MoH autograph signing at Governor's Open House, Pueblo, CO. Sept. 21, 2000. CMOHS Convention. Photo provided by Robert M. "Mick" Bush 2000, CMHS Photographer.

That sentiment echoed across the ranks of Vietnam veterans in Albuquerque who had benefited from the programs Rocco developed.

"Richard was our godfather, the guy who guided us through," said John Garcia, an army veteran and director of the Barelas Community Development Corp. "He was given the Medal of Honor by our country. But I think he also wore a Medal of Honor from the hearts of all the veterans that he helped."

Presidents, generals, CEOs and junkies have hailed Rocco's heroism, his compassion, and his unfailing desire to reach out and help.

At 63, he came full circle. He dragged himself through America's longest war and carried veterans through its awful aftermath.

Helmets, rifles and jungle boots tell a grim tale of the action fought by the 1st Brigade, 101st airborne paratroopers in Operation Wheeler near Chu Lai. This battlefield memorial honors the soldiers killed during the offensive between September 11th and November 25th, 1967. Photo courtesy www.vietnampix.com.

LATINOS NOT YET AWARDED THE MEDAL OF HONOR

■ ■ ■ ■ ■

4

Latinos Not Yet Awarded the Medal of Honor

Note: The following is a compilation of articles written by various writers including; Mike Baird, Gregg K. Kekesako, Elena Gomez, and Joe Olvera. For details please see Bibliography.

There are other Hispanic veterans who also fought valiantly, or as in the case of **Guy 'Gabby' Gabaldon**–used his special skills–to save American soldiers further blood-shed. However, for various reasons these men have never been selected to receive the Medal of Honor.

Many believe "The Pied Piper of Saipan," as Guy Gabaldon is known, has never received proper credit for single-handedly capturing 1,500 Japanese soldiers and civilians during World War II.

But Guy shows no bitterness.

"Life has just been a beautiful experience," says a man who has piloted his own plane throughout the South Pacific, skippered a logline fishing vessel, and worked, as he put it, as "a spy in Mexico."

Guy 'Gabby' Gabaldon was born in Los Angeles and was adopted by a Japanese American family who taught him Japanese. He added, "I came from such a large Latino family that no one objected when I moved in with a Japanese family. They were my extended family. It was there I learned Japanese, since I had to go to language school with their children everyday."

When war broke out with Japan, his 'brothers' joined the U.S. armed forces in Europe and his Japanese American foster parents and sister were sent to a relocation center in Arizona. He went to Alaska and worked in a fish cannery and as a laborer, until he decided to enlist in the Marine Corps at the age of seventeen.

Gabaldon qualified as a mortar crewman, Japanese translator, and scout observer. He then received amphibious training, and was sent to Saipan on June 15, 1944. He was only an 18-year-old Marine Corps private first class when he corralled more than 800 prisoners on July 8, 1944.

"The first night I was on Saipan, I went out on my own," said Gabaldon, who now lives in Old Town, Florida, "I always worked on my own, and brought back two prisoners using my back street Japanese.

"My officers scolded me and threatened me with a court-martial for leaving my other duties,

4.1 Marine veteran Guy Gabaldon wows the crowd with his impromptu comedy and his tales of valor from World War II at a Pentagon ceremony honoring Hispanic World War II veterans Sept. 15, 2004. Photo by Sgt. Adam R. Mancini, U.S. Army.

but I went out the next night and came back with 50 more prisoners. After that I was given a free rein."

His pitch simply was that the Japanese would be treated humanely.

"I was 18, It was a game, and I spoke Japanese," said the now retired Marine.

"People always want to know how one man brings back hundreds of prisoners. Families were committing suicide, tossing their babies off cliffs and jumping behind them. They had been pushed back on a small island until they could go no further," he said. "I told the mothers in Japanese, 'don't kill your babies, come with me, and live.'"

Gabaldon often uses levity to skirt the awful situation. So at times, he says, twitching his thin, silver mustache, "I surrounded them. I told them if they didn't surrender, I'd call John Wayne."

On another day, Gabaldon corralled six Japanese men by holding them at gunpoint. "I sent others to gather family and friends, under the threat of killing the six men if they didn't," he said. "I didn't know if I had 80 or 8,000. I just promised they could live, and we all walked into camp." He had 800 and holds the military record for the most single-handed captures.

The Mariana Islands–specifically Saipan, Tinian and Guam–were considered key strategic Japanese strongholds in World War II, since they were located only 1,250 miles from Tokyo.

The 5th Amphibious Corps carried out the Mariana assault, under the code name Operation Forager. The 2nd and 4th Marine Divisions landed on Saipan on June 15. The U.S. Army's 27th Infantry Battalion later joined those units. The battle of Saipan turned out to be one of the bloodiest confrontations of the Pacific War. It cost the lives of more than 3,000 American Marines and Army soldiers, 30,000 Japanese soldiers and 900 civilians before the island was secured on July 9, 1944. On August 1, after nine days of fighting, Tinian Island, just five miles to the south of Saipan, was under U.S. control.

Gabaldon was recommended for the Medal of Honor by his commanding officer, Capt. John Schwabe, now a retired colonel. However, the Marine Corps initially downgraded the award to a

Silver Star and then upgraded it to the Navy Cross–one medal lower than the Medal of Honor– just as a movie on his exploits, *Hell to Eternity*, was released in 1960.

"I hate to use the race card," Gabaldon said in a phone interview, "but it is so obvious. I don't think the Marine Corps ever awarded the Medal of Honor to any Chicano in World War II. "It was only with a twinge of conscious that they upgraded my Silver Star to a Navy Cross, and to me that indicated they knew they had made a mistake."

He said the campaign to award him the country's

4.2 Marine Pfc Guy Gabaldon received the Silver Star for actions performed on Saipan in 1944 when he captured 1,500 Japanese soldiers. Photo courtesy of the U.S. Army.

highest medal for valor continues with an ongoing congressional investigation on why he was denied the medal, since he captured more than 10 times the number of prisoners taken by Sgt. Alvin York, who won the Medal of Honor in World War I.

Besides the Hispanic communities in the western United States, Gabaldon, who spoke at the National Archives during the dedication of the World War II Memorial in Washington, D.C. on Memorial Day weekend, said he has the support of several congressional members.

"The fight continues," said the World War II hero who loves to fly and sail. "I don't want it. It's not false modesty. I enjoy what I was doing. It was a game to me. I didn't enjoy killing."

Gabaldon returned to Saipan after the war and lived there for more than 40 years with his wife, the former Ohara Suzuki, whom he met while working in Mexico. "I loved the sea," said Gabaldon, who also had the government contract at one time to haul milk on his 95-foot boat from Tinian to Saipan. "God has given me everything."

In 1990, he wrote a book, Saipan: *Suicide Island*, about his wartime exploits. He said there is another movie in the works, with talk of Antonio Banderas in the lead role. Referring to the 1960 movie, *Hell to Eternity*, Gabaldon said, "I had a lot of fun shooting it. But Jeffrey Hunter (who portrayed Gabaldon) doesn't resemble me. He's tall with blue eyes. Me, I am a short Chicano."

Gabaldon said Hollywood "toned the story down. It gave me a sidekick-actor David Janssen-but that wasn't true, I always worked alone." Gabaldon said it's hard to single out any one point in his life, which included being adopted by a Japanese family when he was 12.

"I was kind of a stray as a kid," he said while describing his childhood in the Los Angeles barrios. "Worst thing then we'd fight someone, then later shake hands, but now people say, 'Why you looking at me?'" He said, pointing his finger like a gun. "Bang."

Gabaldon and his Japanese wife raised their five children in Saipan, where he worked for many years to help troubled youths. He came to Corpus Christi, Texas during Memorial Day weekend in 2005 to spread the message of youth crime prevention.

Guy, now 79 years old, was a guest of Hispanic War Veterans of America, Department of Texas, Corpus Christi Chapter No. 1.

"After two years trying to get him here, we're so pleased," said Joe Elizondo, spokesman for the chapter.

"He's an influential person, for all military people, who gives great honor to Hispanic veterans still fighting for recognition."

THREE OTHER HISPANIC MILITARY HEROES WHO ALSO DESERVE THE CONGRESSIONAL MEDAL OF HONOR

Marcelino Serna was born in Chihuahua City, in the Mexican State of Chihuahua in 1896. He enlisted in the Army and was sent to fight in the frontline trenches of France during World War I. On September 12, 1918, the U.S. First Army launched an attack to crash through the St. Mihiel salient near the French-German border. That same day, Private Serna shot a German soldier opposite him in the trenches. The German was wounded by Serna but still managed to return Sernas's fire, grazing him slightly on the head.

Following a trail of blood, Serna tracked the wounded enemy soldier to a dugout. He paused a moment, then tossed a concussion grenade into the bunker. To his surprise, not one but 24 Germans came out.

For this feat, Serna was awarded the Distinguished Service Cross. Although apparently eligible for the Congressional Medal of Honor, he was told by an officer that to be so honored one had to be of a higher rank than a "buck" private, and that he could not be advanced to a higher grade because he could not read or write English well enough to sign reports.

Serna was decorated with the highest military medals of Italy and France. The descriptions of his exploits on the battlefields of Belgium and France read like casebooks of heroism. In recovering from wounds suffered toward the end of the war, he was personally decorated by General John 'Black Jack' Pershing.

Serna earned two French Croix de Guerre with Palm medals, the Italian Cross of Merit, the French Medaille Militaire, the British Medal of Honor, the French Commemorative

4.3 PVT Marcelino Serna, World War I. Photo courtesy of El Paso Community College, Borderlands Project.

Medal, WWI Victory Medal with five stars, the Victory Medal with three campaign bars, the St. Mihiel Medal, the Verdun Medal and two Purple

Hearts. Serna was the most decorated World War I soldier from Texas.

Serna served the remainder of his time with occupational forces in Germany. In May 1919, Marcelino Serna was discharged at Camp Bowie, Texas. He married and settled in El Paso. In 1924, Marcelino Serna became a U.S. citizen. He worked at the Peyton Packing Company and then became a civil service employee at Fort Bliss.

In 1960, he retired as a plumber from William Beaumont Hospital. In 1973, the Marcos V. Armijo VFW Post 2753 honored Serna with a 40-year pin for continuous membership.

During his retirement, Serna spent most of his time tending his flower garden until the family house, and others in the neighborhood, had to be removed to make way for the Chamizal Highway. He moved his family into a new residence on Buena Vista Street and continued his interest in gardening. He participated in Veteran's Day parades for years. On February 29, 1992, Private Marcelino Serna died at the age of 95.

Serna has never received the Congressional Medal of Honor. However in 1995, Texas Congressman Ron Coleman introduced legislation to award Serna the Medal of Honor. It is unclear if any action was ever taken on this legislation.

Gabe Navarrete, who hails from the barrios of El Paso, was a Second Lieutenant during World War II. His mission was to cross enemy lines to determine the strength and position of the enemy, and to find a suitable crossing point. He crossed the freezing cold Rio Rapido (a river aptly named) in Italy in the dark of night, engaged the enemy in close combat and was wounded seven times. Yet, Lt. Navarrete was able to fulfill his mission and reported to his superiors the vast number of waiting German enemy troops on the other side. He warned the generals that forcing the men to cross the river would be suicidal.

However, his superior officers decided to not take his advice, and instead ordered that the crossing take place. In what has been described as one of the most tragic stupidities of World War II, the waiting German forces killed more than 1,700 men. Although he was recognized for his leadership, Lt. Navarrete didn't rest easy.

History has it that he had threatened one of his superior officers by telling him that if his men were sacrificed (more than 300 of them were from El Paso), he would challenge him to a duel. When Navarrete found out about all the casualties, he went looking for that officer. However, he was stopped before he could carry out his threat.

He too has never received a Congressional Medal of Honor.

Command Sgt. Ramon Rodriguez was awarded the Silver Star for his gallantry in action in Vietnam near Hue on January 24, 1968. He was awarded another Silver Star (First Oak Leaf Cluster) for his gallantry in Vietnam on Feb. 5, 1968, and received a third Silver Star for his gallantry in action near Phu Bai, Vietnam, on Feb. 26, 1968.

Sgt. Rodriguez, first distinguished himself when his outpost came under a heavy

4.4 Soldiers load a cannon as they prepare for an attack on a battlefield in Europe. Photo courtesy of the U.S. Army.

4.5 Members of the U.S. 1st Air Cavalry march
through the forest en route to Chu Phong mountain,
in the Ia Drang Valley, Vietnam, 1965.
Photo courtesy of www.vietnampix.com.

barrage of enemy mortars, followed by a ground assault. Rodriguez, although wounded in the arm, and
with complete disregard for his own safety, began
moving through the trench line, giving first aid to
the wounded personnel and returning intense fire
that killed four enemy shooters.

On another mission, Sgt. Rodriguez again distinguished himself while on a search-and-destroy
mission. An unknown-size enemy force had ambushed
his platoon, and the platoon leader and the point
man were seriously wounded. Rodriguez assumed
command. Although wounded himself, and with
disregard for his own safety, he made a sweep of the
area–revealing eight mortally wounded insurgents,
seven AK-47 rifles, and three grenade launchers.

STILL WAITING

These four men, although they served in three
different wars, shared the same courage under fire.
They took risks and they were heroic in carrying
out of their duties. Gabaldon and Navarrete had
been told by their superiors that they were in line
for the Congressional Medal of Honor.

None of them was so rewarded. We do not
know why not.

Four Mexican–Americans, four stories of courage under combat conditions, during three different
wars–World War's I and II and Vietnam. So far, 42
Medals of Honor have been awarded to Latinos,
making them the largest single ethnic group to receive this most prestigious award, in proportion to
the number who served. But still, there should be
even more recipients–four more Medals of Honor,
for four more Hispanic Military Heroes. They've
earned the accolades.

Note: Investigations conducted in 1998 by Congress and the
Navy are still pending and new events may come about which
change Gabaldon's most recent status.

Monument to honor the Hispanos of Hero Street who served the United States of America.
Photo courtesy of the Hero Street Foundation.

HERO STREET USA

. . . . .

5

Hero Street USA

Note: The following is from an article written by John Culhane in the May 1985 Reader's Digest.

In a sense, the fight for Hero Street, U.S.A. began with the revolution that ravaged Mexico from 1910 to 1917. In Mexico, in those days, you could be made to join either side, and you could end up fighting your own father or brother. So thousands of Mexicans fled to the United States.

A few came as far as northwestern Illinois, where the communities of Rock Island, Moline, East Moline and Silvis run into one another along the Mississippi. Some found work at the huge locomotive-repair shop being built by the Rock Island Railroad in the tiny town of Silvis (pop. 2,500).

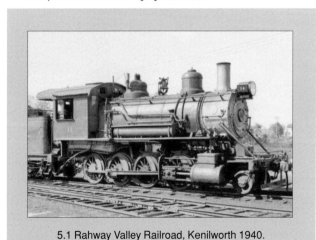

5.1 Rahway Valley Railroad, Kenilworth 1940.
Photo courtesy of www.trainsarefuncom.

The railroad not only gave the Mexicans jobs; it let them live in boxcars in the yard. Elated, the Mexicans sent word back to relatives and friends that there was steady work for adults and uninterrupted schooling for children.

It was a hard life. A railroad laborer was paid just 35 cents an hour. When the Mexicans in their boxcars woke up in the wintertime, the children had to break ice in the washbowls before they could clean up for school. But the hardship was worth it. School meant a chance to learn English and to succeed in sports. And, in those days, success in sports was one of the few ways a Mexican-American could be accepted as equal.

One American who wanted to see the Mexicans make it in the United States was the basketball coach at McKinley School in Silvis, Willard Gauley. On the basketball court and off, Coach Gauley showed the young seventh- and eighth-graders how to achieve their goals: by teamwork.

In 35 years, Gauley led little McKinely to 30 winning seasons against much larger schools, winning 313 games and losing 121. But, more than anything else, the coach gave the young Mexican-Americans opportunities to show what they were made of.

A one-eyed boy badly wanted to play basketball, but Coach Gauley was afraid the kid would injure his other eye. When the youngster kept begging, Gauley finally went to his mother and asked her, "Do you think it's worth the risk?" The mother said, "His whole heart is in it. Let him play."

Gauley gave the boy a uniform, and he was good enough with one eye to make the team. That uniform meant so much to him that when his home burned down he rushed into the burning building to rescue it. "That kind of spirit," Coach Gauley always said, "is why we win."

5.2 Frank Sandoval.   5.3 William Sandoval.

Photos courtesy of the
Hero Street Monument Committee.

By 1928, the Mexicans who lived in boxcars had saved enough money to buy land that no one else wanted at the west end of town. Twenty-two families built their houses on either side of Second Street– little more than a muddy stretch between Honey Creek and Billy Goat Hill. The hill had that name because the children said it was so steep that only Billy goats–and they themselves–could climb it.

And climb it they did, to play war games and to hunt rabbits with slingshots. The older boys, of course, had already given up the hill. They had jobs, and were getting married and having families of their own.

"GREATEST STREET IN THE WORLD"

Then on December 7, 1941, the United States was attacked and went to war, and so did the Mexican-Americans of Second Street.

Tony Pompa lied about his age to get into the Army Air Corps at 17. He loved airplanes, and was honored to have become a B-24 tail gunner in the 449th Bombardment Group. Over Aviano, Italy, on January 31, 1944, Tony's plane was hit. As he was trying to get out of the burning aircraft, his chute opened, trapping him inside. Tony Pompa was the first from Second Street to die. He left a young, pregnant widow and a small son.

The Sandoval family alone sent six young men to defend their country: Frank, Joe, Tanilo 'Tony,' Emidio, Eddie, and Santiago 'Yatch.' Their mother,

Angelina Sandoval, said in Spanish–her English was never good–"They didn't complain about going. This was their country, and they were willing to die for it." Their V-mail letters home eventually filled a canvas bag.

While serving with Company C, 209th Engineer Combat Battalion, Frank was killed in combat on the Burma Road. Ten months later, on April 14, 1945, Frank's brother Joe, fighting with Company I, 41st Armored Infantry Regiment, was killed by German forces on the bank of the Elbe River. His body was never found.

Another Sandoval family, unrelated to the first, lived on Second Street. This family sent seven sons to war, including William. On October 6, 1944, William's unit–Company F, 2nd Battalion, 504th Parachute Infantry–attacked German-held woods near Nijmegen, Holland. Between the Americans and their objective stood a fence. William was going over it when he was shot to death.

Claro Soliz made a will when he went to war. To various members of his family he bequeathed his ring, his typewriter, and the bicycle that often couldn't be ridden along this unpaved street.

"Second Street is really not much–just mud and ruts," he admitted in a letter home. "But, right now, to me it is the greatest street in the world."

Staff Sgt. Claro Soliz, Company E, 120th Infantry Regiment, died on January 19, 1945, of wounds received during the Battle of the Bulge.

Peter Masias wanted to be a singer. Many people on Second Street still remember his sweet, clear baritone. In the

5.4 Claro Soliz.
Photo courtesy of the Hero Street Monument Committee.

war he served with Company C, 139th Engineer Battalion. Enemy bullets cut him down in Wesel, Germany, on March 4, 1945.

5.5 Peter Masias.   5.6 Joe Gomez.   5.7 Johnny Munos.

Photos courtesy of the
Hero Street Monument Committee.

FAR, FAR AWAY

The Mexicans' sacrifice did not end with World War II. Five years later, when war broke out in Korea, Second Street continued to send its sons.

Two of the first Sandoval family's World War II veterans–Eddie and Yatch–went to Korea. Both came home. Five weeks later, Yatch was killed in a car crash.

Joe Gomez had served in World War II and did occupation duty in Germany afterward. Then he came home, joined the Reserves, got married and had a daughter. When the Korean War broke out, he was called up.

On May 17, 1951, Joe Gomez, Company K, 38th Infantry Regiment, charged alone up a hill into point-blank enemy gunfire, to clear the way to a vital position where American and United Nations forces were trapped and being slaughtered. Because of Joe's bravery, many lives were saved, but he lost his own to Communist Chinese bullets. His young widow held their baby daughter in her arms as she received Joe's Silver Star for gallantry.

Johnny Munos had married Mary Bessera only three months before he was called up, and he missed her terribly. By mid-July 1951, Johnny was serving in Company F, 38th Regimental Combat Team, 2nd Infantry, in the mountains of Korea, living in a bunker, eating 'C' rations.

They used to say on Second Street that running up and down Billy Goat Hill was good practice for the battles they had to fight in war. On Monday, August 27, Johnny Munos was killed fighting his way to the top of a hill in Korea–far, far away from Silvis, IL.

OUR FLAG, TOO

After the war, despite their sacrifices, the people of Second Street still hadn't won acceptance by most white Americans in Silvis– as they discovered when they tried to join the local post of the Veterans of Foreign Wars. All were turned down, they later learned, because some members of the post were afraid they would be outnumbered by so many Mexican–American veterans.

"You guys should form your own post," one man said. So they did.

Meanwhile, Second Street itself had become a bitter reminder that the rest of the community still considered Mexican-Americans to be second-class citizens. Some of those who had come home in flag-draped coffins had to be carried up the un-paved street by their military escort on foot, because the hearses had bogged down in the mud.

Even before they went to war these men had been heroes to Joe Terronez, a younger kid who lived on Third Street. Now Joe grew angry at the sight of his heroes being carried into Our Lady of Guadalupe Catholic Church by men with muddy boots just because the town wouldn't pave the street.

Terronez decided to fight the American way– with votes. In the late 1950's, he and a friend began paying for any Mexican-born person's citizenship-application photographs, driving applicants to the Rock Island courthouse and, after they were sworn in, showing them how to register to vote. One year they helped create 27 new voters.

In 1963, the Mexican-Americans of his ward in Silvis helped to elect Joe Terronez to the city council. Soon he was making a motion that Second

Street be paved and renamed, "Hero Street U.S.A.," and that Billy Goat Hill, where his heroes used to play, be turned into a park in their memory.

5.8 Hero Street USA Monument.
Photo courtesy of the Hero Street Monument Committee.

An ugly controversy erupted. The council said it didn't have the money. As for the name change, it was pointed out that Second Street wasn't the only street in Silvis that had sent me to fight and die.

"True," conceded Terronez. But he bet that no other street in America had sent so many men, or lost so many of them in combat. "The most from one family to be killed in World War II were the five Sullivan brothers, and there's a destroyer named after them," he reminded the council. "But the eight guys from Second Street who were killed were like brothers, because they were all raised together. We want their street named after them."

Terronez' fight for Hero Street finally caught the attention of the U.S. Department of Defense, which looked into the matter. The department's director of military equal opportunity made it official: 57 men from Second Street fought in both World War II and Korea. As far as he could determine, this was the largest number of servicemen of the same ethnic background to come from any area of comparable size during those conflicts.

"When you are willing to fight–even die–for your country, who can say 'It's my flag more than yours'?" asks Joe Terronez. "Those boys could have

said, 'I'm going back to Mexico so I don't have to risk my life.' Instead, fifty-seven put their lives on the line for the United States, and eight of them died."

SPIRIT OF SILVIS

Finally, on Memorial Day, 1971, Second Street officially became Hero Street, U.S.A. A red-white-and-blue sign was unveiled at the corner of Second Street and First Avenue (the main street) to proclaim it, and the Los Amigos marching band swung into 'America' from *West Side Story*.

U.S. Rep. Thomas Railsback of Moline told the crowd, "I am proud to represent this neighborhood whose families generously gave the best they had to this country. I question whether any group in this country has done more."

Railsback had been working to obtain a federal grant to make the Billy Goat Hill Park possible. Finally, the Department of Housing and Urban Development agreed to pay half the $88,000 cost if the town would match the funds.

Volunteers swung into action. Local 1304 of the United Auto Workers collected money at factory gates all over the area. Other local Mexican-American communities raised money with fiestas. The John Deere and International Harvester companies contributed machinery, as did the city of Silvis.

Gradually, a third of Billy Goat Hill was cut away and a concrete monument shaped like an Aztec temple was fashioned into it. Where the heroes once dropped a rubber ball into a hoop nailed to a tree, there was a full basketball court. And where they once played in the mud, there was a playground with a jungle gym.

Hero Street Park was dedicated October 30, 1971, and Hero Street, U.S.A. was finally paved in 1975. Claro Soliz' family could at last ride their bicycles in all seasons.

5.9 Tony Pompa.
Photo courtesy of the Hero Street Monument Committee.

Ironically, in the late 1950's, the Silvis VFW post, which had blackballed the Mexican-American veterans, was forced to sell its building because it could no longer afford the mortgage payments. So the Mexican-American veterans asked the "Anglos" if they wanted to meet in their building, an abandoned church they had bought and converted themselves. Today, all of Silvis's Veterans of Foreign Wars meet there.

VICTORY IN PEACE

In the winter of 1984, already planning the 1985 V-E Day observance in Hero Street, U.S.A. Memorial Park, Joe Terronez climbed the snowy hill to the plaque that bears the names of the eight heroes from Second Street. As he climbed, he talked about his children and the children of other Mexican-Americans born in Silvis, kids who are now lawyers, chemists, nurses, teachers—working at better jobs than their grandfathers would have thought possible.

But of course Terronez was really talking about his dead heroes—Tony Pompa; Frank, Joe and William Sandoval; Claro Soliz, Peter Masias; Joe Gomez; Johnny Munos—because suddenly he said: "Coach Gauley, who died in January 1984, used to say the problem was that most people wouldn't give us a chance to show what we're made of." He pointed to the names of the plaque. "They showed what we're made of."

What the citizens of Silvis celebrated on May 8, 1985, the 40th anniversary of the end of the war in Europe, was more than a victory in war. It was also a victory in peace: a victory over prejudice and a victory for democracy. Most of all, it was a victory for the principle that all men are created equal. That is the bedrock of the American way of life for which the men of Hero Street, U.S.A., like so many others, fought and died.

The street has contributed more men to military service than any street of comparable size in the United States—84 men from 26 families serving in World War II, Korea, and Vietnam.

The flag of Puerto Rico.

THE
BORINQUENEERS

■ ■ ■ ■ ■

6

CHAPTER 6

"The Borinqueneers"

Note: The following text is a compilation of articles written by Lt. Col. Gilberto Villahermosa and the Borinqueneers website. For details please see Bibliography.

The U.S. Army National Guard 65th Infantry Regiment in Puerto Rico was organized in 1899; a year after the United States seized Puerto Rico from Spain. At the time, the U.S. Army considered the regiment to be "colonial troops" for the defense of the island.

In 1908, the regiment was attached to the Regular U.S. Army. Its nickname, "The Borinqueneers," honors Puerto Rican native warriors.

In August 1950, the Korean War was less than two months old, and Puerto Rico's 65th Infantry Regiment was on its way to the combat zone. The regiment landed at the port city of Pusan on the Korean Peninsula's southern tip, where U.S. forces had been holding a perimeter against the Communist

6.1 The Borinqueneers, a National Guard Heritage painting by Domenick D'Andrea.
The battle portrayed in this painting was the last recorded battalion-sized bayonet attack by the U.S. Army.
Image courtesy of the Army National Guard.

95

North Korean invaders. Sent into action immediately, the Puerto Ricans took part in the U.S. breakout and drive to the north.

6.2 65th battle weary troops return to safety behind the lines after two days of being trapped north of the Han River. Photo courtesy of the U.S. Army.

Following the brilliantly planned and executed surprise landings at Inchon, U.S. and other United Nations forces drove deep into the mountains of North Korea. At that point a huge Chinese Army entered the war. The U.S. Eighth Army was overrun, and the 1st Marine Division, with attached U.S. and British Army Units, was completely encircled.

In one of the greatest fighting retreats in history, the outnumbered Marines battled their way south to the coast. The first friendly troops they saw on the frozen ridge tops were the Puerto Ricans of the 65th Infantry Regiment, sent to hold the perimeter around the vital port of Hungnam. The Puerto Ricans supervised the evacuation of Hungnam, finally sailing themselves on Christmas Eve, 1950. The 65th landed in Pusan as they had five months before, and again fought their way northward.

Late January 1951, found them south of the Korean capital of Seoul, under orders to take two hills being held by the Chinese 149th Division. The assault began on January 31, and took three days. On the morning of the third day the top of the hills were within reach, and two battalions of the 65th fixed bayonets and charged straight at the enemy positions. The Chinese fled.

The 65th Infantry Regiment established a reputation as one of the 3rd Infantry Division's most dependable formations in Korea. Manned by Puerto Rican troops and commanded by predominantly white officers, the regiment was a well-led, well-trained, and disciplined formation.

"The Puerto Ricans forming the ranks of the gallant 65th…are writing a brilliant record of heroism in battle," wrote Gen. Douglas MacArthur, "and I am indeed proud to have them under my command."

By the end of 1951, the officers and men of the regiment had garnered four Distinguished Service Crosses and more than 125 Silver Stars. "The Borinqueneers" were also awarded the Presidential and Meritorious Unit Commendations, two Korean Presidential Unit Citations and the Greek Gold Medal for Bravery.

The 65th Infantry Regiment's gallant service in a difficult war is exemplified by its regimental motto, "Honor and Fidelity," and the regiment itself exemplifies the National Guard's leading role in our nation's military history.

"Its performance was superb. We were very proud of our regiment's action," recalled Capt. Fernandez–Duran, a Puerto Rican officer of the 1st Battalion. "There was never any fear or cowardice displayed by anyone in our unit. Leadership was

6.3 Borinqueneers man a machine gun position south of burning Oro-ri. December 1950. Photo courtesy of the National Archives.

superb, and most of the soldiers were veterans and Regular Army. As to discipline, nothing was left to be desired."

A BORINQUENEER CHRISTMAS CAROL

All the excitement and gut-tightening anticipation behind, the 65th prepared to enjoy the most unforgettable Christmas Eve many had ever had. They had proven to the toughest skeptics that the Borinqueneers were a fighting force to be reckoned with. It had earned a place of honor in Marine Corps history. It had survived the Korean winter at its worst. It had safeguarded the largest sealift since World War II.

The evacuation itself took 193 shiploads using 109 ships. Two CCF armies (37,500 men) were annihilated by X Corps and/or the weather during the withdrawal from Changjin. More than 3,600 wounded soldiers and 200 vehicles were airlifted out. Hungnam was destroyed. In Harris' opinion, the overall venture constituted "a logistic and strategic miracle."

On board the USS Freeman, the exhausted Puerto Ricans were treated like honored guests. Many, after enjoying their first hot showers and hot meals in months, had much to thank the Lord for. Regimental Catholic chaplain Father Ryan said a Mass, and the men sang "Noche de Paz" ("Silent Night") while their Continental comrades sang "Adeste Fideles." Colonel Harris commended

6.4 Elements of the 65th Infantry Regiment "Borinqueneers" withdraw from Hungnam. Onboard the USS General H. B. Freeman. Christmas Eve 1950. Courtesy of the National Archives.

his men on an unparalleled performance, reiterating his "complete and unbending confidence in [their] fighting ability." Christmas Day in the morning treated the warriors with a unique breakfast resembling nothing of the cold C rations the men got used to, in a preamble to the heavenly evening banquet of roast turkey.

The influx of troops in Pusan initially overwhelmed that port's capacity, but by New Year's Day the 3rd Division was on the ground again and ready to assume its duties under EUSAK's I Corps.

The Borinqueneers stood tall and ready for future triumphs in the Land of Morning Calm.

ESCUADRON 201, "THE AZTEC EAGLES"

■ ■ ■ ■ ■

7

Escuadron 201, "The Aztec Eagles"

Note: The following is a compilation of articles written by David Uhler, Sig Unander and Lucy Guevara. For details please see Bibliography.

World War II was a turning point for America and the world. America realized its potential as an industrialized nation and the world recognized that international alliances were essential for the progress of humanity. Two nations that experienced this at a closer level were the United States and Mexico.

On December 8, 1941, the day after the attack at Pearl Harbor, Mexico severed its ties to Germany, Italy and Japan. In May 1942, Nazi submarines sank two Mexican tankers, and Mexico declared war against the Axis powers. Soon thereafter, President Manuel Avila Camacho offered, unofficially, to send Mexican troops to join with the United States in their war effort.

The United States responded to his proposal in the spring of 1944 and Roosevelt offered the Mexican Air Force an opportunity to fight in the war with the United States. That spring, Mexico formed the *Fuerza Aerea Expedicionaria Mexicana*, a three hundred man Air Force Squadron, known as Squadron 201.

Squadron 201 flew fifty-nine combat missions from Porac and Clark Fields on the island of Luzon in the Philippines against Japanese positions until the war ended in August 1945. Five 201 pilots died in the Philippines. One was shot down by enemy anti-aircraft fire; one died in a crash, and three ran out of fuel, crashed and died at sea after being lost in bad weather.

Escuadron 201 made a contribution to the war effort that was more than merely symbolic, helping the Allies liberate Luzon and Formosa (Taiwan)

7.1 Squadron 201 pilots during their training in the U.S. Photo courtesy of www.integrate.com.

while logging 59 missions and 1,290 hours of combat flight time. The service of these 300 Mexican soldiers changed how Mexico was perceived by the world immediately following the war.

Chosen by Mexican officials from numerous volunteers, this event marked the first time that Mexican troops were trained for overseas combat. Among the 300 men were 38 experienced pilots and 250 ground crewmen. Measures for the development of the Mexican Fighter Squadron 201 were soon taken by both nations.

After meetings between President Camacho, General William E. Hall, U.S. Deputy Chief of Air Staff, and Mexican Air Force chief, General Salinas, specifications for the participation of the squadron were established. The Mexican Fighter Squadron 201 would receive training in an American air base for a minimum of five months. After completing training on the P-47, they would be assigned to the Pacific Theater.

After a modest farewell in Mexico, the Mexican Fighter Squadron 201 left Mexico to receive training in the United States on July 24, 1944. The men arrived at Laredo, Texas on July 25, 1944.

7.2 Mexican maintenance mechanics prepare the plane for a mission. Photo courtesy of www.portalaviacion.com.

They would become part of the first Mexican military organization to leave the country with a war mission.

They soon arrived at Randolph Air Field in San Antonio, where they received medical examinations, as well as weapons and flight proficiency tests. The men went on to Pocatello Army Air Base in Pocatello, Idaho.

In Pocatello, the men were given extensive training in their area of specialty such as armament, communication, or engineering. They arrived at Majors Field in Greenville, Texas on November 30, 1944. Here, the pilots received further aviation instructions and training. Training included combat air tactics, formation flying, and gunnery. The men were honored with graduation ceremonies on February 20, 1945 where they were presented with their battle flag.

The largest groups went to Pocatello, Idaho and the Republic Aviation Corporation in Farmingdale, Long Island, and N.Y. Others went to Boca Raton, Florida, and Scot Field, IL. Training for the ground echelon consisted basically of instruction in English, basic military subjects, and on the job training in different specialties. Instructors and trainees worked hard to accomplish the mission. In the opinion of their instructors, "the Mexican maintenance men were demonstrating a commendable seriousness of purpose, initiative, and comprehension."

The pilots commenced refresher training in Foster Field, TX that terminated in October 1944. Twenty-seven pilots were needed to fill the Tables of Organization, and the original training plan included eleven replacements. They flew transition, formation, instruments, navigation, night flying, and strafing missions in the AT-6 and P-40 aircraft. Finally, the men left for the Philippines on the *Liberty Ship Fairisle* on March 27, 1945.

Also known as the 'Aztec Eagles,' the squadron arrived in Manila Bay on April 30, 1945. The Mexican air-group was greeted by General C. Kenney, the commanding officer of the Far East Air Force, as well as by the Philippine General Consul, Alfredo Carmelo. Consul Carmelo welcomed the men with a small celebration that included Mexican music, and fiesta costumes. The Mexican Fighter Squadron 201 received pre-combat training from the pilots of the 58th. After this instruction period, the men were ready to participate in combat.

Although, in the Philippines for only six months, the squadron actively participated in 59 combat missions, totaling more than 1,290 hours of flight. Some mission results mention secondary

7.3 This is a rare photo of Squadron 201 P-47s on a mission over enemy territory in the Pacific. Photo taken by Mexican Lt. Amadeo Castro Almanza.

explosions and silenced machine gun nests. One daily report indicated: "The Mexican P-47s bombed and strafed enemy concentrations and motor convoy north of PAYAWAN on route #4. All bombs were in the target area and two trucks were left burning."

The 201 successfully participated in the Allied effort to bomb Luzon and Formosa in an attempt to push the Japanese out of the islands. Assigned to the 58th Fighter group of the U.S. 5th Air Force, the "Aztec Eagles" were also used as ground support after the aerial threat from Japan weakened. During these ground assignments, the men of the squadron saw first hand the fearlessness and war mentality of the Japanese soldiers. Japanese soldiers were often captured after trying to come into U.S. military campsites for food.

Captain P. A. Reynaldo Perez Gallardo had his day in the sun at a bridge over the Marikina River. The Japanese, defending this key link in their transportation network, concentrated their anti-aircraft fire at the incoming Allied fighter planes. Ignoring the bullet bursts, Gallardo swooped in low and toggled his bomb switch, perfectly timing the release of three 500-pound bombs that knocked the steel span out of commission.

"Luck and fate were with me that day," he says. Some of Gallardo's fellow fliers weren't so fortunate. Five of them died overseas, including one flier whose remains were recovered by a team that included Gallardo.

"All we found were his bones," Gallardo says. On Aug. 6, 1945–11 days after the Mexican pilot's fatal crash–an American B-29 dropped the atomic bomb on Hiroshima. World War II ended a short time later.

Before leaving the Philippines, the members of Escuadron 201 erected a monument, topped by a statue of the Mexican eagle, in commemoration of their fallen comrades.

After a year of training and six months of active duty, the 'Aztec Eagles' were able to return home. Mexico greeted them with a hero's welcome on November 18, 1945 and the leader of the squadron handed the unit's battle flag to Mexican President Avila Camacho.

The Mexican president decorated the entire squadron with a medal for *Servicio en el Lejano Oriente*, the commendation for "Service in the Far East." This was the only medal for valor ever awarded to a Mexican military unit for overseas combat. In addition, each of the pilots later

7.4 Capt. Reynaldo Gallardo wearing the uniform of Escuadron 201, May 7, 2004. Photo courtesy of La Prensa San Diego, CA.

7.5 The Thunderbolt P-47 in this photo was flying one of the last missions for Squadron 201 in July 1945. Photo courtesy of www.portalaviacion.com.

received the U.S. Air Medal from Gen. George C. Kenney, as well as the Philippine Presidential Unit Citation from the president of the Philippines. Other medals awarded were the Mexican Medal of Valor, and World War II Victory Medals.

After the war, Gallardo continued to serve in the Mexican air force, selecting and training new pilots. Later, he served as a pilot for the Mexican state of Michoacan and as director of security for Mexican Social Security. In 1984, Gallardo and his wife, Angelina, moved to Austin, TX. They have two children. At age 77, Gallardo still works in the trucking business.

On Veteran's Day, Carlos Foustinos, a former member of the Squadron, flies a Mexican flag in his home instead of 'Old Glory.'

This flag is flown in commemoration of the men of the 201st Mexican Fighter Squadron who fought and died in aerial combat along with Americans in the South Pacific.

Faustinos flew approximately 25 missions, recording six Japanese zero kills. This feat brought him the distinction of a flying ace and he was awarded the "La Cruz de Honor" (The Cross of Honor), which is equivalent to the U.S. Medal of Honor, by the Mexican government.

Today, monuments to Escuadron 201 still stand all over Mexico. The names of the fallen pilots are inscribed in a marble amphitheater below Chapultepec Castle in Mexico City, where survivors of the

squadron gather every year on the anniversary of their return to Mexico.

The American GI Forum has recently honored these veterans and they have participated in several oral history projects. Today, squadron members reminisce about their experience and the friendships they made. They feel undeserving of heroic admiration, but rather feel they were simply completing their responsibility to serve their country.

The men of the 'Escuadron 201' give praise to the united efforts of the Allied Nations during World War II and feel that it was a common desire for democracy that won the war. They expressed their sentiments with hopes that future generations realize that fighting a war is useless.

Relations between the United States and Mexico strengthened with the formation of agreements such as the U.S. and Mexico Defense Commission, which allowed military conscription of

7.6 This group of Mexican officers are posing at their base in the Phillipines. Photo courtesy of www.rathbonemuseum.com.

Mexican citizens living in the United States. The other major agreement between the two countries was the Bracero Program.

From 1943 to 1945, the Bracero Program brought more than 100,000 Mexican laborers to work the fields and railways in order to alleviate Americas manual labor shortage. This agreement allowed the two neighboring countries to use each other's resources as efficiently as possible during this time of need. World War II marked the first time that these countries had combined both their industrial and armed forces to conquer a common threat.

From June 1 to July 10, 1945, the 201st:
(1) Flew 50 missions and 293 sortie,
(2) Dropped 181 tons of bombs,
(3) Fired 104,000 rounds of ammunition, and
(4) Seven pilots were killed in action.

The aircraft carrier USS Essex underway during World War II, May 1943.

FIGHTER ACES FROM WWII AND THE KOREAN WAR

■ ■ ■ ■ ■

8

Fighter Aces from World War II and the Korean War

Note: The following is a compilation of articles written by: Santiago A. Flores, Roger A. Freeman, MSgt Sarah Hood, Mary Scott, Edward Sims, and Barrett Tillman. For details please see Bibliography.

The term "Ace" has been used since World War I. It is used to designate a fighter pilot who destroys five or more enemy aircraft in aerial combat. The term originated in the French escadrilles (squadrons) of World War I.

1ST LT. OSCAR PERDOMO
LAST ACE IN A DAY, WWII

Born in El Paso, Texas, on June 14, 1919, Oscar F. Perdomo graduated from James A. Garfield High School in Los Angeles, California, in 1937

8.1 First Lt. Oscar Perdomo. Photo courtesy of the U.S. Air Force.

and joined the Army Air Forces in February 1943 as an aviation cadet. After earning his wings at Williams Field, Arizona, in January 1944, he was eventually assigned to the 464th Fighter Squadron in October 1944. Part of the 507th Fighter Group, the squadron did not move overseas until late in the war, arriving at the island of Ie Shima off the west coast of Okinawa in June 1945.

Flying Republic P-47N "Thunderbolt" fighters specifically designed for service in the Pacific, the

8.2 The P-47 Thunderbolt was heavily used as both a fighter and fighter-bomber; the later of these two roles is where the plane really proved its capabilities. Photo courtesy of jetplanes.co.uk.

unit participated in the final air offensive that ended World War II. On August 13th, a week after the atomic bomb had been dropped on Hiroshima, Perdomo achieved one of the ultimate measures of a combat pilot; he became the last ace of the war by shooting down five enemy aircraft.

Perdomo, along with nearly 50 other Army pilots, took off from Ie Shima on the 13th. Leading an element from the 464th, he took after five Japanese "Franks," Nakajima Ki-84 aircraft, and was credited with shooting down three of them. By then, Perdomo had become separated from the rest of his squadron when he spotted two "Willows," Japanese Navy trainer aircraft. He was able to shoot one down before being "jumped" by three more Franks.

In the ensuing dogfight, Perdomo scored his last victory, his fifth confirmed kill of the day. During his 8-hour sortie, which covered 1,800 miles, this Hispanic American hero joined the most elite of the elite in the fighter community, an ace in a day. For "his outstanding skills and courage, coupled with his unfaltering determination to destroy the enemy at all costs," Perdomo received the Distinguished Service Cross.

Perdomo remained in the service until January 1950 when he joined an Air National Guard unit in California and then an Air Force Reserve unit. Recalled to active duty in January 1952 during the Korean War, Perdomo remained on active duty until January 1958.

Two of his sons fought in Vietnam, with one, Kris, being killed in action on May 9, 1970, while serving as a gunner aboard a UH-1C "Huey" helicopter.

Oscar Perdomo died in Los Angeles, California, on March 2, 1976, at the age of 56.

COMMANDER EUGENE A. VALENCIA, JR. LEADER OF VALENCIA'S "FLYING CIRCUS," WWII

Aboard the USS Yorktown was the most successful fighter division (4 planes) of the war, known as "Valencia's Flying Circus." They shot down 50 enemy planes and they hold the record as being the highest-scoring fighter division in Navy history.

Eugene Valencia was born in San Francisco in 1921. He joined the Navy as an aviation cadet in mid-1941, and trained until April 1942. After a stint as an instructor, he was assigned to the brand-new Navy carrier, USS Essex in February 1943. With Essex, he scored his first aerial kill, shooting down three enemy planes over Rabaul and one over Tarawa in November 1943.

Over Truk on February 16, 1944, he became separated from his wingman,

8.3 CDR Eugene A. Valencia.
Photo courtesy of www.acepilots.com.

Bill Bonneau, and was attacked by several Zeros. They chased him at length and fired repeatedly, but couldn't hit him. Figuring that their poor gunnery didn't threaten him too much, Valencia swung around to face his attackers, and shot down three in short order. On his return to Essex, he shouted out for his Hellcat, saying, "I love this airplane so much that if it could cook, I'd marry it."

The "Mowing Machine"

At Truk, he spotted a weakness in the enemy's fighter tactics, from which he developed his famed "Mowing Machine." The intense and mercurial Valencia strove to build an 'esprit de corps' in his division: requesting purple lightning bolts on their Hellcats (denied), decorating their helmets flamboyantly, and securing mint juleps

8.4 F6F Hellcat fighter.
Photo courtesy of www.btinternet.com.

or champagne for the division's pre-flight refreshment. They worked relentlessly, flying over 100 hours a month.

On February 15, VF-9 escorted a raid on Tokyo (the first in 3 years). Valencia spotted a bogey high and behind them. He racked his Hellcat around and challenged the "Tojo" head-on, first firing his rockets. Mitchell came up to help, flamed the bandit, and saw the pilot bail out. The division reformed and continued hunting both aerial and ground targets. Valencia got two more, while James French and Clinton Smith got three between them. The "Flying Circus" came back from its first combat mission with six confirmed kills, with no damage to their Hellcats.

In March VF-9 joined USS Yorktown, CV-10 (a new Essex-class carrier, the first Yorktown being sunk at Midway), a part of Task Force 58. TF 58 participated in the difficult Okinawa campaign, which the Japanese defended fiercely from March until June 21.

Okinawa

On the morning of April 17, his squadron, the VF-9 was flying Combat Air Patrol (CAP); Japanese air attacks were expected. Before dawn Valencia and the other Hellcat pilots launched and began the climb to 25,000 feet. Patrolling to the north, Valencia had a good chance of encountering the Japanese. The Hellcats circled on reaching altitude, and continued uneventfully for an hour. But then *Yorktown's* radar room reported contacts to the north, which Smith soon spotted. "Tally ho! Bogeys! Three o'clock!"

The closest pilot, French (a wingman), headed toward them; the division had trained so that any one of the four could take the lead. From ten miles out, the enemy seemed to number about 20 or 30. But as the distance closed, Valencia estimated 35 or 40. "Closing further," French called out "There must be fifty of 'em!" French and Smith led the first diving attack, with Valencia and Mitchell as top cover. The enemy formation didn't react; French and Smith both fired and hit the bomb-carrying Franks, which disintegrated when their high explosives were hit. These two crossed and pulled up to cover Valencia and Mitchell, who then rapidly closed with the enemy gaggle and exploded two more Franks.

The four Hellcats then reversed direction, while the Japanese continued on their southern course, gambling that they could reach the American fleet before the Hellcats decimated their planes. Valencia and Mitchell led the return, closed in, and exploded two more Franks. After this, the Japanese dispersed, and Valencia radioed, "break tactics, select targets of opportunity!" The Franks, Zeros, and Oscars scattered widely, and Valencia's division split into pairs, pursuing as well as they could.

To his relief, some other Hellcats joined the interception, as the Japanese were closing in on *Yorktown.* Valencia got onto another Franks' tail, and opened up from one hundred yards. Smoke streamed back and the Frank exploded. Victory number three for Valencia! So far his division had scored nine kills and two probables!

Valencia spotted three other Franks, and was briefly distracted by tracer fire, which turned out to

8.5 The F6F Hellcat was built specifically to counter the Japanese Zero, and earned the nickname "ace maker." Artwork courtesy www.acepilots.com.

be from Mitchell. Recovering, Valencia walked up on his fourth victim, and fired.

He stayed with his smoking target, while Mitchell clobbered another Frank from the same trio. Soon these two went down, upping the division's total to eleven, and Valencia's to four. Maneuvering, he then went for the remaining plane in the division, and poured shells into it. Victory number five!

All over the sky, American planes were downing the Japanese attackers. Valencia spotted a Frank on the tail of two unsuspecting Hellcats (intent on their own targets); he picked up speed, came within range, and pulled the trigger. His win number six saved the other Hellcat pilot. By this time his division had racked up 14 kills.

At this point, low fuel forced Valencia to head back for the *Yorktown.* He rendezvoused with Mitchell, and circled, hoping to pick up French and Smith. A stray Japanese fighter came too close, and Valencia stood on a wing and made for him. But as he pressed the trigger, nothing happened. His guns were empty! Valencia radioed the *Yorktown* and received permission for him and Mitchell to land. They thumped down their dirty, but unhurt fighters, followed shortly by Smith and French. The division had scored seventeen confirmed kills and four probables–their best day of the war.

The 'Flying Circus' continued its deadly work. Seventeen days later, they knocked down eleven enemy aircraft. Then on May 11, they scored another 10 kills, all in defense of the fleet.

By the end of the war, all had become aces, Navy Fighter Ace, also known as, 'Okinawa Ace', Commander Valencia leading them with 23 kills, receiving the Navy Cross for his heroism and leadership.

RICHARD GOMEZ CANDELARIA FIGHTER ACE, WWII

World War II Captain Richard Gomez Candelaria Air Force Fighter Ace was assigned to the 479 Fighter Squadron and fought in the European Theatre. He shot down six German aircraft. On April 13, 1945, he was shot down by anti aircraft fire in East Prussia and finished the war in a German prisoner of war camp.

8.6 Capt. Richard Gomez Candelaria. Photo courtesy of the U.S. Air Force.

The Top Scorer

Candelaria, was born on July 14th, 1922 in Pasadena, California, he joined the U.S. Army Reserves, was commissioned a 2nd Lt. and received his wings on February 8th, 1944 at Williams Field, Arizona. He joined the 479th Fighter Group on September 22, 1944.

This particular fighter group was assigned to the 8th Air Force since its arrival in May 1944 in Scotland. The unit initially flew the Lockheed P-38J twin-engine fighter, and the group was assigned to the 65th Fighter Wing and was the last fighter group to be assigned to the VIII Fighter Command.

Lt. Candelaria opened his scorecard on December 5th, 1944 on a mission to support the bombers to hit targets in the Berlin and Munster area. On that day, Lt. Candelaria shot-down two FW-190's, NW of Berlin. While his squadron, the 435th, shot-down three more German aircraft.

8.7 P38 Lightning fighter.
Photo courtesy of www.btinternet.com.

On March 3rd, 1945, Lt. Candelaria with Lt. B.C. Means attacked German aircraft on the ground at Dummer Lake. Candelaria claimed three BF-109's damaged on the ground, while Lt. Means claimed a BF-109 destroyed on the ground.

But his big day would be on April 7th while protecting the bombers from Schulungslehrgang Elbe.

"I Have A Bunch of Germans Cornered!"

This statement is reportedly what Lt. Candelaria radioed to his squadron mates on that particular day as noted in the book: *The Last flight of the Luftwaffe*, by Adrian Weir.

> *…One of the 435th FS pilots searched the sky around him for signs of contrails. Already feeling alone, Lt. Candelaria had lost contact with the rest of his flight, and on reaching the rendezvous with the bombers had decided to attach himself to the low squadron of Liberators. Finding no signs of the German fighters, Candelaria held his position. Little did he know that he was about to experience a day to remember.*

While other elements from his squadron were engaging a group of Me-262's, in which a jet fighter was shot-down by Capt. Verner E. Hooker, Candelaria would be in the fight of his life.

> *…From his position alongside the lower bombers, Lt. Candelaria was at last alerted to the presence of the jets when the bombers began to fire flares as a general warning to the rest of the group.*
> *Spotting a pair of Me-262's who had started to climb back towards the bombers, he turned towards*

the jets, facing the leading aircraft head-on. Hoping to divert the jets from their approach, Candelaria must have begun to have doubts as to the wisdom of his move as the rotten made no attempt to alter its course.

With only fractions of a second separating the fighters from a collision, the Me-262 pushed his aircraft into a shallow dive beneath the Mustang. In a very unusual move, Lt. Candelaria tried to drop his tanks onto the jet below, then half-rolled his fighter into a position on its tail just as the German pilot opened fire on the bombers.

With the drop tanks tactic having no effect, Candelaria opted for his more conventional armament and let loose a burst, which scored direct hits on both fuselage and wings. With the fighter still in his sights, his concentration was broken by the sight of streams of red and white tracers, the size of golf balls flashing past him.

At that moment a second Me-262 was coming up right behind him, firing away. Before he could free himself from the danger, he received hits on his aircraft right wing; luckily the damage was not serious.

…At the same time, the leading jet broke to the left and entered a half-roll that became a steep dive with smoke trailing behind. Hoping to catch the second jet, Candelaria attempted to haul his fighter into a turn, but the jet was diving at high speed, perhaps in an attempt to assist his crippled Kamerad.

Candelaria was given a 'probable' Me-262 destroyed, it later appeared that the jets were being used to draw the escort fighters away from the bombers so that the Elbe pilots would commence their attack runs with no problems from the escorting P-51's.

At that particular moment, the 434th Fighter Squadron received a warning from a lone pilot who had spotted a formation of about 15 BF-109's heading directly towards the bombers. The pilots of the 434th and Lt. Candelaria immediately headed at full speed to meet the attack and assist the lone pilot that had given the warning.

The enemy formation consisted of three, four aircraft flights lead by an experience leader. Candelaria decided to attack the nearest flight leader, but he turned out to be a very competent German fighter pilot.

Candelaria tried to put himself in the best firing position as he followed after the German. He noted that the rest of the flight did not attempt to fire on him or even the bombers they simply followed the leader. As Candelaria made several passes on the bombers, he shot-down one of them.

It's guessed that the flight was formed from pilots of the Elbe group, and the aircraft that Candelaria was following had enough conventional ammunition to carry out a standard attack on the bomber formation. But Candelaria failed to notice the P-51 that was right behind him as he was firing on the bombers.

…With mounting frustration Candelaria chased the BF-109 and for a split moment found him in his sights. The luck of the Luftwaffe pilot had finally run out: the brief burst of fire struck this German.

Now the subject of attention of the many German BF-109's, Candelaria continued to fight it out.

…Able to out-turn his pursuers, he again opened fire and almost instantly a third BF-109 stalled out and the pilot jumped free. A fourth BF-109 followed only seconds later as the pilot lost control of his fighter attempting to follow the Mustang. This

8.8 Messerschmitt ME-262 German jet fighter.
Courtesy of www.ares.cz.

Luftwaffe pilot was trapped in his wildly spinning machine as it crashed to earth.

As Candelaria claimed the fourth BF-109 in this dogfight, his actual fifth victim of the day, help finally arrived as other P-51's reached the bombers. The first pilots to arrive included 1st Lt. Charles Heathman and William Barksky who were both in position to observe the final moments of Candelaria's combat and confirm the burning wreckage of four BF-109's, all within a radius of less than five miles.

After his hectic aerial combat, Candelaria decided not to risk it and stayed with this group of

8.9 P-51 Mustang fighter.
Photo courtesy of www.seymourjohnson.af.mil.

pilots for the remainder of the mission, later in his 'after combat report', he credits the arrival of these P–51's that saved him from the surviving BF-109s.

For this particular mission Lt. Candelaria achieved the status of "Ace" with a score of six German aircraft destroyed plus one probable.

But on April 13, 1945 the Germans got even with Lt. Candelaria, while strafing a German airfield South of Tarnewitz, he was shot-down by ground fire, while flying his P-51K, "My Pride and Joy," as reported by Capt. Theo J. Sowrby of the 435th fighter squadron:

...I was leading lakeside on a dive strafing pass on Tarnewitz airfield at 1630 hours on the 13th of April. On pulling up after the first run Lt. Candelaria called me on the radio and asked if he could make another pass as he had something spotted. I OK'd him and he started a shallow dive 30 degrees from the bay toward the airfield.

We picked up a lot of flack and Candeleria soon called on the radio that he had been hit and had no oil pressure and asked for the best steer to friendly territory. I told him to fly 200 degrees, which he did for about five minutes. He them called and said his ship was pretty hot and guessed he would have to bail out. This was right near the town of Wittenburg. He bailed out O.K. and on reaching the ground ran into some nearby woods. There was no traffic or persons seen in the area. His plane exploded in the woods some ways to the north of where he landed in his chute. I think that Lt. Candelaria had made a good chance to escape.

But Lt. Candelaria did not escape. He was captured and reportedly taken to a POW camp. Other sources say that he and a RAF aircrew man managed to escape by taking a German Officer hostage and driving his staff car westward, reaching an approaching British armor unit.

After the war, it was reported that Candelaria became a restaurant owner in California, serving better food than he had at the POW camp. He later served in the Air National Guard, reaching the rank of Colonel. He is reported to be living in California.

CAPTAIN MICHAEL BREZAS
AIR FORCE FIGHTER ACE, WWII

Michael Brezas arrived at Lucera, Italy during the summer of 1944, to join the 48th Fighter Squadron of the 14th Fighter Group. He came to

8.10 P-38 Lightning fighter.
Photo courtesy of home.teleport.com.

the 48th Fighter Squadron as a 2nd Lieutenant. He was promoted to 1st Lieutenant in July and to Captain in November. Brezas was only 21 years old. Flying a P-38 aircraft, Lt. Brezas downed 12 enemy planes within two months. On July 8, he destroyed an ME 109 over Vienna, Austria.

On a mission to Budapest on July 12, he downed one ME 109 and two FW 190's. He became an ace on July 19 when he destroyed an FW 190 on a mission to Munich, Germany.

Then on July 20, he shot down another ME 109 while flying against Menninger, Germany. Six days later he destroyed two FW 190's near Buzau, Romania. Lt Brezas also downed two ME 109's on August 7 while flying a mission to Blechhammer, Germany.

His final two victories were scored on August 25 against two FW 190's while on a mission to Kurin, Czechoslovakia. Brezas received the Distinguished Flying Cross, the Air Medal with eleven Oak Leaf Clusters, and the Silver Star.

LT. COL. DONALD S. LOPEZ, USAF (RET.) FIGHTER ACE

Donald Lopez was born in Brooklyn, NY in July 1923, and flew a Curtiss P-40 Warhawk with the 14th Air Force's 23rd Fighter Group, known as The Flying Tigers. Lopez served in the U.S. Army Air Force in China and Burma defending China.

Lopez became an "ace" after downing five Japanese aircraft in aerial combat. Lopez' other military assignments included five years as a fighter test pilot, a short combat tour flying North American F-86s in Korea, and five years at the U.S. Air Force Academy as an Associate Professor of Aeronautics and Chief of Academic Counseling.

Following a tour in the Pentagon, he earned a bachelor's degree in aeronautical engineering at the Air Force Institute of Technology and a master's degree in aeronautics from the California Institute of Technology.

After his retirement from the U.S. Air Force in 1964, Lopez worked as a Systems Engineer on the Apollo-Saturn Launch Vehicle and the Skylab Orbital Workshop for Bellcomm, Inc. In 1972,

8.11 Donald Lopez, shown here as a lieutenant in a U.S. fighter unit. Photo courtesy of smithsonianeducation.org.

Lopez joined the National Air and Space Museum, Smithsonian Institution, as assistant director for the Aeronautics Department. Lopez was instrumental in developing the exhibits that welcomed visitors at the Museum's opening on July 1, 1976, and that have made it the most visited museum in the world. More recently, he was appointed Deputy Director of the museum from 1983 to 1990, and then reappointed in 1996.

Lopez is a member of the American Fighter Aces Association, the Experimental Aircraft Association, and is a Fellow of the Royal Aeronautical Society. In 1995, he was named an Elder Statesman of Aviation by the National Aeronautic Association.

COLONEL MANUEL J. FERNANDEZ, JR. AIR FORCE FIGHTER ACE, KOREAN WAR

The only Latino fighter ace during the Korean War, Capt. Manuel J. Fernandez is credited with 14.5 kills during the Korean War and was also the 3rd leading ace of the Korean War.

Col. Fernandez was born on April 19, 1925 in Key West, Florida, and in 1943 graduated from Andrew Jackson High School, Miami, Florida. He enlisted as an aviation cadet and in 1948 piloted a C-47 in the Berlin Airlift. For his actions Great Britain made him an honorary member of the Most Excellent Order of the British Empire.

From September 1952 to May 1953, Captain Manuel J. Fernandez, Jr. shot down 14.5 MIGs and flew 125 combat missions with the 4th Fighter Interceptor Wing in Korea.

Flying F-86 aircraft, his first MIG victory occurred on October 4, 1952. On May 10, 1953 he had

8.12 Col. Manuel F. Fernandez, Jr.
Photo courtesy of U.S. Air Force.

his last Korean victory and shared a one-half victory over a MIG aircraft the same day.

In 1956 Colonel Fernandez was awarded the Bendix Trophy for setting a record with an average speed of 667 mph flying an F-100C from George Air Force Base, California to Tinker Air Force Base, Oklahoma. He was also a member of the Nellis Air Force Base, Nevada Mach Riders aerobatics flying team.

Later Fernandez became a test pilot for the F-100 Super Sabre and an advisor for the Argentine Air Force. He achieved the rank of Major before resigning in 1963. He died in a flight in the Bahamas during October 1980.

MAJOR GENERAL EDWARD W. SUAREZ FLIGHT INSTRUCTOR, WWII

While those who served on the front lines during World War II received most of the attention, those who trained the pilots, bombardiers, gunners, mechanics, and engineers also deserve recognition. One such individual was Edward W. Suarez.

Born in Biloxi, Mississippi, on March 11, 1909, Suarez attended West Point and received his commission as a second lieutenant in the Infantry in June 1932. While at West Point, Suarez earned All-American status as a tackle on the Army football team. Twenty-four years later, he would be honored with a *Sports Illustrated* magazine's silver anniversary All-American Award for his accomplishments on the football field and in his professional life.

Suarez began his flying career at Randolph Field, in San Antonio, considered the Army's "West Point of the Air," in October 1932 and graduated from advanced flying school at nearby Kelly Field a year later. After an initial assignment with the 11th Bombardment Squadron at March Field, California, Suarez was transferred to Hawaii in June 1937.

Returning stateside in June 1939, Suarez became a flying instructor at Randolph Field, and served in that capacity for three years. With America's entry into the World War II, military training programs exploded, and the Army Air Forces Training Command (AAFTC) grew to include programs at some 600 locations. Through his intense and committed involvement with flying training, Suarez would play a significant role in the defeat of the Axis powers, though he never made it to Europe, the Middle East, or the Pacific.

From Randolph, Suarez traveled to the newly opened flying school at Blackland Air Base, Waco, Texas, as the Director of Training, then moved to Del Rio, Texas, renamed Laughlin Army Airfield in March 1943, as commander of the just-activated B-26 "Marauder" bomber school.

From Del Rio, Suarez joined the AAF Flying Training Command headquarters staff at Fort Worth, Texas, in December 1942, where he served until August 1945.

In 1944, when production was greatest, Training Command graduated more than 87,000 pilots and nearly 40,000 navigators from its flying programs. For the outstanding performance of his flying training management duties, Suarez received the

8.13 MG Edward W. Suarez.
Photo courtesy of the U.S. Army.

Legion of Merit. One of his major accomplishments was writing the first official training manual for instruction in basic flying training.

In a career that lasted 17 years after the end of World War II, Suarez served in a wide variety of posts, including chief of the Policy Branch of Supreme Headquarters, Allied Powers in Europe and as the chief of staff for Allied Air Forces in Southern Europe. Between 1957 and 1959, he worked closely with the elite of the nation's military thinkers while serving as deputy commandant for Military Affairs and then Deputy Commandant for Academic Affairs at the National War College. Suarez retired in 1962.

After having served on the front line of the Cold War in Europe in the early 1950s, and in Turkey from 1959-1962, he lived to see the end of the Cold War before Gen. Suarez died on November 4, 1994.

SATOR "SANDY" SANCHEZ
GUNNER, WWII

Born on March 22, 1921, Sator "Sandy" Sanchez grew up in a Hispanic community in Lockport, Illinois, near Chicago.

Just growing up was an ordeal as Sanchez's mother died from tuberculosis when he was only two, and his father was murdered when Sandy was eight. Adopted by his grandparents, Sanchez dreamed of flying and often walked or rode his bicycle to watch the planes come and go at Lewis Airport.

In high school, he belonged to a junior reserve officer training corps unit and worked for the Civilian Conservation Corps after graduation. In December 1939, he joined the Army and became an aircraft mechanic in May 1941.

After the outbreak of war, Sanchez moved to England and joined the 334th Bombardment Squadron at Horhan, Suffolk, where he served as a tail gunner in a Boeing B-17 "Flying Fortress" bomber. During a mission over Munster, Germany, on October 10, 1943, one of the most concentrated air battles in the early days of the war, he shot down two enemy aircraft, a Messerschmitt ME-109 and a Junkers JU-88.

For his actions during the mission, in which 30 American planes were shot down, Sanchez received a Silver Star. After completing 25 missions and gaining eligibility to go home, he volunteered to stay on and completed a total of 44 missions before he was forced to return to the United States in June 1944.

Listed among his many accomplishments was the destruction of six enemy aircraft. Because

8.14 B-17, the Flying Fortress bomber flying over Europe during World War II.
Photo courtesy of hsgm.free.fr/b17.jpg.

bomber crewmembers usually did not receive credit for kills due to the difficulty identifying which of the gunners shot down the enemy aircraft, Sanchez is not recognized as an ace. However, he did have the unique honor of having a plane named for him, the "'Smilin' Sammy Sanchez," the only known case of a B-17 having been named for an enlisted man.

After six months in the states, Sanchez returned to combat, assigned to the 353rd Bombardment Squadron based at Lucera, Italy. Sanchez died on March 15, 1945, during a mission in which he served as the top turret gunner. While attempting to bomb an oil plant deep inside Germany, his B-17 bomber was hit by bomb flak.

As the rest of the crew bailed out, Sanchez stayed with the aircraft manning his gun, the plane exploded and broke into several pieces. The Germans captured the nine surviving crewmembers that jumped and told pilot Dale Thornton they had buried Sanchez next to the B-17.

One of the most highly decorated Army Air Forces enlisted crewmembers, Sanchez earned the Silver Star, Distinguished Flying Cross, Soldier's Medal, Air Medal with 10 Oak Leaf Clusters, and the Purple Heart.

In March 1996, the United States Air Force Museum personnel recovered the tail section of the plane in which Sanchez died and brought it home to Wright-Patterson Air Force Base. Former crewmembers Thornton, co-pilot Ted Narracci, navigator Les Tyler, and bombardier Steve Stofko accompanied the recovery effort. Sanchez's body was not found at the crash site near Bad Muskau, about 80 miles southeast of Berlin.

MAX BACA, JR.
GUNNER, WWII

Not much is known about Max Baca, Jr., who grew up in Albuquerque, New Mexico. Assigned to

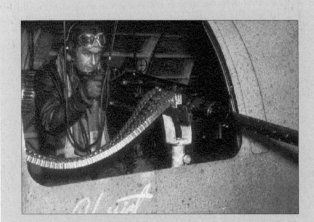

8.15 Gunner Max Baca, Jr. Photo courtesy of Air Training Command History Office, Randolph AFB Texas.

the 93rd Bombardment Squadron, Baca flew as a crewmember in B-17 Flying Fortresses in the Pacific.

He served as an aerial engineer and gunner and received his first Silver Star for "unusual gallantry in action, calmness under fire, and a high sense of devotion to duty," during operations on the morning of December 22, 1941, barely two weeks after Pearl Harbor.

A formation of American bombers took off from its base in Australia, sank several Japanese ships in the Gulf of Davao in the Philippines, and destroyed supplies that had been off-loaded to the beach.

Landing after dark at a friendly field after traveling nearly 1,500 miles, the crews caught a quick rest before continuing to the next objective, a huge

concentration of enemy transports in the Lingayan Gulf of Luzon. After 13 hours of flying through enemy fire and stormy weather, four planes reached safe haven. They refueled and returned to their home base.

The order awarding the Silver Star recognized not only the superior skills of the pilots, but also "the courage and determination of every man on the combat crew." In August 1942, Baca received a second Silver Star "for gallantry in action over Simpson Harbor, Rabaul, New Britain."

The citation included a comment that Baca had participated "in numerous combat missions in the Philippine Islands, Java and Australia, and on every occasion has displayed outstanding courage."

FRANCIS X. (FRANK) MEDINA,
TAIL GUNNER, WWII

Francis X. (Frank) Medina from Kansas City, Missouri, was a 20-year old tail gunner in the 459th Bomb Group of the 756th Bomb Squadron, when he was shot down over northern Italy in July 1944. Hit by anti-aircraft fire, the crew of nine bailed out; all but Medina was captured, and he was believed to be missing in action. On his own in unknown territory, he was befriended by Italians who helped him link up with the partisans with whom he was active for eight months. In 1945, the British rescued Medina.

8.16 B-24 bomber dropping bombs over Germany in WWII. Photo courtesy of www.military.cz.

JOSE RAMIREZ
CREW CHIEF, WWII

Jose R. Ramirez, born of Mexican parents in Bowie, Arizona, in May 1915, served as crew chief for a B-24 'Liberator' bomber known as Witchcraft.

Assigned to the 790th Bombardment Squadron stationed at Rackheath, England, this aircraft flew an amazing 130 combat missions without an abort. One of the plane's pilots, John Oder, noted that Ramirez was totally devoted to his aircraft and kept the B-24 immaculate.

Because of the loving care the ground crew lavished on Ramirez's charge, the *Witchcraft* was the first B-24 in the Eighth Air Force to participate in 100 consecutive missions. For his diligence and attention to detail, Ramirez received the Bronze Star and an Oak Leaf Cluster.

He was also concerned about the comfort of his crew and arranged to have a wooden shed built next to the *Witchcraft*. This allowed the men to

8.17 B-24 from the 790th Bombardment Squadron. Photo courtesy of hometown.aol.com.

avoid a long walk back to the barracks after a hard day's work.

It should also be noted that the *Witchcraft* ground crew represented a colorful cross-section of America, consisting of George Dong of Chinese heritage, Raymond Belcher of Dutch extraction, Joseph Veller of German ancestry, the 'American' Walter Elliot, and Mexican-American Ramirez.

This mural titled, *Women in the Military*, was painted by Nancy E. Rhodes. © Copyright 2005 Nancy E. Rhodes.
Reproductions and Note Cards available at nancyerhodes.com. All Rights Reserved.

HISPANIC
SERVICEWOMEN

■ ■ ■ ■ ■

9

Hispanic Servicewomen

Note: The following is a compilation of articles written by Karen Anderson, Dr. Judith Bellafaire, Melvin Ember, Richard Hall, Jenny Haugh, Elizabeth Leonard, Manuel Servin, and SPC Felicia Whatley. For details please see Bibliography.

Richard Hall, in *Patriots in Disguise*, takes a hard look at *The Woman in Battle* and analyzes whether its claims are accurate history or largely fictionalized. Elizabeth Leonard in, *All the Daring of the Soldier*, assesses *The Woman in Battle* as largely fiction, but based on real experience. From *Documenting the American South*, University of North Carolina.

THE CIVIL WAR

Loreta Janeta Velazquez, also known as Lt. Harry T. Buford (1842-?)

In 1876, the American public was introduced to an astonishing and controversial figure by the name of Madame Loreta Janeta Velazquez. Like so many others, she wrote a Civil War memoir, *The Woman in Battle: A Narrative of the Exploits, Adventures, and Travels of Madame Loreta Janeta Velazquez, Otherwise Known as Lieutenant Harry T. Buford Confederate States Army.*

> To My Comrades of the Confederate Armies...
>
> Who, although they fought in a losing cause succeeded by their valor in winning the admiration of the world, this narrative of my adventures as a soldier, a spy, and secret service agent, is dedicated with all honor, respect, and good will.
>
> –Loreta J. Velazquez

...*Within three days I managed to provide myself with a very complete military outfit; quite sufficient to enable me to commence operations without delay, which was the main thing I was after, for I was exceedingly anxious to carry out a magnificent idea I had in my mind, and to present myself before my husband, under such auspices that he could no longer find an excuse for refusing his consent to my joining the Southern army as a soldier.*

My uniform suit having been arranged for, it was an easy matter for me to procure the rest of my outfit without unduly attracting attention, and I soon had in my room a trunk well packed with the wearing apparel of an army officer, and neatly marked upon the outside with the name I had concluded to adopt.

9.1 Loreta Janeta Velasquez as Lt. Buford on the left side and as herself on the right side. Image from *The Woman in Battle*. Courtesy of University of South Carolina at Chapel Hill.

When I saw the trunk with this name upon it as large as life, my heart fairly jumped for joy, and I felt as if the dream of my life were already more than half realized. There was a good deal, however, to be done before I could move any farther in this momentous affair, and while waiting for the tailor to send my uniform suit, I thought and planned until my head fairly ached.

At length I hit upon a method of arranging my financial matters which I judged would prove satisfactory, and concluded to call in a gentleman who was a very old and intimate friend of both my husband and myself, and demand his assistance…

Loreta Velazquez claimed four marriages, though she never took any of her husbands' names. Her second husband enlisted in the Confederate Army at her urging, and, when he left for duty, she raised a regiment for him to command. He died in an accident, and the widow then enlisted–in disguise– and served at Manassas/Bull Run, Ball's Bluff, Fort

9.2 Loreta Janeta Vasquez as Lt. Buford in a bar.
From *The Woman in Battle*.
Courtesy University of South Carolina at Chapel Hill.

Donelson, and Shiloh under the name Lieutenant Harry T. Buford.

Needless to say, this was no ordinary war story, for Madame Velazquez claimed to have so fervently supported the Southern cause that she donned the Confederate uniform as Lieutenant Harry Buford

and fought at the battles of First Bull Run, Fort Donelson, and Shiloh.

Madame Velazquez maintained that she had always wished for the privileges and status granted to men and denied to women. Comparing herself to Deborah of the Hebrews and Joan of Arc, she explained her desire for martial adventures by asserting that her girlhood was spent "haunted with the idea of being a man." She demonstrated unusual independence for a pre-civil war adolescent when, at the age of 14, she ran away from her school in New Orleans to marry an American soldier named William.

When William's state seceded from the Union, he resigned his commission and joined the Confederate Army. At that point Madame Velazquez again fell victim to her old desire to be a man. Unable to persuade her husband to let her fight in the Confederacy, she simply waited for him to leave, adopted the name Lieutenant Harry T. Buford, was measured for two uniforms by a tailor in Memphis, and proceeded to Arkansas to raise a battalion for the Southern cause.

She claimed that she enrolled 236 men in four days and shipped them to Pensacola, Florida, where she presented them to her astonished husband as his to command. Unfortunately he was killed a few days later demonstrating a weapon to his troops. The bereaved widow turned the men over to a friend and proceeded to search for military adventure at the front.

Claiming that she was serving the Confederate Army as an independent, she crossed the South from Virginia to Tennessee, searching for an opportunity to display her military talents. After the First Battle of Bull Run she grew weary of camp life and borrowed female attire from a farmer's wife so that she could go to Washington, D.C. to gather intelligence for the Southern Cause. She finally returned to the South, where she was rewarded for her services by being assigned to the detective corps. But again she grew weary of her assignment and left her duties to go fight in Tennessee. She arrived in Fort Donelson just in time to see it surrendered.

After Fort Donelson she was forced to face the possibility that someone would discover her disguise when she was wounded in the foot and examined by an Army doctor. Apparently she escaped detection, but decided to flee to New Orleans, where

9.3 Loreta Janeta Vasquez as Lt. Buford in a battle leading a charge. From *The Woman in Battle*. Courtesy University of South Carolina at Chapel Hill.

ironically she was arrested on suspicion of being a woman in disguise.

And so the charade continued until April 1862, and the Battle of Shiloh, the scene of her greatest military triumph. Here she found the battalion she had raised in Arkansas and joined them for the fight. She was wounded by a shell while burying the dead after the battle, and an Army doctor discovered her identity.

She fled again to New Orleans and was there when Major General Benjamin F. Butler took command of the city in May 1862. Believing that her military career was at an end because too many people now knew her true identity, she gave up her uniform.

She claimed to have been hired by the authorities in Richmond to serve in the secret service corps and began to travel freely throughout the North, as well as the war-torn South, pausing only long enough to marry her beloved, Captain Thomas DeCaulp.

Widowed shortly after the wedding when her new husband died in a Chattanooga hospital, she traveled north, gained the confidence of Northern officials and was hired by them to search for herself. During her search she continued to serve the Southern cause by trying to organize a rebellion of Confederate prisoners held in Ohio and Indiana. She spent a number of months after the war traveling through Europe and the South.

She also married for the third time. She and her new husband, a Major Wasson, left the United States as immigrants to Venezuela. But when her husband died in Caracas, she returned to America. Again she began to travel, this time through the West, stopping long enough in Salt Lake City to have a baby and meet Brigham Young.

In Nevada, she claimed to have married again for the fourth time to an unnamed gentleman. Then she was off again.

> *…With my baby boy in my arms, I started on a long journey through Colorado, New Mexico, and Texas, hoping, perhaps, but scarcely expecting, to find the opportunities which I had failed to find in Utah, Nevada and California.*

Her story ends at this point. Her final plea was that the public would buy her book so that she could support her child. She was not ashamed of her behavior and hoped that her conduct would be judged with "impartiality and candor" and that credit would be given her for 'integrity of purpose.' "I did what I thought to be right," she said.

According to the book, her father was the owner of plantations in Mexico and Cuba and a Spanish government official, and her mother's parents were a French naval officer and the daughter of a wealthy American family.

The historical validity of the Velazquez claims remains to be determined. Historians themselves are divided on the issue. In the end, we will probably never know conclusively if Madame Loreta Janeta Velazquez was a brave soldier and spy or merely a literary opportunist–or both.

The veracity of the account was attacked almost immediately, and remains an issue with scholars. Some claim it is probably entirely fiction, others that the details in the text show a familiarity with the times that would be difficult to completely simulate.

A newspaper report mentions a Lieutenant Bensford arrested when it was disclosed 'he' was actually a woman, and gives her name as Alice Williams, which is a name, which Loreta Velazquez apparently also used.

Elizabeth Leonard identifies Loreta Janeta Velazquez's published biography as a work of fiction. She believes, however, that this fictional biography may actually be "rooted in real experience." She notes that the Records of the Confederate Secretary of War contain a reference to a request for an officer's commission from a soldier named "H.T. Buford," which was Velazquez's reported pseudonym.

Leonard also cites several newspaper articles that can be interpreted to support Velazquez's story. Whether these newspaper accounts were the inspiration for Velazquez's biography or whether they actually reflect her true experiences is impossible to determine. Leonard's dispassionate examination of the pros and cons of this case will be helpful as future historians attempt to make a final determination on the veracity of Velazquez's service.

PRE WORLD WAR II

In the Pre World War II Era, women began to question the traditional female roles expected of them, and were faced with a dual challenge in order to achieve change. They had to overcome oppression of their ethnicity and their sex, and the war served as a perfect opportunity for such changes to occur. Prejudice and cultural roles had an immense impact on the social status Mexican-American women held in American society before and during World War II.

Prior to World War II, the United States became the destination for countless immigrants. Despite the fact that much of the Southwest once belonged to the Mexicans, they became the targets of overwhelming prejudice. This fact became so evident that even European immigrants, whose accents clearly revealed their recent arrival to the United States, did not hesitate to consider Mexican-Americans of another class, even less American than themselves.

Mexicans were seen as a lazy, nonproductive, dirty, and uneducated people, and as a result they encountered difficulties when looking for work. To support their families, the men were forced to take the lowest paying jobs as well as the hardest work. They worked countless hours in occupations such

as railroad construction, meatpacking, and agriculture, yet made hardly any money for food and shelter.

Despite the need for money, these men would not allow their wives and daughters to enter the workforce. Women were expected to uphold traditional familial roles, such as sewing and cooking,

9.4 Mexican-American women working in a rail-yard during WWII. From *Mexican-American Women on the Home Front Before and During World War II*, by Jenny Haugh.

and if they did try to work outside of the home, they were met with ridicule and pressure because in Mexican culture, a woman's place is in the home. Sadly, even when these women tried to make money off these skills, it was very little.

World War II eventually offered women the truly equal experience they were looking for. With their men on the war front, it was up to them to take care of things at home. Wartime labor demand promoted opportunities for Mexican-American women, especially those who lived near aircraft and shipbuilding industries. Young Mexican-American women found themselves free to take advantage of wartime opportunities not offered to previous generations. Previous discrimination made it hard for their mothers to find work, yet these American born women found it a much easier task to secure all sorts of employment.

However, discrimination was nowhere near over despite these new opportunities. Some areas were just slower in opening their doors to Mexican-American women. Discrimination against Hispanics in general, and women in particular, persisted in many communities and in those areas where large numbers of migrant workers were located. Women were hired later in the war and in smaller numbers than Anglos and experienced most of their gains in service and unskilled manufacturing work.

When the military first began accepting women into its ranks in the early 20th century, only small numbers of Hispanic women joined the services. Traditional Hispanic cultural values discouraged women from traveling any distance from or working outside the home. These prohibitions began to change during World War II, when the nation needed the contributions of all of its citizens. Finally, Hispanic women began joining the military.

WORLD WAR II

Carmen Contreras Bozak joined the Women's Army Auxiliary Corps (WAAC) in 1942. The Army was looking for bilingual Hispanic women to fill assignments in fields such as cryptology, communications and interpretation. Bozak volunteered to be part of the 149th WAAC Post Headquarters Company–the first to go overseas–and went to North Africa in January 1943. Serving overseas was dangerous for these women. If captured, WAACs, as–"auxiliaries" serving with the Army rather than in it, did not have the same protections under international law as male soldiers. Tech 4 Bozak worked as an interpreter at Army Headquarters in Algiers, and dealt with nightly German air raids.

Sergeant Mary Valfre Castro, the first Hispanic woman from San Antonio, TX, to join the WAAC, signed up to help bring home the seven men in her family who were fighting in the Southwest Pacific. The Army sent her to radio school in St. Louis, MO, where she learned to transcribe encoded radio messages. After Castro completed radio school, the Army assigned her to Barksdale Air Force Base (AFB), LA. Instead of working in a position for which she had been trained, she became a drill sergeant for new Women's Army Corps (WAC) recruits.

In 1944, the Army sent three WAC recruiters to Puerto Rico to organize a unit of 200 WACs. The young women of the island responded enthusiastically, and over 1,500 applications were submitted. The women selected were trained at Ft.

Oglethorpe, GA, and assigned, as a single unit, to the New York City Port of Embarkation.

They worked in the military offices that planned the shipment of troops around the world. When the war ended, the women helped millions of soldiers to return home before they themselves returned to Puerto Rico in 1946. Private First Class Carmen M. Medina, born in San Sebatian, was a member of this WAC detachment. Private Medina worked as a clerk typist in an Army post office at the port. She is proud of her service and believes that it was the most important thing she has ever endeavored to do.

Hispanic women also served as nurses during World War II. Army nurse Carmen Salazar of Los Angeles, CA, was assigned to a hospital train unit at the Presidio in San Francisco. The unit transported wounded servicemen from Letterman General Hospital to military hospitals across the United States. Second Lieutenant Salazar's patients included ex-prisoners of war who had survived the Bataan Death March.

When large numbers of Puerto Rican troops were inducted into the Army in 1944, the Army Nurse Corps decided to actively recruit Puerto Rican nurses so that Army hospitals would not have to deal with language barriers. Thirteen women submitted applications and were accepted into the Army Nurse Corps.

They were Venia Hilda Roig, Rose Mary Glanville, Asuncion Bonilla-Velasco, Elba Cintron, Casilda Gonzalez, Olga Gregory, Eva Garcia, Marta

9.5 Verneda Rodriguez, Women Airforce Service Pilots (WASP). Photo courtesy of the U.S. Air Force History Museum, Randolph AFB Texas.

Munoz-Otero, Margarita Vilaro, Medarda Rosario, Aurea Cotto, Julie Gonzalez, and Carmen Lozano. Eight of the nurses were assigned to the army post at San Juan, and four worked at the hospital at Camp Tortuguero, a training center near Vega Baja.

Carmen Lozano Dumler, one of the thirteen, knew that she wanted to be an Army nurse when she graduated from the Presbyterian Hospital School of Nursing in the spring of 1944. She was sworn in as a second lieutenant on August 21, 1944, and remembers it as the proudest day of her life. Her first assignment was at the 161st General Hospital in San Juan. The Army then sent her to Camp Tortuguero. The patients were happy to have a Spanish-speaking nurse to whom they could relate.

Lieutenant Dumler assisted as an interpreter whenever necessary. Her next assignment was at the 359th Station Hospital at Fort Read, Trinidad, British West Indies. While there, she nursed soldiers recovering from wounds they had received at Normandy. The soldiers appreciated being able to talk out their anxieties and nightmares with someone who shared their language.

Lieutenant Maria Garcia Roach served as a flight nurse with the Army Nurse Corps in the China-Burma-India Theater of Operations, and

9.6 U.S. Army nurses fill and place sandbags around their living quarters in order to provide better protection against German bombs and shrapnel. Photo courtesy www.randomhouse.com.

received an Air Medal and two Bronze Stars for her heroic actions. First Lieutenant Jovita (Soto) Mounsey joined the Army Nurse Corps in 1945, and was assigned to the William Beaumont Army Hospital in El Paso, Texas, where she worked on the surgical ward and cared for orthopedic patients.

After the war, Lieutenant Mounsey was sent to Europe, and served with US forces in Belgium, France, and Occupation Germany.

A small number of Hispanic women served in the Naval Women's Reserve, known as the WAVES (Women Accepted for Volunteer Emergency Service), during World War II. Maria (Rodriguez) Denton, a native of Guanica, Puerto Rico, was one of these women. Lieutenant (jg) Denton worked in New York City. Maria (Ferrell) Menefee, born in Guadalajara, Mexico, joined the WAVES in 1944, and was sent to Bronson Field, Florida where she met her future husband, a naval aviator.

The Marine Corps Women's Reserve also had the aid of Hispanic women during the war. Corporal Maria (Torres) Maes joined the Marines specifically to 'free a man to fight.' After completing boot camp at Camp LeJeune, NC, she was sent to Quartermaster School and assigned to the Marine Corps Base at Quantico, Virginia.

THE 1950s AND THE KOREAN CONFLICT

At the end of World War II, many women left the service. When the Korean War began in June 1950, the services of women were needed once again and the Department of Defense instituted a nation-wide recruitment campaign aimed at encouraging more women to join the armed forces. The American people, however, were tired of war and recruitment campaigns faltered. The Korean situation did not appear to be a direct threat to the U.S. and most women were more interested in raising families than in embarking upon careers, military or otherwise. Nevertheless, some patriotic women joined up.

First Lieutenant Celia Perdomo Sanchez joined the Army Nurse Corps in 1949. While stationed at the 343rd General Hospital, Japan, she nursed soldiers and Marines who had been wounded on the Korean battlefields.

Julia Benitez Rodriguez-Aviles, the first Puerto Rican servicewomen to obtain the rank of captain, joined the Army Nurse Corps in 1950. She served as a nurse anesthetist in Occupation Germany; Washington, D.C.; Texas and Puerto Rico.

Lieutenant Colonel Nilda Carrulas Cedero Fuertes was born in Toa Baja, Puerto Rico, and joined the Army Nurse Corps in 1953, serving on active duty until 1964. She then joined the Reserves and served until 1990. Her most memorable

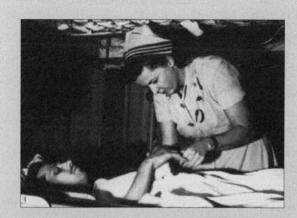

9.7 A U.S. Navy nurse examines a wounded serviceman aboard the U.S. Navy Hospital Ship *USS Haven* during Korean War. Photo courtesy http://korea50.army.mil.

experience in the military was teaching the latest modern nursing techniques to Nicaraguan Army nurses while on temporary duty (TDY) in Nicaragua for six months.

Alicia (Gutierrez) Gillians joined the WAC in 1948. While serving as a recruiter in Los Angeles, California, then Staff Sergeant Gutierrez rescued a young boy whose clothes had caught fire. Her actions earned her the Commendation Ribbon for Meritorious Service. In August 1955, she was named the All-Army Women's Singles Tennis Champ. Master Sergeant Gillians retired from military service in 1980.

Rose Franco was one of the few Puerto Rican women to join the Marine Corps during the 1950s. Born in Ensenada, she joined at the age of 20 and became a supply administrative assistant at Camp Pendleton, CA. Franco returned to Puerto Rico at the end of her four-year enlistment, intending to work for an airline company, but missed being a Marine so much that she decided to re-enlist. She was sent to the First Marine Corps District in Garden City, Long Island, NY, and was later assigned to Parris Island, SC.

In 1965, Franco was selected for a job at the Pentagon as the Administrative Assistant to the

Secretary of the Navy. On his recommendation, she was appointed as a warrant officer, one of only 11 women warrant officers in the Marine Corps at that time. Franco went on to hold several notable positions throughout the country. She retired from the Marine Corps in 1977 as a Chief Warrant Officer 3.

THE 1960s AND VIETNAM

During the 1960s, the number of women entering the military remained fairly small. Although the armed forces permitted relatively few women to serve in Vietnam, nurses, medical specialists, and civilians (such as those with the Army's Special Services) were desperately needed. Mary Agnes Trujillo-McDonnell joined the Army Nurse Corps in 1963. As a first lieutenant she served at the 85th Evacuation Hospital north of Qui Nhon, Vietnam, from 1965 to 1966.

Air Force flight nurse Lieutenant Colonel Lupita Cantu Perez-Guillermety served on active duty from 1962 to 1971 and then entered the active Reserve. While stationed at Clark Air Base in the Philippines, from 1968 to 1970, she flew aeromedical evacuation missions in South Vietnam, Thailand, South Korea, Japan, Taiwan, and the Philippine Islands, in a variety of aircraft and medical evacuation helicopters.

Major Aida Nancy Sanchez, Army Medical Specialist Corps, served at the 95th Evacuation Hospital near Da Nang, from December 1970 to December 1971. As the first physical therapist (PT) assigned to the hospital, she had to set up a clinic in a quonset hut that had previously served as the Post Exchange (PX). In the meantime, Sanchez treated as many as 70 patients a day, using a ward storage area as an office.

During Tet, the Vietnamese lunar New Year, hospital personnel were issued "frag" (bulletproof) jackets and helmets. The protective gear was required to be kept close at all times in case of a reoccurrence of the 1968 Tet Offensive. When she left Vietnam she was assigned as the chief of the Physical Therapy Section, Fort Gordon, Georgia. In 1976, Lieutenant Colonel Sanchez retired after serving 24 years.

Cathleen Cordova joined the Army Special Services after graduating from college, and volunteered for service in Vietnam. Her first assignment was to the Free World Service Club in Tay Ninh. She then became the club director assigned to DiAn and Vinh Long. Eventually, she served with 15 different units, performing duties such as managing Army service clubs and libraries, working in orphanages, participating in Medical Civilian Action Programs (MEDCAPs), and assisting with visiting dignitaries and USO shows.

THE 1970s AND THE ALL-VOLUNTEER FORCE

When the Department of Defense established the All Volunteer Force during the 1970s, more women of every race began entering every branch of the service. Navy Petty Officer Margarita Rodriguez enlisted in the Army in 1972, and served as a medical specialist until 1975. She nursed soldiers returning from Vietnam, and felt that she was

9.8 Saigon, South Vietnam.
Staff Sergeant Ermalinda Salazar, a woman Marine, has been nominated for the 1970 Unsung Heroine Award presented annually by the Ladies Auxiliary to the veterans of foreign wars. Staff Sergeant Salazar, determined to help the children of the St. Vincent de Paul Orphanage in Vietnam in her off-duty hours, holds two of the youngsters. June 1970. Photo courtesy of 20th Century History, http://history1900s.about.com.

making a significant contribution. Rodriguez then joined the Navy as a hospital corpsman.

In 1977, while at Naval Facility (NAVFAC) Eleuthra in the Bahamas, she was named "Sailor of the

Quarter." She was honored as "Sailor of the Month" in 1981, while stationed at Oakland Naval Hospital, CA. Rodriguez completed her military career by serving in the Naval Reserve from 1982 to 1984.

Staff Sergeant Norma Alvarado of El Campo, TX, enlisted in the Marine Corps in 1973. She served for six years, three of which she spent as a drill instructor and depot inspector at the Women Recruit Training Command at Parris Island, SC.

In 1975, Ophelia Rodriguez De La Garza enlisted in the Air Force. She was the first female from her family to join the military. De La Garza became a contract specialist in procurement, and for years was one of the few women in the Air Force to hold this traditionally male job. She then became the only female member of the Honor Guard at Langley AFB, Hampton, VA. At first, her colleagues doubted her ability to handle the job, but she proved herself and held the position for two years. Staff Sergeant De La Garza served in the Air Force until 1986.

Sergeant Brunilda Cofresi-Toro joined the Army in 1979. She received her basic training at Ft. Dix, NJ, and then went to Ft. Lee, VA, for specialist training as a material supply specialist. The Army then sent her to the 535th Engineer Company at Grafenwohr, West Germany, for three years where she served as a clerk with The Army Maintenance Management System (TAMMS). Sergeant Cofresi-Toro then left active duty. As a Reservist, Cofresi-Toro was assigned to the 464th Transportation Company in Alexandria, VA, as a dispatch clerk.

As of September 1977, there were about 3,640 Hispanic women in the military—260 officers and 3,380 enlisted women. They represented about 3 percent of all enlisted women and 2 percent of the female officers at a time when Hispanics comprised five percent of the U.S. population. During the 1980s, the percentage of Hispanic female enlisted and officer personnel began to increase.

THE 1980s AND OPERATION DESERT SHIELD/DESERT STORM

Many Hispanic servicewomen served overseas during Operations Desert Shield and Desert Storm. Petty Officer Sandra Villarreal Hormiga served aboard the ship USS *McKee*. One day, while performing a General Quarters Drill, she realized that, "We were no longer 'just doing drills' we were practicing saving our own lives. From that moment on, I began to treat each drill as an actual chemical attack."

In 1978, Sergeant Gianna Fimbres Nenna Church joined the Air Force and served for five years. After a four-year hiatus, she joined the Army in 1987. During the Gulf War, Church was sent to Saudi Arabia, as a petroleum supply specialist. She drove fuel trucks in convoys, traveling day and night to supply fuel to units scattered across the desert. Church recalled one mission during which she and several other soldiers got stuck in the sand and encountered enemy fire. On another occasion, they were lead into a tank fight. "Rounds were going in between the trucks," remembered Church.

THE 1990s AND THE END OF THE MILLENNIUM

Overseas service often entails personal risk, even when it is not tied to an official military operation. Captain Wanda Ortiz Thayne, the only military woman in a family with a proud tradition of military men, joined the Air Force in 1989. One of her assignments, as a social worker in the Biomedical Services Corps, sent her to Clark AFB in the Philippines.

Upon her arrival, Thayne learned that, only three days before, the National People's Army had killed three Americans. The base was in "THREAT CON Charlie" for most of her tour. Service personnel were forbidden from wearing their uniform off base, a curfew was put into effect, and off-base travel was strictly limited.

Although her tour was stressful, Thayne received a great deal of satisfaction helping handicapped and learning disabled military family members. Another memorable experience in Thayne's career was briefing departing troops in stress management during Operation Desert Storm.

Five years after the Gulf War, Hispanic women comprised approximately six percent of enlisted women in the military, and three percent of female officers. Today, Hispanic women are serving throughout the armed forces and breaking traditional barriers.

Army Major Sonia Roca, born in San Juan, Puerto Rico, was proud to have been the first Hispanic female officer to attend the Command and General Staff College. Iris Rodriguez, a sergeant with the United States Army, was the Military District of Washington's Soldier of the Year in 1996. During an assignment at the Pentagon, she was selected to work for the Defense Advisory Committee on Women in the Services (DACOWITS).

A FAMILY AFFAIR

We often hear stories of sons following their fathers into the service or of brothers enlisting together to fight the enemy. As women establish their own military tradition, daughters now follow in their mother's footsteps and sisters serve together. The experiences of one woman can inspire those around her to pursue a military career.

Diana Ruiz Werts joined the Women's Army Corps (WAC), in 1955, "to see the world." After her first assignment in Chicago, she was sent overseas and stationed in Germany. During her tour, Corporal Werts was a member of the Women's Army Volleyball Team. "I was fortunate to travel to other European countries, sampling their cultures. Truly an experience not to be forgotten," she recalls. Werts was honorably discharged from the WAC in 1958.

Encouraged by the experiences of her sister Diana, Diamantina (Ruiz) Jannone enlisted in the Air Force in 1960 and served until 1963. During her career, she served as a flight traffic specialist with the Military Air Transport Service (MATS). She routed air traffic when President Kennedy deployed thousands of troops to West Berlin and assisted in the transportation of soldiers and cargo en route to Vietnam. Airman First Class Jannone also participated in Showtime McGuire, an entertainment group of personnel from McGuire Air Force Base, NJ, and performed at northern bases including Thule, Greenland.

Their sister, Geraldina Ruiz Zore, joined the Army in 1970, and attended Officer's Candidate School at Fort McClellan, AL. As a second lieutenant, she was a WAC Detachment Commander and the first female commander to whom a male

soldier was assigned. She served as a recruiting operations officer and was the first female account
officer with responsibility for two finance officers
and a forward support team. As a captain, Zore was
assigned to the Department of the Army Quality
Assurance Team. She then served as an inspector
general for a joint command, and was the first female finance officer to be selected and serve as battalion commander and account holder. Lieutenant
Colonel Zore, who retired in 1994, believes that
her success in traditional male jobs has paved the
way for other women to follow.

Lillie Werts-Smith, following the example of
her mother Diana and two aunts also chose to serve
her country in the armed forces. In 1977, she joined
the Air National Guard. Werts-Smith served until
1988, at which time she became a nurse in the
Army National Guard. Her unit was activated during Operation Desert Storm. In 1997, Werts-Smith
retired as a major after serving 20 years.

Twins Rosalia and Rosana Maldonado, with
the Florida Army National Guard's 260th Military
Intelligence Battalion from Miami, were promoted
to captain while serving on active duty at Eagle Base.

The sisters enlisted in the Florida Army
National Guard with their older sister Melissa in
1990. Now, all three sisters are captains in the
same battalion.

After achieving identical scores on the
ASVAB test, the twins began their military careers
training together at the same basic training post,
and continued on together during Advanced Individual Training, the Primary Leadership Development Course and Officer Candidate School. Although they always served in different training platoons, they somehow scored the same. During each
phase of their training, the sisters continued to
achieve identical scores on all their tests.

"Basic training was the hardest. We were in
the same battery but different platoons. We weren't
allowed to confer with one another. We were
dropped often for just looking at one another,"
said Rosalia.

The twins always found a way to communicate
with one another though–their mother–who would
update each one on how the other twin was doing.

9.9 Rosalia Maldonado is promoted to captain by
Brig. Gen. James R. "Ron" Mason. Photo courtesy of the
U.S. Army, by Sgt. 1st Class Ray Simmons.

"Our parents were concerned about us getting deployed but since we are together they are com-
forted," said Rosana.

Rosalia and Rosana share similar parallel lives
in their civilian careers as well. They are both
middle school science teachers at the same school
and they are roommates

"People think we do everything together but in
the Army we have different companies to lead, and
in our civilian lives we have separate classes to
teach," said Rosalia.

Although the twins lead separate lives in the
260th they both find time to enjoy their off-duty
interests together, which includes running and
drinking coffee at Alma's Juice Bar on Eagle Base.
Overall, they've enjoyed their time on Eagle Base
and know that much of that enjoyment comes from
their being able to spend the deployment together.

"Everyone says that deployments are supposed
to be hard because you're so far from home and
family, but it hasn't been like that for me," Rosana
said. "And I know that's because my sister's here
with me."

Looking forward to the future, the twins will
lead side-by-side but independently as sisters,
teachers and soldiers. The September 2004 Defense
Manpower Data Center Report shows that there

are 1,789 Hispanic women commissioned officers in the American armed forces.

The Women In Military Service For America Memorial Foundation, Inc. honors all women who have served or are serving in or with the U.S. Armed Forces from the creation of this nation to the present day. The Women's Memorial is asking descendants, family, friends, and all servicewomen (veterans, active duty, Guard and Reserve) to register women's military experiences. Every woman's story is important and without them our history will never be complete.

THE
AMERICAN
GI FORUM
AND
DR. HECTOR

■ ■ ■ ■ ■

10

The American GI Forum and Dr. Hector

Note: The following is a compilation of articles written by Carl V. Allsup, Libby Averyt, and Ron George. For details please see Bibliography.

Hector Garcia was born January 17, 1914, one of the seven children of Jose and Faustina Perez Garcia of Llera, Tamaulipas, Mexico. When revolution swept across Mexico in 1918, the family moved to Mercedes, in the Rio Grande Valley of Texas.

His father, a strict, proud man who made his seven children study hard, was a professor who ran a dry-goods store in Mercedes. Hector eventually went to the University of Texas at Austin and received his bachelor's degree in zoology in 1936.

He received his medical degree in 1940 from the University of Texas Medical Branch at Galveston. Since no Texas hospital would offer him an internship, he completed his surgical internship in 1942 at St. Joseph's Hospital, Creighton University, in Omaha, Nebraska.

Dr. Garcia joined the Army immediately after finishing medical training and earned the Bronze Star with six battle stars for service during World War II and emerged with the rank of major in the Medical Corps. Then in Naples, Italy, Garcia met the woman he would soon marry, Wanda Fusillo, in late 1944. At the time, she was a student at the University of Naples.

The couple was married on June 23, 1945, less than a month after she finished her doctoral studies in liberal arts. They had three daughters, Wanda, Cecilia and Susana. A son, Hector, died at age 13 after falling while running down the stairs at their mountain home in Mexico.

After the war, Garcia started his medical practice in Corpus Christi in 1946. He contracted with the Veterans Administration to treat World War II veterans with service-connected disabilities.

In 1948, Dr. Hector was quarreling with the Naval Air Station in Corpus Christi, Texas, which refused to accept sick Hispanic World War II veterans. After this effort, Garcia founded the American GI Forum. While many veterans advocacy groups were already in operation, very few allowed Hispanics membership, and none actively fought for Latino veterans' rights. The approximately 500,000 Latinos who honorably served in World War II now had a leader in Garcia, and within months of inception, the American GI Forum was opening branches across the nation.

Garcia today remains a central figure of the Hispanic civil rights movement, due to his refusal

10.1 Dr. Hector P. Garcia graduated from High School in 1932, then for two years he hitchhiked thirty miles to the nearest Junior College in Edinburg. Photo courtesy of the Dr. Hector Garcia Papers, Special Collections, Bell Library, Texas A&M University, Corpus Christi.

to stand idle while Mexican-Americans were being dehumanized in the post-World War II society.

Garcia organized back-to-school drives for Mexican American children. He launched case after case against Texas school systems for discrimination, and won many of his efforts. He and others instigated court cases to sue for the right of Mexican-Americans to serve on juries (winning one such case in the Supreme Court).

10.2 In June, 1945, Army PVT Felix Longoria of the small South Texas town of Three Rivers was killed in action in the Philippines. Photo courtesy of the Dr. Hector Garcia Papers, Special Collections, Bell Library, Texas A&M University, Corpus Christi.

He established schools to teach veterans how to access the benefits under the new G.I. Bill, and advocated for the welfare of Mexican-Americans everywhere, especially in areas of health care. While making him heroically revered among the Mexican American culture, these actions also made him the most hated man in Texas by discriminating parts of society.

In 1948, an incident known as, **'The Felix Longoria Affair,'** boosted the American GI Forum into the national spotlight. Three years after the conclusion of the war, the remains of Army Private Felix Longoria, a native of Three Rivers, Texas, killed on duty during a volunteer mission in the Pacific, were being returned home for burial. However, the owner of the town's sole funeral parlor would not allow a Mexican-American to have chapel services there. He stated, "The Anglo people would not stand for it." Then, Longoria's widow approached Dr. Garcia for assistance.

The deceased Private Longoria quickly became a symbol of racism in Texas. Latinos were outraged that an American soldier, after giving the supreme sacrifice of his life to his country, was not allowed to be buried in his own hometown. The national media huddled around the story. Walter Winchell, a radio journalist, said on the air, "The great state of Texas, which looms so large on the map, looks mighty small tonight."

Soon after, the citizens of Three Rivers, in an attempt to defend their good name and dispel protests that racism was rampant in the town, gave a hero's welcome to Longoria's remains. However, most of America viewed this action as too little, too late. As if this act of racism wasn't enough, during this ordeal, Dr. Garcia's wife and daughters were denied service at a local restaurant because they were Mexican American.

Ultimately, Longoria was interred at Arlington National Cemetery with the sponsorship of then U.S. Senator Lyndon Baines Johnson. The story of Longoria made him a martyr for the dignity of Mexican-Americans everywhere. The story also gave the fledgling American GI Forum respect and national media focus. Lastly, it was the beginning of a long, powerful association between Dr. Hector and the future president, Lyndon Baines Johnson.

The Three Rivers incident shocked Dr. Garcia, and from then on, he and the American GI Forum focused on combating discrimination, segregation, and exploitation of Mexican-Americans. GI Forum attorneys went to the U.S. Supreme Court in 1954 to argue the case of Pete Hernandez, a Jackson County farm worker convicted of murder and sentenced to life in prison.

10.3 PVT Felix Longoria was buried in Arlington National Cemetery. Photo courtesy of the Dr. Hector Garcia Papers, Special Collections, Bell Library, Texas A&M University, Corpus Christi.

The GI Forum contended that Hernandez had not received a fair trial because Hispanics were systematically excluded from the jury. The Supreme Court, headed by Chief Justice Earl Warren, found unanimously for Hernandez.

"Dr. Hector gave the system integrity and direction," attorney and Dr. Hector's cousin, Amador Garcia said. "He gave the minorities a lot of hope that the system worked for all of us. He was the personification of leadership. He led by example. He would not expect people to do anything that he wouldn't do."

DR. GARCIA IN NATIONAL POLITICS

In 1954, Garcia was on the Advisory Council of the Democratic National Committee.

In 1957, the Texas forum ended a ten-year struggle when a federal court agreed that school segregation of Mexican-American children in Texas schools was unjustified. In the same decade the forum helped thousands of Mexican Americans in the Rio Grande valley to register to vote, and

10.4 Dr. Garcia formed Viva Kennedy clubs to get Mexican-Americans to support JFK in his election. He is seen here with other national leaders of the Viva Kennedy organization, meeting with JFK in October 1960. Photo courtesy of the Dr. Hector Garcia Papers, Special Collections, Bell Library, Texas A&M University, Corpus Christi.

incidents of police brutality were confronted in forum efforts.

In the 1960s, Garcia negotiated a resolution to the Chamizal dispute between the United States and Mexico.

10.5 With their long-time friend Lyndon Johnson in the White House, Dr. Garcia and the American GI Forum anticipated what might be possible in LBJ's Great Society. Photo courtesy Dr. Hector Garcia Papers, Special Collections, Bell Library, Texas A&M University, Corpus Christi.

He also was chairman of the Mexican-Spanish section of the Nationalities Division of the Democratic National Committee in 1960.

In the 1960 presidential election, Garcia helped organize 'Viva Kennedy' clubs in support of Democratic candidate John Fitzgerald Kennedy, who in turn made Garcia a member of the American delegation to sign a treaty between the United States and the Federation of West Indies in 1961.

Robert Kennedy stated that the Spanish-speaking voters won the election for his brother. Although the Kennedy administration did not reciprocate with much federal aid, the Johnson administration did. Dr. Garcia helped LBJ get elected to the presidency and kept close ties with him throughout his administration.

The GI Forum played a significant role in the application of Great Society programs in the Latino barrios, and for the first time Hispanic Americans were appointed to influential federal and state government positions and agencies. When Johnson established the first cabinet-level office for Hispanic issues, he selected a former national chairman of the G.I. Forum, Vicente Ximenes, for the position.

President Johnson appointed Dr. Hector to the National Advisory Council on Economic Opportunity and later as U.S. ambassador to the United

Nations. He also was a commissioner of the U.S. Commission on Civil Rights in 1968. And, later that year was named ambassador to the U.S. delegation to the United Nations under President Johnson.

In February 1972, Garcia was appointed to the Texas Advisory Committee on Civil Rights.

In 1978, he was a member of the White House conference on Balanced National Growth and Economic Development in Washington, D.C.; and in 1979, a member of U.S. Attorney General Benjamin Civiletti's Hispanic Advisory Committee on Civil Rights.

President Jimmy Carter invited Garcia to participate in a high-level briefing on Iran and Afghanistan in January 1980.

"Dr. Garcia was a tremendously decent man and his legacy to us is to treat each other decently as human beings," said U.S. Rep. Solomon Ortiz, D-Corpus Christi. "There are a host of people in South Texas who received free medical care from Dr. Hector because they simply couldn't afford to pay him."

"Today, Dr. Garcia's message is the political gospel to which we all adhere," Congressman Ortiz said. "While others fought the system, often unsuccessfully, Dr. Garcia worked within the system to open it up for everyone to participate. He amazed us all with his wisdom, foresight and longevity."

GARCIA ALSO WAS INVOLVED IN TEXAS POLITICS

In the 1960s, Dr. Hector fought to get the poll tax repealed in Texas. The tax required every voting Texan to pay $1.75 per year to participate in state, regional or local elections.

In 1987, Garcia spoke out against a bill in the Texas Legislature to make English the official language of Texas. He also lobbied hard for a four-year university in Corpus Christi. His efforts won him respect from lawmakers statewide.

"Dr. Hector was a great person, not only for South Texas, but for the entire country," said state Rep. Todd Hunter, D-Corpus Christi.

"His accomplishments will be known throughout the country, as well as our area, for many years to come. He was a great person and he did a tremendous job uniting people throughout our great state."

DR. GARCIA RECEIVED SOME OF THE NATION'S MOST PRESTIGIOUS HONORS

In 1984, President Reagan awarded Garcia the Presidential Medal of Freedom, America's highest honor given a civilian by the president. Established in 1963, the award is given to those who have made outstanding contributions to U.S. security or national interest, world peace or cultural endeavors.

Garcia was honored extensively in Corpus Christi. A city park and post office are named after him, and a bronze sculpture of him was placed on the campus of Texas A&M University-Corpus Christi.

In May 1991, the university awarded Garcia its first honorary doctorate in recognition of his efforts as a scholar, teacher and leader. The following year, Garcia donated his papers to the university library's Special Collections and Archives Department.

Memorial Medical Center named its indigent health clinic after Garcia, as a tribute to his 47 years of care for the most needy.

However, he had health problems of his own. He was stricken with a serious kidney ailment when he returned to civilian life after World War II. He suffered a heart attack in

10.6 Dr. Hector P. Garcia in the late 1950's. This image appears on the face of the U.S. Treasury $75 I Bond series honoring great Americans. Photo courtesy of the Dr. Hector Garcia Papers, Special Collections, Bell Library, Texas A&M University, Corpus Christi.

1980 and had open-heart surgery shortly thereafter and again in 1985. He also had half of his stomach removed after doctors found a cancerous tumor.

10.7 Dr. Garcia supported Bill Clinton in his 1992 presidential campaign. Photo courtesy Dr. Hector Garcia Papers, Special Collections, Bell Library, Texas A&M University, Corpus Christi.

In 1996, the legendary civil rights advocate, adviser to presidents and hero to Hispanics nationwide, died after a long illness. He was 82.

"Although it was not unexpected, his death was a shock to all of us," said Ken DeDominicis vice president for institutional advancement and alumni affairs at Texas A&M University-Corpus Christi.

DeDominicis helped coordinate the drive to build the university's $500,000 plaza where the nine-foot bronze statue of Garcia is located. The committee that oversaw the campaign to build the plaza is continuing work to enlarge a scholarship endowment connected to the project. The endowment already has $60,000.

"He was a great man, a visionary man whose work made a difference in the lives of millions of people," DeDominicis said. "He won't be forgotten."

Dr. Garcia was known in the power circle capitols of Austin, Texas and Washington, D.C., and in the poorest regions of South Texas, where he was known to dispense free medical care to those who could not pay. Although he never aspired to elected office, Garcia carried clout among national, state and local politicians, who sought his counsel and his blessing.

President Clinton, in a statement faxed to the family called Dr. Garcia 'a national hero.' "Those

who knew him, and looked up to him as a hero, called him Dr. Hector."

Clinton said, "Dr. Hector fought for half a century for civil and educational rights of Mexican-Americans…. Hillary and I extend our deepest condolences to his family and to all the Latino community."

Amador Garcia said, "It is difficult to describe what the doctor's loss will mean to the community, the state and the United States."

"It's something you can't put your finger on," said Garcia, his voice cracking. "He was so many things, to so many people. He represented honesty and integrity. He loved his country. He loved us, and he loved the Constitution."

"His favorite phrase was, 'We the people.'"

"Texas and the world are better places because of Hector Garcia's selfless service, hard work and dedication," Gov. George W. Bush said. "He will be missed."

Dr. Hector prided himself in working for change within the system. The American GI Forum, now centered in Austin, Texas, remains an active veteran's organization and continues its advocacy in a medley of fields.

10.8 Dr. Hector with his wife, Wanda Fusillo Garcia upon Dr. Hector's being awarded the Presidential Medal of Freedom by President Bush. Photo courtesy of the Dr. Hector Garcia Papers, Special Collections, Bell Library, Texas A&M University, Corpus Christi.

10.9 With his health permitting during the 1990's, Dr. Garcia attended community events to talk about the Forum and its history, as well as current political events. Photo courtesy of the Dr. Hector Garcia Papers, Special Collections, Bell Library, Texas A&M University, Corpus Christi.

"The biggest impact I had was that I never pushed or favored any demonstrations or revolt to tear down the system," Garcia told the Corpus Christi Caller-Times in 1993. "I always thought the system would work with us."

Before it was closed on March 29, 1996, Garcia's medical office at 1315 Bright St. in Corpus Christi, was a journey through history, its walls blanketed with photos of him with U.S. presidents and various state and international figures.

Mixed with the photos were dozens of awards given to Garcia for his humanitarian work–awards he said he didn't deserve, but appreciated.

"His death will be a tremendous loss because we all came to love, respect and admire Dr. Hector for who he was, but also for what he did," said Corpus Christi attorney Jorge Rangel.

"Fortunately, because of his efforts, we now have individuals in high-ranking positions in government, in education and in industry. If he has a legacy he has left with us, it's that those of us who are in whatever positions should carry forward his efforts to make sure all Americans are treated with dignity and respect."

Despite his actions and many accomplishments, "Garcia shied from public recognition, such as the recent statue erected at Texas A&M University-Corpus Christi," said Gilbert Jasso, civil rights official with the GI Forum and Dr. Hector's executive assistant for the past three years.

"We are very grateful we were able to have the statue made before he died," Jasso said. "He at first did not want it. I had to go to his brother in order to convince him to allow that to be made. And then Dr. Hector gave the OK. Dr. Hector said he didn't feel like he deserved it.

"But he said that about everything. More than anything, that statue is a symbol of freedom," he said. It's also a symbol of success in the fighting for civil rights.

Friends and foes alike described Garcia as a short-tempered, aggressive man who was unwilling to reason at times. The physician also was called a

10.10 Dr. Hector P. Garcia breaks new ground at U.N. in 1967. Dr. Garcia was the first member of the U.S. delegation to address the U.N. General Assembly in a language other than English, speaking in Spanish on the issue of nuclear weapons in Latin America. Photo courtesy of the Dr. Hector Garcia Papers, Special Collections, Bell Library, Texas A&M University, Corpus Christi.

natural leader, a self-appointed boss, kind and generous, and a believer in democracy and equality. He was fluent in Spanish, English, French and Italian, and also knew a smattering of Arabic, Portuguese and German.

Among his close friends, he was an avid devotee of dominoes.

Survivors include his wife, Wanda; three daughters, Wanda Garcia of Austin, Cecilia Akers of San Antonio and Susie Garcia of Louisiana; a brother, Dr. Xico P. Garcia of Corpus Christi; and three sisters, Dr. Cuitlahuac P. Garcia of San Antonio and Dr. Dahlia P. Garcia and Dr. Clotilde Garcia, both of Corpus Christi.

HISPANIC GENERALS AND ADMIRALS

■ ■ ■ ■ ■

11

Hispanic Generals and Admirals

Note: The following is a compilation of articles written by SSG Marc Ayallin, Sgt. Jimmie Perkins, Joseph Galloway, Carlos Guerra, Mark Holston, Ken Rodriguez, and Rudi Williams. For details please see Bibliography.

Hispanics have served as general and flag officers in the military since the American Revolutionary War. According to the Defense Manpower Data Center Report of September 2004, there were 11,198 Hispanic commissioned officers in all branches of the U. S. military.

Admirals are the highest-ranking officers in the U.S. Navy. The term 'admiral' comes from the Arabic term amir-al-bahr, meaning "commander of the seas."

The U.S. Navy had no admiral rank until 1862, when Congress appointed nine rear admirals to fulfill the needs of the rapidly expanding Navy in the Civil War. Two years later, a Hispanic American named David Glasgow Farragut was appointed as the first vice admiral in the Navy, and within another two years was appointed as the first "full" admiral in the history of the U.S. Navy.

- **Admiral David Glasgow Farragut** was appointed as the first vice admiral in the Navy, and two years later was appointed as the first "full" admiral in the history of the U.S. Navy."
- **Admiral Horacio Rivero** was the first Hispanic four-star admiral in the U.S. Navy.
- **General Richard E. Cavazos** was the first Hispanic four-star general in the U.S. Army.
- **Lieutenant General Elwood R. Quesada** was the first Hispanic general in the U.S. Air Force.

- **Brigadier General Luis R. Esteves** was the first Puerto Rican graduate of West Point and founder of the Puerto Rican National Guard.
- **Maj. General Ricardo S. Sanchez** commanded the U.S. Army's V Corps and all coalition ground forces in the Iraqi Freedom War.

DAVID GLASGOW FARRAGUT ADMIRAL, U.S. NAVY

On July 25,1866 David Glasgow Farragut, was given the rank of Admiral, the very first Admiral of the United States Navy. Farragut was among the first truly American hero of Hispanic descent.

Admiral Farragut was born July 5, 1801 near Knoxville, Tennessee. He was the son of a seafaring family. His father, Jorge Farragut emigrated from Minorca, Spain in 1776, served both in the Revolutionary War and the War of 1812. David's mother was a North Carolinian, Elizabeth Shine.

11.1 Admiral David Glasgow Farragut.
Photo courtesy www.civil-war.net.

David went to sea at eight years of age, as the adopted son of David Porter. He joined the Navy when he was only 10 years old–the youngest person ever to enlist! In the War of 1812, Farragut was made prize master of a captured British ship. He was 12 years old. Some fifty years later, he became the most famous Hispanic soldier in the Civil War.

Admiral Farragut's place in naval history became assured in August 1864 at the Battle of Mobile Bay. Leading the attack on this Confederate supply port, Farragut lashed himself to the maintop of his flagship, the *Hartford*, so that he could better direct the battle. While maneuvering his fleet of ships through a field of floating explosive mines, the ship in front of his struck one of the mines and sank. Not to be deterred, Farragut urged on his crew, shouting, "Damn the torpedoes…full speed ahead–Four bells (full speed)!" His fleet of ships fought on and captured the Confederate ships in the harbor and won the battle.

HORACIO RIVERO
ADMIRAL, U.S. NAVY

In his lengthy career of service to his country, Horacio Rivero not only attained the rank of Admiral in the Navy, but also served as U.S. Ambassador to Spain.

Rivero was born in Ponce, Puerto Rico, in 1910. At that time, residents of Puerto Rico, a possession of the United States since the Spanish-American War in 1898, were not U.S. citizens and were ruled by a civilian governor appointed by the President of the United States.

Horacio Rivero received an appointment to the U.S. Naval Academy in 1927, ten years after the people of Puerto Rico attained U.S. citizenship. Four years later, he graduated third in his class of 441. Rivero was a

11.2 Admiral Horacio Rivero.
Photo courtesy of the U.S. Navy.

veteran of World War II and the Korean War. In 1962, as Commander of Amphibious Forces, Atlantic Fleet, he played a key role in the Cuban Missile Crisis.

First Hispanic Four-Star
Officer in the U.S. Military

In 1964, Horacio Rivero made history as the first Hispanic to become a four-star Admiral in the United States Navy. From 1968 until his retirement from the Navy in 1972, Admiral Rivero was the Commander of Allied Forces in Southern Europe. After bringing to a close a military career spanning six decades, Admiral Rivero remained in public life as the U.S. Ambassador to Spain from 1972 until 1975.

Following his retirement, Admiral Rivero served as the Honorary Chairman of The American Veterans' Committee for Puerto Rico Self-Determination, an independent, and non-profit national veterans' organization working to help Puerto Rico obtain a permanent political status.

Admiral Horacio Rivero died September 24, 2000, at 90 years of age. Admiral Rivero reached the highest rank of any Puerto Rican in the U.S. military.

The Chairman of the Veterans' Committee, Major General William A. Navas, U.S. Army (Retired), said, "the passing of Admiral Rivero closes a brilliant chapter of Puerto Rico's military history. Admiral Rivero epitomized the dedication, commitment and loyal service of Puerto Ricans to our Nation. He will be missed, his service honored, and his legacy remembered."

RICHARD E. CAVAZOS
BRIGADIER GENERAL, U.S. ARMY

Cavazos made military history by becoming the first Hispanic to attain the rank of brigadier general in the United States Army. Less than 20 years later, the native Texan would again make history by being appointed the Army's first Hispanic four-star general. Cavazos rose on to become one of the most respected generals–Hispanic or otherwise–in the military. He also worked with military luminaries such as General Colin Powell and General H. Norman Schwarzkopf, the latter of whom wrote in his autobiography, *It Doesn't Take a Hero*, that

11.3 Brigadier General Richard E. Cavazos. Photo courtesy of the U.S. Army.

Cavazos was one of the finest division commanders he ever worked for.

Cavazos was born on January 31, 1929, in Kingsville, Texas, and raised on a ranch. He attended Texas Tech University, graduating with a bachelor's degree in geology in 1951. During college he was an active member of the ROTC program and through it received an officer's commission as a second lieutenant in the United States Army on June 15, 1951. He topped off his degree with officer basic training at Fort Benning in Georgia and then completed Airborne School before heading off to Korea with the 65th Infantry. He joined Company E as a platoon leader and eventually became a company commander.

Cavazos proved to be a fearless soldier, especially in the Korean War. On February 25, 1953, a large enemy force attacked Cavazos' platoon. A fierce battle ensued, yet Company E managed to overcome the enemy.

According to *Frontiernet*, as the battle was winding down, "By the light of a flare, Lieutenant Cavazos observed an enemy soldier lying wounded not far to the front of his position. He requested and obtained permission to lead a small force to secure the prisoner. Intense enemy mortar and small arms fire completely blanketed the route to be covered. Nevertheless, Lieutenant Cavazos, with complete disregard for his personal safety, continued alone through the enemy fire to capture and return with the enemy soldier."

For his actions Cavazos received a Silver Star, one of the military's highest honors. He later received the Distinguished Service Cross for another battle fought on June 14, 1953.

U.S. Army's First Hispanic General

Following the Korean War, Cavazos joined the 1st Armored Division as an executive officer. In 1957 he returned to his alma mater, Texas Tech, where he worked as an ROTC instructor. His next post was in West Germany as an operations officer at the U.S. Army's European headquarters.

Meanwhile, Cavazos continued his military training. He attended the U.S. Army Command and General Staff College, the British Army Staff College, and the United States Armed Forces Staff College where he graduated in 1965. By this time the Vietnam War was underway and in February of 1967, Cavazos–who had since achieved the rank of lieutenant colonel–was appointed commander of the 1st Battalion of the 18th Infantry Division.

In September and October of that year, Cavazos' unit engaged in heavy sporadic fighting near the border of Cambodia culminating in a ferocious two-day assault–now known as the Battle of Loc Ninh–during which the 1st Battalion lost five soldiers. In contrast, the enemy troops suffered more than 100 deaths. For his personal actions during these battles, Cavazos received his second Distinguished Service Cross.

With his tour of duty in Vietnam complete, Cavazos returned stateside and resumed his peacetime career path with fervor. He became the director of concept studies at the U.S. Army Combat Developments Command Institute and in 1969 completed additional military training at the Army's famed War College. His next post was from 1970 to 1971 at Kansas's Fort Leavenworth where he served as the chief of the Offense Section in the Department of Division Operations at the Army Command and General Staff College.

In the early 1970s Cavazos held several positions including assistant deputy director of operations at the Pentagon, defense attaché in Mexico, and director of the Inter-American Region, Office of the Assistant Secretary of Defense for International Security Affairs.

In 1976, 25 years after receiving his military commission, Cavazos was promoted to the rank of brigadier general and pinned one gleaming star on his uniform lapel. In doing so, he became the first

Hispanic general in the Army and a role model for the thousands of minority recruits who join the military each year.

Cavazos' first post after becoming a general was as assistant division commander of the 2nd Armored Division. He then assumed a larger leadership role as commander of the 2nd Brigade in the 1st Infantry Division. In 1977 he took over the top spot of the 9th Infantry Division. One of the officers in this division at that time was Norman Schwarzkopf who was appointed to brigadier general under Cavazos.

Schwarzkopf later went on to military fame as the commander of U.S. forces in Desert Shield and Desert Storm in Iraq. Meanwhile Cavazos continued moving up in rank and by 1978 he was promoted to major general. In 1980 he became the commander of III Corps based in Fort Lewis, Washington.

Cavazos' final military post was overseeing the U.S. Army Forces Command (FORSCOM). He assumed this role in 1982, the same year that he received his fourth star, becoming a full general. According to the website of the Fort Leavenworth Hall of Fame, "At FORSCOM Cavazos' early support for the National Training Center and his involvement in the development of the Battle Command Training Program enormously influenced the war fighting capabilities of the U.S. Army."

Under his command at FORSCOM, combat troops were deployed to Grenada, West Indies, in 1983. On June 17, 1984, after a brilliant military career that spanned three decades, Cavazos retired with his wife and four children to Texas.

In his retirement Cavazos remained busy. In 1985 he was appointed by President Ronald Reagan to serve on the eight-member Chemical Warfare Review Commission. Back in Texas, he served on the board of regents of Texas Tech University. He also regularly advised the Army on leadership, serving as a mentor to younger generals.

The *Killeen Daily Herald*, a mostly military paper based out of Fort Hood, Texas, described one such program that Cavazos participated in: "To help train its leaders, the Army reaches into its past by pairing each general with a senior retired

general…. [Passing] along the special experiences of the retired generals to their successors."

One of the planners of this training session noted, "General Cavazos comes here with a reputation that inspires everyone who sees him."

Well into 2003, that reputation persisted as Cavazos continued to lend his military expertise to the U.S. Army–and as a result, the United States.

ELWOOD "PETE" QUESADA MAJOR GENERAL, U.S. ARMY

Gen. Quesada and his tactical air forces helped the Allies win the ground war in Europe in WWII. An advocate of close air support and air supremacy over the battlefield, Quesada went on to become an Air Force lieutenant general and the first commander of Tactical Air Command.

He was an aviation pioneer, and an organizer of Allied victory during World War II.

Quesada was the son of a Spanish businessman and an Irish-American mother. His military career spanned aviation history from post-World War I era biplanes to supersonic jets. He was born in Washington, D.C., in 1904, a few months after the Wright Brothers flew at Kitty Hawk, N.C. He grew up with aviation.

World War I imposed hothouse growth on all things connected with planes. In 1914, when the war began, primitive aircraft scouted enemy forma-

11.4 Major General Elwood 'Pete' Quesada. Photo courtesy of the U.S. Air Force.

tions. They did not fire at each other, nor did they drop bombs on the enemy troops. The aviators themselves began the first moves toward arming the craft. The pilots shot at each other first with pistols and rifles and then machine guns. Bombs and rockets came next. The U.S. Army used aircraft to good effect during the St. Mihiel offensive of 1918.

All through the war, the opposing sides developed planes that flew longer, farther, faster and could do more things. After the war, aircraft development continued. The 1920s were a time of experimentation. Plane design changed from biplanes at the beginning of the decade to sleek monoplanes by the end.

Quesada started his military career in the middle of these turbulent times. He entered the Army Air Service as a flying cadet in 1924. He went through flight school at what is now Brooks Air Force Base, Texas (then called Brooks Field) and advanced training at neighboring Kelly AFB, both at San Antonio.

Having only a reserve commission, Quesada found the active Army Air Service had no space for him. He returned to civilian life, playing baseball for the St. Louis Cardinals. In 1927, he returned to the Air Service and received a Regular Army commission. He reported to Bolling Field in Washington.

Bolling AFB is now an administrative center, but its runways in 1927 were full of aircraft flown by some of the most innovative thinkers in the Army Air Corps. Pete Quesada joined then–Maj. Carl "Tooey" Spaatz and then–Capt. Ira Eaker in developing air-to-air refueling. On Jan. 1, 1929, a three-engine Fokker C-2A rose into the air from Metropolitan Airport in Los Angeles. It did not land again until Jan. 6, 1929. Quesada, Spaatz and Eaker shared piloting duties aboard the plane, dubbed the 'Question Mark.'

Throughout their five days aloft, the Fokker crew took in fuel from a Douglas C-1C that passed a hose in flight–as well as oil, water and food. In all, the Fokker crew made 37 mid-air transfers and flew more than 11,000 nonstop miles.

Today, air-to-air refueling is almost routine. The United States bases the B-2 bomber in Missouri, knowing that no spot on the globe is too far away thanks to in-flight refueling. This started with the flight of the 'Question Mark."

But Quesada's larger contribution came during World War II. The fabulous Allied air-ground machine that chewed up Nazi forces in Europe didn't just materialize. It was Quesada's baby.

Even before the war, Quesada–like many others–had been thinking of the place of air power. But where others looked to strategic bombing, Quesada concentrated on the tactical application of air power. During classes at Maxwell Field, Alabama, and at the Command and General Staff College at Fort Leavenworth, Kansas, Quesada began to build the concept of close air support. He predicted the next war would require "all sorts of arrangements between the air and the ground, and the two will have to work closer than a lot of people think or want."

He got the chance to put his theories into practice. In December 1942, he was promoted to brigadier general and sent to North Africa to command the 12th Fighter Command. He put his ideas through the crucible of combat, and they evolved into Army Air Forces field regulations "Command and Employment of Air Power," published in July 1943.

At the heart of these regulations is the premise that air superiority is the prerequisite for successful ground operations. Further, he said, "the air and ground commanders must be equals and there had to be centralized command of air assets to exploit the flexibility of air power."

In October 1943, Quesada went to England and assumed command of the 9th Fighter Command and readied that unit for the Normandy invasion. During the build-up and breakout that followed the invasion, Quesada was at his best. He placed forward air observers with divisions on the ground, and they could call for air support. He mounted radios in tanks so ground commanders could contact pilots directly. He pioneered the use of radar to vector planes during attacks. This was particularly helpful during the Battle of the Bulge in December 1944, when bad weather hid many German targets.

The air–ground apparatus he put together was the best in the world. After the war, he was the first commander of TAC–the Tactical Air Command.

He moved the headquarters from Tampa, Fla., to Langley AFB, Virginia, so he could be close to the headquarters of the Army Ground Forces. When the Air Force became a separate service in 1947, he went along as a lieutenant general.

Quesada retired from the Air Force in 1951. He was disillusioned with the emphasis placed on Strategic Air Command at the expense of tactical air. He served as the first head of the Federal Aviation Administration and held positions in private firms.

Quesada died in Washington in 1993.

RICARDO S. SANCHEZ
MAJOR GENERAL, U.S. ARMY

Gen. Sanchez took command of the U.S. Army's V Corps and all coalition ground forces during the war in Iraq on June 14, 2003.

11.5 Major General Ricardo S. Sanchez. Photo courtesy of the U.S. Army.

It was the second tour in Iraq for Gen. Sanchez who thrives on tough jobs. In his first tour, as an armor battalion commander, Sanchez fought his way almost to the gates of Basra in 1991 in Operation Desert Storm.

Gen. Sanchez and the nearly 200,000 American and British troops in Iraq worked to make peace and keep it among a fractious and feuding 24 million people in a country the size of California.

Success Story

His rise to high command is an American success story. He grew up poor in the poor South Texas town of Rio Grande City. The son of a single mother who struggled to obtain education for her six children and for herself.

Sanchez remembers how excited he and his brothers and sisters were on the two Thursdays each month when his mother would go to the relief center and draw their food rations. "That meant we would have some meat, cheese and butter in the house for at least a couple of days," he said recently. "With a family of six that didn't last long, and there were many days when we had only beans and rice."

Sanchez began working after school, sweeping and cleaning his uncle Raul Sanchez's dry-cleaning and tailor shop, and making deliveries in the first grade. By the fourth grade he had a second after-school job, sweeping and cleaning at a pharmacy. The money helped keep the family afloat.

He focused strongly on schoolwork, especially math. When he was in the sixth grade, his math teacher called him a dummy. He struggled to prove her wrong, and became a whiz at math. He graduated eighth in his high school class of 300, and was voted most likely to succeed.

A professor of military science helped Sanchez, a high school ROTC standout; earn a four-year Army/Air Force college scholarship at Texas A&I College in Kingsville. This is where he earned his Bachelor of Science degree in mathematics.

Sanchez was commissioned a second lieutenant in the Army in 1973. When someone told him he should avoid the 82nd Airborne Division "because ROTC lieutenants didn't stand a chance there, much less a Mexican," he promptly volunteered for the 82nd and served there for the next five years.

Back then his highest ambition was to be an armor battalion commander, something he achieved in the first Persian Gulf War. Sanchez led three of his companies in a stunning raid on Tallil Airfield in southern Iraq, destroying at least 10 MIGs fighter planes on the ground, and earning a Bronze Star with a V for valor.

Sanchez's commanding general, Maj. Gen. Barry McCaffrey, who retired a four-star general and served as the nation's drug czar, said of him: "An officer of enormous personal competence, humility and a terrific tactical sense of organizing and leading combat operations."

Principled Leader

Lt. Gen. Eric Olsen, a fellow armor battalion commander in the first Gulf War, said: "Sanchez is one of the most principled, ethical commanders I have ever met. He is not afraid to offer an opinion or take an action that might be perceived as unpopular

11.6 Major General Ricardo S. Sanchez answering a question during a press conference. Photo courtesy of the U.S. Army.

if it was the right thing to do. I'd trust my flank to him anytime."

Retired Col. Bill Chamberlain, another Gulf War armor battalion commander who served with Sanchez, said: "He's one of the true achievers in our Army. He got what he got through hard work, lots of ability and some luck."

Sanchez is one of nine Hispanic generals in U.S. Army history. Six of them hail from South Texas. Asked why this is so, Sanchez said: "It is love of country, a hardworking ethic and a value system that is totally compatible with military life. The Hispanic family is all about loyalty, taking care of each other, perseverance, courage and a willingness to sacrifice. Hard work in the Army is easy compared to being out in the fields picking cotton."

By nature an introvert, if Lt. Gen. Ricardo Sánchez was struggling with his newfound fame a year later in San Antonio in 2004, it wasn't evident at a breakfast salute to the military at the 75th national convention of the League of United Latin American Citizens (LULAC).

Wading through the adoring throngs with seeming disregard for the uniformed entourage that accompanied him, he greeted his fans with a disarming smile and honored every request for photos or autographs until he met Medal of Honor

recipients Rodolfo P. Hernandez and José M. Lopez, for whom he made special time as the crowds withdrew respectfully.

"It's remarkable to see José Lopez's service to the country when Hispanics were being discriminated against," Sánchez marvels.

"I think of the tremendous willingness of Hispanics to stand up and fight for a country that at times did not appreciate our service."

Then, he stopped to shake a young boy's hand and gave him a commander's medallion, leaving the kid with a face so awe-struck I will never forget it. "It's very humbling," Sánchez muses. "People in airports now come up and say, 'Ricardo, how are you doing?' and I have no idea who they are. And sometimes they're from other nations."

Some LULAC conventioneers expressed concern that Sánchez will be made the scapegoat of the Abu Ghraib prison abuse scandal.

"It's not an issue to me," he says.

"Abu Ghraib was a defeat for our Army and our America; it was horrible and totally unacceptable. We walked away from the warrior ethic and the value system we worked so hard to establish and defend in that country. But the investigations will establish the facts very objectively, and they will be laid out for America to judge."

Maria Elena Sánchez, his 77-year-old mother, still lives in Rio Grande City, in the same neighborhood where Sánchez and his five brothers and sisters were born and raised. "She was very disciplined

11.7 Major General Ricardo S. Sanchez (right) talking to Secretary of Defense Donald Rumsfeld during the war in Iraq. Photo courtesy of the U.S. Dept. of Defense.

and focused and taught us about perseverance and dedication and definitely about family," he recalls of her firm hand and unwavering counsel.

"Those are also the values that the Hispanic community embraces," he adds. "It's patriotism, service to country, and being very loyal to your family. When I became a soldier, the ethics and the value system of the military profession fit almost perfectly with that ethic. It made it very easy for me to adapt to the military value system."

The Rio Grande City native earned a history and math degree at Texas A&I University in 1973, only because an ROTC scholarship paid his tuition, he says, and gave him "a uniform I could wear twice a week and enough money to take María Elena out to dinner every now and then."

They married and he rose quickly through the ranks, earning a master's degree in operations research and systems analysis engineering that he now credits, with math, for the detached perspective it gave him to successfully solve problems.

"In the early days, being a Hispanic was sometimes a detriment," he recalls. "But our Army has come a long way in my 31 years, (and now) it truly rewards an individual's performance with a very objective, fair promotion process."

As the highest-ranking Hispanic in the U.S. Army in 2004, and only the ninth Hispanic general in the history of the army, Gen. Sánchez is closely attuned to the cultural and social factors that make military service so attractive to Hispanics. He keeps in touch by regularly mixing with the troops.

His 14-month command, he says, "was more than a hardship, I spent 10 years in Iraq last year (2003), working 18-hour days when your troops are in combat every day, and getting killed or wounded." And worse was the separation from his family, he adds.

Walking with him through the Convention Center were María Elena and two of their children. "His body language and demeanor are slowly returning to normal," she says, adding, She looks forward to returning to their home in Heidelberg, Germany, where he recently visited very briefly to attend his son's high school graduation.

"And some things changed," she says, recalling that during his short visit, "he didn't want to drive

because he hasn't driven for so long. So I was driving and we stopped somewhere and got out of the truck and he left his door open," she laughs, "like I was going to close it for him."

Yes, Ricardo, you may be a general. But that's in the Army.

LUIS R. ESTEVES
BRIGADIER GENERAL, U.S. ARMY

Gen. Esteves was born in Aguadilla, Puerto Rico, in 1893. Esteves was the first Puerto Rican to graduate from West Point. He earned a Bachelor of Science degree in engineering from this military academy in 1915.

"He was the first person out of his West Point class of 1915 to become a general officer," Gen. Myers said. "That's notable because Gen. (Dwight) Eisenhower and (Gen.) Omar Bradley were also in that class. Gen. Esteves was the founder of what is today the Puerto Rican National Guard."

General Esteves organized the first units of the Puerto Rico National Guard in 1919, commanded its first battalion and its first regiment. When a second regiment was added he commanded both units. Then in 1937 he was made Adjutant General of Puerto Rico.

In October 1940, he was ordered to active duty and commanded the 92nd Infantry Brigade until summoned by the governor, with Army approval, to organize a State Guard that in a short time consisted of nine well-trained and equipped regiments. He reverted to National Guard status for the reorganization of the Puerto Rico National Guard in November 1946, at which time he resumed his position as Adjutant General, a position he held until his retirement in June 1957.

11.8 Brigadier General Luis R. Esteves. Photo courtesy of the Puerto Rico National Guard.

Esteves died on March 12, 1958 in San Juan, Puerto Rico, at the age of 64.

CHARLES G. RODRIGUEZ
MAJOR GENERAL,
TEXAS NATIONAL GUARD

Major General Charles "Chuck" Rodriguez is the son of Col. (retired) Joseph "Joe" C. Rodriguez, recipient of the Congressional Medal of Honor during the Korean War.

The state's first Hispanic adjutant general took charge of the Texas National Guard in June 2005. Rodriguez will oversee thousands of Texans fighting in Iraq, Afghanistan, and soon, Kosovo.

"Today, our challenges are many because we support thousands of our deployed and deploying soldiers and airmen in the 'away game'–that is, in multiple assignments overseas," he said. "In addition, we simultaneously prepare to respond domestically, in the 'home game'–to natural disasters and even acts of terrorism inside Texas."

11.9 Major General Charles G. Rodriguez. Photo courtesy of the UT Health Science Center at San Antonio.

"Most of the 5,200 Texans on active duty are in Iraq," said Col. John Stanford, spokesman for the Guard. About 500 are in Afghanistan. More will go to Kosovo, Bosnia, Iraq and the Sinai desert starting next year. Rodriguez said he wants to create a broad sense of diversity in the Guard's leadership positions.

"We're not fighting World War II anymore, and this is a different kind of challenge we face and a different kind of world we live in," he said. "So it's going to take a whole lot of different people in senior leadership, and we have to find them and grow them, and we've got to help them along."

The San Bernardino, CA native left his job as chief fundraiser for the University of Texas Health Science Center at San Antonio to take the command post. Rodriguez, 51, who was promoted from brigadier general at the installation ceremony, moved from San Antonio to Camp Mabry, the Texas National Guard headquarters in Austin.

BERNARDO C. NEGRETE
BRIGADIER GENERAL, U.S. ARMY

Gen. Negrete had a message for young Hispanic Americans in 2003, "The military is a perfect place to build your future!

"I think I'm an example. I'm a Cuban refugee who came to this country when I was 10 years old and flunked the sixth grade because I couldn't speak English," said Negrete, an Army brigadier general who speaks unaccented English. "So you can make a difference, and the system can make a difference for you. The key is, you've got to make a difference."

Negrete is the deputy-commanding general of Army Recruiting Command West, which covers everything west of the Mississippi River and South Korea.

His remarks came during an interview in San Antonio at the Department of Defense's first observance of Hispanic American Heritage Month outside the Pentagon. Charles Abell, Assistant Secretary of Defense for Force Management Policy, hosted the symposium and luncheon in 2003 as part of DoD's ongoing initiatives to increase Hispanic representation and to improve access to information and opportunities.

11.10 Brigadier General Bernardo C. Negrete. Photo courtesy of the U.S. Army.

Emphasizing that the military doesn't reward anyone for where their parents came from, the one-star general said, "The military is going to reward you for what you do, who you are and how you do it. As long as you know those rules, you've got an equal chance. It doesn't matter if you're Hispanic, Chinese or from any other ethnic group."

Negrete ran the Army program that aims to attract more Hispanics to serve. "The Army has an underrepresented Hispanic population," he noted. "When I started this program about 15 months ago, we were about 8 percent. We're about 10 percent now. We've made a significant improvement (by) going after Hispanics in a manner we've never done before. We're giving our recruiters goals to meet in order to bring the Hispanic population of the Army to par with the general population of the country. The Army's plan seems to be working well and calls for achieving parity by 2006," Negrete said.

"This year (2003) our goal was 12 percent and we hit 13 percent. Next year, 2004, our goal was 13 percent–I just raised it to 14 percent."

Gen. Negrete passed away suddenly Sept. 16, 2005 at his home in San Antonio while handling a handgun.

ALFRED VALENZUELA
MAJOR GENERAL, U.S. ARMY

After 33 years in the U.S. Army, after tours in Europe and Asia, the Middle East and Africa, Central America and South America, Maj. Gen. Alfred Valenzuela is turning his heart toward home, toward the streets of his youth, toward San Antonio's West Side in 2005.

On the West Side, at 23rd and Salinas, Valenzuela decided he would become a soldier–at age 5.

On the West Side, on Matamoros and Frio streets, Valenzuela joined the Boys Club–at age 10.

On the West Side, Valenzuela found inspiration and a vision. He found trouble, too. Speeding tickets, brushes with the law, and finally an appearance in court.

"When I was 17, a judge told my parents, this guy is going to get himself into trouble," Valenzuela says. Young Freddie, the judge told Alfred and Sara Valenzuela, had two options: jail or the Army.

No one could have imagined then that young Freddie would grow up to become a two-star general.

No one could have imagined that Freddie, now 55, would grow up and catch a vision for the West Side.

But after he retires from the Army, Valenzuela wants to start a school for troubled youths. A special school for delinquents, dropouts, pregnant teens, and kids running on the wrong side of the law. A school of last resort that would funnel teens into the military and college.

11.11 Major General Alfred Valenzuela. Photo courtesy of the U.S. Army.

Why the special school?

Because, Valenzuela says, "a large number of West Side San Antonio Hispanic youths don't finish high school. Because today, in 2003, troubled kids on the West Side can't enlist in the Army unless they have a high school diploma.

"A four-year enlistment gets you up to $65,000" for college, Valenzuela says. "My goal is to get kids in the Army and then get them to go to college."

Valenzuela holds four degrees from St. Mary's University, but he was not a gifted student. He flunked an entrance exam at Central Catholic High School and enrolled at Jefferson High School, where he graduated with "a 2.5 GPA" in 1966.

As he awaits his next assignment from the Army, Valenzuela is discussing his vision with local businessmen and political leaders. Unlike retired Spurs center David Robinson, who used part of his own money to start the Carver Academy on the East Side, Valenzuela does not have the resources to start his own school on the West Side.

What he does have is the same drive that propelled him from an aspiring soldier at age 5 to commanding general of the U.S. Army South–an area that covers Central and South America and the Caribbean. On his visit to San Antonio,

Valenzuela observed the anticipation of Toyota's arrival on the South Side, the energy and excitement of Carver Academy on the East Side, the affluence and wealth on the North Side.

"But what do we have on the West Side," he asked. "*Nada.* The West Side is not part of the game."

Valenzuela also has noted the city's changing boundaries. When he was in eighth grade, his parents moved from the West Side to the 'North Side,' where he attended Mann Middle School.

Today, what then was considered the North Side–Zarzamora and Huisache–is now inner city.

As San Antonio has grown, so has Valenzuela's career.

"When he went into the Army," recalls Valenzuela's mother, Sara, I said, "If you make general, I promise you I'll buy you a Corvette. I never thought he'd become a general. It was a joking matter. I haven't bought it yet."

Valenzuela can wait for the Corvette. But he hardly can wait to pursue his West Side vision. He doesn't know where he'll get the money to build, or how he will recruit students, or when he will begin setting the project into motion.

All he knows is that the desire to build a school is as strong his desire to serve in the Army. "I have a vision," he says, "to satisfy a new calling."

CHRISTOPHER CORTEZ
MAJOR GENERAL, USMC

Major General Christopher Cortez relinquished his final command and he retired after 33 years of service to the Marine Corps. Cortez retired in 2004 as the highest-ranking Hispanic American currently serving in the Corps.

"My time here at the Recruiting Command has been extremely rewarding as I have been blessed to lead some of the finest Marines our Corps has to offer," said Cortez.

"For these last 25 months you have been nothing short of awesome."

Every month, since Cortez assumed command of MCRC in August of 2002, MCRC has successfully met its recruiting goals and has exceeded in attaining the required number of quality recruits.

Under his command, the Marine Corps shipped more than 75,000 young men and women to recruit training.

Cortez' commitment to strengthening the Marine Corps' image with young people and its message with the broader society is rooted in his own beginnings. "I grew up working on farms and orchards with my father," he says.

Born the son of an immigrant sharecropper and raised in Vacaville, California, Cortez recounts that opportunities were rare when he graduated from high school. "College was almost a dream," he says of the chances of low-income high school graduates obtaining a higher education in the 1960s. "It seemed beyond my reach. But I wanted it, and did get into college."

The general then joined the Marine Corps by entering the Platoon Leaders Program. He was commissioned a 2nd Lieutenant in the Marine Corps upon graduating from Marietta College.

Cortez will be leaving the Marine Corps with a long and distinguished career. Entering the Marine Corps as an infantry officer, Cortez served in command of infantry Marines at the platoon, company, battalion, and regimental levels.

"I've been proud to wear this uniform. I am grateful my father came to America for the opportunities this great country offered to my family, and I am also grateful to the Marine

11.12 Major General Christopher Cortez. Photo courtesy of the U.S. Marine Corps.

Corps for the opportunities that it has offered me," said Cortez.

Shortly after retiring from the corps, Gen. Cortez joined Coors Brewing Company as area vice president of sales.

MICHAEL J. AGUILAR
BRIGADIER GENERAL, USMC

Michael J. Aguilar was in the seventh grade when he decided he wanted to be a military pilot and fly combat missions.

He became a pilot, but never flew a combat mission. However, Aguilar became a brigadier general in the Marine Corps, one of three Hispanic Americans to reach that rank in the corps' history. His advice to young Hispanic's who want to succeed in the military and life as a whole, is a resounding "stay in school!

"My biggest concern with the Hispanic community is our poor record in education," he said. "We make a lot of news about the future size of the Hispanic community. I wish we, as a group, would make as much news about our educational achievements."

Aguilar pointed out that the Hispanic community has the lowest high school and college graduation rate of all groups in the nation. He went on to finish college while in the Marines and holds a bachelor's degree in business administration and a master's in strategic studies and national security affairs.

Gen. Aguilar contented himself flying helicopters throughout his career. He served as officer in charge of a Cobra detachment and has held a variety of jobs at aviation squadron, group and wing levels.

"We were the first Marine unit to fly into Saudi in 1990," he said. "But I didn't fly any combat missions." During Operations Desert Shield and Desert Storm, he was executive officer of Marine Aircraft Group 16.

After being promoted to brigadier general, Aguilar became deputy director for operations in the Joint Chiefs of Staff National Military Command Center. In July 1999, he was assigned as commanding general, Joint Task Force Panama. That December, he became deputy commander, U.S. Marine Corps Forces South, Miami, and commander of Fleet Marine Forces South.

11.13 Brig. Gen. Michael J. Aguilar. Photo courtesy of the USMC.

He retired in January 2002 and then moved back to California.

Admirals are the highest-ranking officers in the U.S. Navy. The term "admiral" comes from the Arabic term amir-al-bahr, meaning "commander of the seas."

In the tradition of Admiral Farragut, Hispanic Americans are serving and leading the U.S. Navy as admirals today.

JOSE LUIS BETANCOURT, JR.
REAR ADMIRAL, US NAVY

Hometown: Brownsville, Texas

Family Heritage: Mexican

Education: Graduate of Pan American University; master's degrees from the Fletcher School of Law and Diplomacy, Tufts University, and from the Industrial College of the Armed Forces, Washington, D.C.

Date of Commission: March 1972

Decorations & Awards: Defense Superior Service Medal, the Legion of Merit, the Bronze Star, the Meritorious Service Medal, the Navy Commendation Medal, the Humanitarian Service Medal and others.

11.14 Rear Admiral Jose Luis Betancourt, Jr. Photo courtesy of U.S. Navy.

Current Assignment: Commander, Mine Warfare Command, headquartered at Naval Air Station (NAS) Corpus Christi, TX, with subordinate units based at NAS Corpus Christi, NAS Kingsville and home ported at Naval Station Ingleside.

Current Responsibilities: As Commander Mine Warfare Command, Admiral Betancourt is in charge of making sure the Navy's mine countermeasure forces locate and destroy sea mines and identify and mark safe passage routes for the Navy's ships. Commander Mine Warfare Command is also responsible for the development of the Navy's mining strategy and the Navy's inventory of underwater mines.

Commander Mine Warfare Command has worldwide responsibility for 27 ships, including USS INCHON (MCS 12), the Navy's only mine countermeasures command and control ship; 14 mine countermeasures ships (MCMs) and 12 coastal mine hunters (MHCs).

Commander Mine Warfare Command also serves as operational commander of Helicopter Mine Countermeasures Squadron FOURTEEN (Norfolk, VA), Squadron FIFTEEN (Corpus Christi, TX) and dozens of explosive ordnance disposal (EOD) detachments during mine countermeasures operations.

ALBERTO DIAZ JR.
REAR ADMIRAL, US NAVY

Hometown: Gaithersburg, Maryland

Birthplace: San Juan, Puerto Rico

Family Heritage: Puerto Rican

Education: Bachelor of Arts degree from George Washington University; master's degree from Butler University; master's degree from the University of Barcelona School of Medicine in Barcelona, Spain

Date of Commission: April 1976

Decorations & Awards: Legion of Merit with Gold Star, the Meritorious Service Medal with Gold Star and the Navy Commendation Medal and others.

Current Assignment: Commander, Naval Medical Center San Diego and Lead Agent TRICARE Region Nine.

Current Responsibilities: As Commander, Naval Medical Center San Diego, charged with providing leadership and management of the Command; planning, directing and administering the operation of NMCSD to ensure efficient, effective and economic accomplishment of the Command mission. Responsible for the

11.15 Rear Admiral Alberto Diaz, Jr. Photo courtesy of the U.S Navy.

professional care and services provided to the patients in the Medical Center and for the safety and well being of the entire Command.

As Lead Agent TRICARE Region Nine, his role is to advance the partnership and communication between the military health system leadership, military treatment facilities, the managed care support contractor, and the civilian network to provide our beneficiaries access to a high-quality integrated healthcare delivery system.

RODRIGO C. MELENDEZ
REAR ADMIRAL, U.S. NAVY

Hometown: Los Angeles, California

Family Heritage: Mexican, Spanish, and Latvian

Education: Bachelor of Science and Doctor of Dental Surgery degrees, University of Southern California; Master of Science degree from George Washington University

Date of Commission: April 1965

Decorations & Awards: Legion of Merit (with two gold stars), Meritorious Service Medal, and Navy Commendation Medal. He is a Fellow in both the American and International College of Dentists and the Academy of General Dentistry.

11.16 Rear Admiral Rodrigo C. Melendez. Photo courtesy of the U.S Navy.

Current Assignment: Assistant Chief for Education, Training and Personnel, Bureau of Medicine and Surgery in Washington D.C. He was selected for promotion to Rear Admiral in 2000.

Current Responsibilities: Responsible for Navy Medical Department enlisted technical training, officer and enlisted education programs and officer personnel accession and scholarship programs. Over 40,000 personnel attended Navy Medical Department schools and courses during the year 2000. Additionally, as the Tri-Service Medical Department representative for inter-service training, he coordinates cooperative medical training initiatives between the Army, Navy, Air Force and Coast Guard.

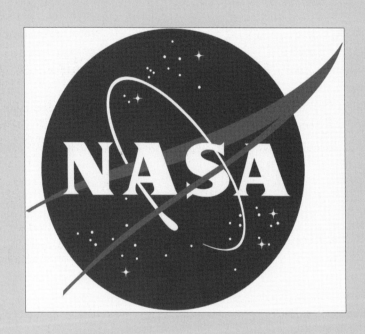

HISPANIC
ASTRONAUTS

■ ■ ■ ■ ■

12

Hispanic Astronauts

Note: The following is a compilation of articles written by Dean Acosta, Renee Juhans, Terry Hudson, and NASA. For details please see Bibliography.

The contributions of Hispanic-American space explorers begins with trailblazers such as:

- **Rodolfo Neri-Vela**, the first Hispanic payload specialist,

- **Franklin R. Chang-Diaz** and **Ellen Ochoa**, the first Hispanic male and female astronaut in space, and

- **Michael Lopez-Alegria**, the first Hispanic American to walk in space.

There have been a total of 13 (eight astronauts, two candidates in training, one retired, two international space agencies) Hispanic men and women who have participated in the National Aeronautics and Space Administration (NASA) Career Astronauts program and are members of the NASA astronaut corps. Currently (2005), nine Hispanic Americans have been chosen to represent our Nation in space.

RODOLFO NERI VELA, PH.D. PAYLOAD SPECIALIST

Born February 19, 1952, in Chilpancingo, Guerrero, Mexico. Vela received a bachelor's degree in mechanical and electronic engineering, University of Mexico, 1975; studied the master's program in science, specialized in telecommunications systems, 1975-1976, University of Essex, England; received a doctoral degree in electromagnetic radiation, University of Birmingham, England, 1979; and one year of postdoctoral research in wave-guides, University of Birmingham, England.

Space Flight Experience: Dr. Neri Vela flew on the crew of STS-61B *Atlantis* (November 26 to December 3, 1985), conducted two six-hour spacewalks, conducted several Mexican Payload Specialists Experiments for the Mexican Government, and tested the Orbiter Experiments Digital Autopilot (OEX DAP). At mission conclusion, Dr. Neri Vela had traveled 2.4 million miles in 108 Earth orbits, and logged over 165 hours (seven days) in space.

Experience: The Institute of Electronic and Electrical Engineers, USA; The Institution of Electrical Engineers, England; Asociacion–Mexicana de Ingenieros en Comunicaciones Electricas y Electronicas, Mexico; and Colegio de Ingenieros Mecanicos y Electricistas, Mexico.

Dr. Neri Vela has worked at the Institute of Electrical Research, Mexico, in the Radio-communications Group, doing research and system planning on antennas and satellite communications systems; he had also been Head of the Department of Planning and Engineering of the

12.1 Astronaut Rodolfo Neri Vela. Photo courtesy of NASA.

Morelos Satellite Program at the Mexican Ministry of Communications and Transportation, and is now a full time post-graduate lecturer and researcher at the National University of Mexico on antenna theory and design, satellite communications systems, and Earth station technology.

MICHAEL E. LOPEZ-ALEGRIA CAPTAIN, ASTRONAUT, US NAVY

Captain Lopez-Alegria was born in Madrid, Spain on May 30, 1958, and grew up in Mission Viejo, California where he graduated from Mission Viejo High School in 1976. He then graduated from the U.S. Naval Academy in 1980 with a Bachelor of Science degree in systems engineering and later earned a Master of Science degree in aeronautical engineering from the U.S. Naval Postgraduate School in 1988. Astronaut Lopez-Alegria is also a Graduate of Harvard University's Kennedy School of Government Program for Senior Executives in National and International Security.

12.2 Capt. Astronaut Michael E. Lopez-Alegria. Photo courtesy of NASA.

Captain Lopez-Alegria reported for training to the Johnson Space Center in August 1992 and was the first Hispanic to walk in space in 1995 aboard the space shuttle Columbia. Lopez-Alegria served as the flight engineer and was responsible for all operations of the mission, which was completed in 15 days, 21 hours and 52 minutes and traveled more than 6 million miles in 256 Earth orbits.

He is a veteran of three space flights and has logged more than 42 days in space, including five EVAs (Extra-Vehicular Activity) totaling 33 hours and 58 minutes. Following his first space flight he served as NASA Director of Operations at the Yuri Gagarin Cosmonaut Training Center, Star City, Russia.

He next flight was on Discovery from October 11-24, 2000. During the 13-day flight, the seven-member crew performed four space walks. Lopez-Alegria totaled 14 hours and 3 minutes of EVA time in two space walks.

Endeavour was Captain Lopez-Algeria's last flight on November 23 to Dec 7, 2002. This was the sixteenth Shuttle mission to visit the International Space Station. During the mission Lopez-Alegria performed three EVAs totaling 19 hours and 55 minutes. Endeavour brought home the Expedition-Five crew from their 6-month stay aboard the Station.

ELLEN OCHOA, PH.D. ASTRONAUT

NASA's First Female Hispanic Astronaut

The first Hispanic woman to fly in space has traveled the United States sharing her groundbreaking experience with students and educators. But when they meet her, they don't even notice her gender or cultural heritage. All they see is an astronaut.

Ochoa was born May 10, 1958 in Los Angeles, California, but considers La Mesa, California, to be her hometown. She graduated from Grossmont High School, La Mesa, California, in 1975; received a Bachelor of Science degree in physics from San Diego State University in 1980, a Master of Science degree and doctorate in electrical engineering from Stanford University in 1981 and 1985, respectively.

Before becoming an astronaut Ochoa, was a researcher at Sandia National

12.3 Astronaut Ellen Ochoa. Photo courtesy of NASA.

Laboratories in Livermore, Calif., and a researcher and manager at NASA's Ames Research Center in California.

She is the recipient of numerous awards, including the Women in Aerospace Outstanding Achievement Award, The Hispanic Engineer Albert Baez Award for Outstanding Technical

Contribution to Humanity, and the Hispanic Heritage Leadership Award.

"The kids are interested in hearing what an astronaut does and understanding what it's like to live and work in space," Ochoa said.

"They don't act surprised to see me." This is encouraging to Ochoa, who remembers a time when there were no female or Hispanic astronauts. Today, 27 members of NASA's Astronaut Corps are female, and nine are Hispanic.

She is a co-inventor on three patents for an optical inspection system, an optical object recognition method, and a method for noise removal in images. As Chief of the Intelligent Systems Technology Branch at Ames, she supervised 35 engineers and scientists in the research and development of computational systems for aerospace missions. Dr. Ochoa has presented numerous papers at technical conferences and in scientific journals.

Selected by NASA in January 1990, Dr. Ochoa became an astronaut in July 1991. Her technical assignments in the Astronaut Office includes serving as the crew representative for flight software, computer hardware and robotics, Assistant for Space Station to the Chief of the Astronaut Office, lead spacecraft communicator (CAPCOM) in Mission Control, and Acting Deputy Chief of the Astronaut Office.

She is currently Deputy Director of Flight Crew Operations, helping to manage and direct the Astronaut Office and Aircraft Operations. A veteran of four space flights, Dr. Ochoa has logged over 978 hours in space. She was a mission specialist on her first flight, the *Discovery* shuttle (April 4-17, 1993) that was a 9-day mission. Dr. Ochoa used the Remote Manipulator System (RMS) robotic arm to deploy and capture the Spartan satellite, which studied the solar corona.

Dr. Ochoa was the Payload Commander on the shuttle Discovery flight in 1994, and was a mission specialist and flight engineer on Discovery in 1999. The *Atlantis* mission from April 8-19, 2002 was the 13th Shuttle mission to visit the International Space Station. Dr. Ochoa, along with Expedition-4 crewmembers Dan Bursch and Carl Walz, operated the station's robotic arm during three of the four space-walks.

12.4 Astronaut Ellen Ochoa. Photo courtesy of NASA.

Ochoa has spent nearly 1,000 hours in space during her four missions. While most of her time was occupied using a suite of complex instruments to better understand the impact of the sun's cycle on Earth, Ochoa found a few minutes to use another instrument, the flute she brought from home.

A classical flutist, Ochoa found playing a musical instrument in space is not much different than playing it on Earth. Because the Shuttle cabin is pressurized, the flute worked the same in space, with one exception: in the near-weightless environment, the flute practically held itself aloft. And she had the rare experience of playing the instrument while gazing down at the entire planet 160 miles below.

Her other hobbies include aviation closer to Earth. She's also a pilot, an interest she picked up after applying for the Astronaut Corps. "I realized how important it was to know something about aviation, and it was something I was interested in, so I followed my brother's footsteps and obtained my pilot's license," she said.

Ocha and her husband are the parents of two young sons, and would encourage them to become astronauts, if they choose. "Being an astronaut is a wonderful career," Ochoa said. "I feel very privileged. But what I really hope for young people is that they find a career they're passionate about, something that's challenging and worthwhile."

Relishes Being Role Model

Being a role model is no burden for astronaut Ochoa. In fact, she thinks of it as a benefit.

"It's not something I thought about when I applied for the astronaut program, but it's a wonderful benefit of the job," Ochoa said when reached at the Johnson Space Center in Houston. "I really enjoy the opportunities to talk all around the country and even outside the country about my job and the space program and the importance of education."

Being the first Hispanic woman to reach outer space, Ochoa is an inspiration to many. "I'm certainly asked by both women's groups and Hispanic groups to come speak to them," Ochoa said. "To me, it's an opportunity to reach a new audience. If anyone in the audience is thinking about an exciting career, maybe my visits are worthwhile."

Ochoa was able to reach outer space by being well grounded in schoolwork. "The most important thing is getting a good education.

"Specifically for my job, you need a college degree in a technical field," Ochoa said. "You need to prepare for college by doing well in school and taking school seriously at an early age. And prepare to load up on the math and science.

"Even if you're not considering a career in a technical field, it's so important to take math and science," Ochoa said. "It can affect almost anything you do in life, but the biggest thing is it opens a lot more options for you."

One of five children, Ochoa grew up in La Mesa, CA, in a middle-class neighborhood. She credits her mother with passing on her passion for knowledge.

"My mother was always interested in learning," Ochoa said. "She certainly impressed upon all of us the importance of education, and all five of us have college degrees, and most of us have an advanced degree, too."

That education and an inner drive to reach her goals resulted in Ochoa being the first Hispanic woman in space.

JOSE HERNANDEZ MISSION SPECIALIST, 2004 ASTRONAUT CANDIDATE

NASA engineer Jose Hernandez remembers exactly where he was when he heard the first Hispanic American had been chosen to travel into space.

"I was hoeing a row of sugar beets in a field near Stockton, CA, and I heard on my transistor radio that Franklin Chang-Diaz had been selected for the Astronaut Corps," says Hernandez, 41, who was a senior in high school at the time.

"I was already interested in science and engineering," Hernandez remembers, "but that was the moment I said, 'I want to fly in space.' And that's something I've been striving for each day since then."

Hernandez's work is now paying off. He has been selected to begin training as a mission specialist this summer as part of the 2004 astronaut candidate class.

One of four children in a migrant farming family from Mexico, Hernandez–who didn't learn English until he was 12 years old–spent much of his childhood on what he calls 'the California circuit,' traveling with his family from Mexico to southern California each March, then working northward to the Stockton area by November, picking strawberries and cucumbers at farms

12.5 Astronaut Candidate Jose Hernandez. Photo courtesy of NASA.

along the route. Then they would return to Mexico for Christmas, and start the cycle all over again come spring.

"Some kids might think it would be fun to travel like that," Hernandez laughs, "but we had to work. It wasn't a vacation."

After graduating high school in Stockton, Hernandez enrolled at the University of the Pacific in Stockton, where he earned a degree in electrical engineering and was awarded a full scholarship to the graduate program at the University of California in Santa Barbara, where he continued his engineering studies. In 1987 he accepted a full-time job with Lawrence Livermore National Laboratory, where he had worked as a co-op in college.

In the early 1990s, his work at Lawrence Livermore with a commercial partner led to development of the first full-field digital mammography imaging system, a tool in the early detection of breast cancer. Most recently, he has worked as a NASA engineer at Johnson Space Center in Houston, supporting Space Shuttle and International Space Station missions.

During the astronaut application process, Hernandez had to meet with a review board. That's where he came face-to-face with his original inspiration: Franklin Chang-Diaz.

"It was a strange place to find myself, being evaluated by the person who gave me the motivation to get there in the first place," Hernandez says. "But I found that we actually had common experiences–a similar upbringing, the same language issues. That built up my confidence. Any barriers that existed, he had already hurdled them."

Hernandez smiles. "Now it's my turn."

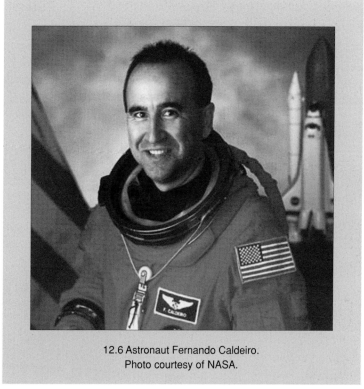

12.6 Astronaut Fernando Caldeiro.
Photo courtesy of NASA.

FERNANDO (FRANK) CALDEIRO ASTRONAUT

Fernando Caldeiro joined NASA in 1991 as a cryogenics and propulsion systems expert for the Safety and Mission Assurance office at the Kennedy Space Center, FL. Selected as an astronaut candidate in April 1996, he is qualified for flight assignment as a mission specialist and is serving as the lead astronaut for Shuttle software testing at the Space Shuttle Avionics Integration Laboratory.

Born June 12, 1958 in Buenos Aires, Argentina, but considers New York City and Merritt Island, Florida, to be his hometowns. Graduated from W.C. Bryant High School, Long Island City, New York, in 1976; received an associate degree in applied science in Aerospace Technology from the State University of New York at Farmingdale in 1978, a bachelor of science degree in mechanical engineering from the University of Arizona in 1984, and a master of science degree in engineering management from the University of Central Florida in 1995.

NASA hired him in 1991 as a cryogenics and propulsion systems expert for the safety and mission assurance office. Selected by NASA as an astronaut candidate in April 1996, Caldeiro reported to the Johnson Space Center in August 1996.

Having completed two years of training and evaluation, he is qualified for flight assignment as a mission specialist. Initially assigned to the Astronaut Office Station Operations Branch, he served as lead astronaut for the European-built station modules. Currently, Caldeiro is the lead astronaut in charge of Shuttle software testing at the Shuttle Avionics Integration Laboratory

FRANKLIN R. CHANG-DIAZ, PH.D. ASTRONAUT AND DIRECTOR, ADVANCED SPACE PROPULSION LABORATORY, JOHNSON SPACE CENTER

Chang-Diaz became an astronaut in August 1981, and is a veteran of seven space flights: which included Discovery in 1998, and Endeavour in 2002. He has logged more than 1,601 hours in space, including 19 hours and 31 minutes in three space walks. He is currently serving as the director of the Advanced Space Propulsion Laboratory at the Johnson Space Center.

Born April 5, 1950, in San Jose, Costa Rica. Graduated from Colegio De La Salle in San Jose, Costa Rica, in November 1967, and from Hartford High School in Hartford, Connecticut, in 1969; received a bachelor of science degree in mechanical engineering from the University of Connecticut in 1973 and a doctorate in applied plasma physics from the Massachusetts Institute of Technology (MIT) in 1977.

In December 1993, Dr. Chang-Diaz was appointed Director of the Advanced Space Propulsion Laboratory at the Johnson Space Center where he continues his research on plasma rockets. He is an Adjunct Professor of Physics at Rice University and the University of Houston and has presented numerous papers at technical conferences and in scientific journals.

He also worked for 2 1/2 years as a house manager in an experimental community residence for de-institutionalizing chronic mental patients, and was heavily involved as an instructor/advisor with a rehabilitation program for Hispanic drug abusers in Massachusetts.

From October 1984 to August 1985 he was leader of the astronaut support team at the

12.7 Astronaut Franklin R. Chang-Diaz. Photo courtesy of NASA.

Kennedy Space Center. His duties included astronaut support during the processing of the various vehicles and payloads, as well as flight crew support during the final phases of the launch countdown. He has logged more than 1,800 hours of flight time, including 1,500 hours in jet aircraft.

Dr. Chang-Diaz was instrumental in implementing closer ties between the astronaut corps and the scientific community. In January 1987, he started the Astronaut Science Colloquium Program and later helped form the Astronaut Science Support Group, which he directed until January 1989.

CHRISTOPHER J. "GUS" LORIA LIEUTENANT COLONEL, USMC

Prior to joining NASA's Astronaut Corps in 1996, Loria was assigned as a test pilot and project officer for the Department of the Navy on the X-31 Program at the NASA Dryden Flight Research Facility at Edwards Air Force Base, CA. He was also a test pilot on Dryden's F/A-18 High Alpha Research Vehicle.

In 2002, Loria was assigned to pilot the Space Shuttle on STS-113. However, an injury prevented him from completing his training and resulted in a reassignment.

Loria served as the Chief of Flight Test for the Orbital Space Plane Program from September 2002 through July 2003.

Born July 9, 1960 in Belmont, Massachusetts, he considers League City, Texas, his hometown. Loria graduated from Belmont High School (1978), and the US Naval Academy Preparatory School (1979). He has a Bachelor of Science degree in general engineering from the U.S. Naval Academy (1983). Loria also has 30 credits from Florida Institute of Technology towards completion of a Master of Science

12.8 Astronaut Lt. Col. Christopher J. 'Gus' Loria. Photo courtesy of NASA.

degree in aeronautical engineering, and a Master in Public Administration from John F. Kennedy School of Government, Harvard University (2004).

CARLOS I. NORIEGA
LIEUTENANT COLONEL, USMC, RET.
ASTRONAUT

Selected by NASA in December 1994, Noriega flew as a mission specialist on STS-84 in 1997, NASA's sixth Space Shuttle mission to rendezvous and dock with the Russian space station Mir, and on STS-97 in 2000. He has logged in excess of 460

12.9 Astronaut Col. Carlos I. Noriega (Ret.). Photo courtesy of NASA.

hours in space, including more than 19 EVA hours in three space walks. Following STS-97, Noriega trained as the backup commander for ISS Expedition Six, and is currently assigned to the crew of STS-119.

Born October 8, 1959, in Lima, Peru, Noriega considers Santa Clara, California to be his hometown. He graduated from Wilcox High School, Santa Clara, California, in 1977. He holds a Bachelor of Science degree in computer science from University of Southern California, 1981, a Master of Science degree in computer science from the Naval Postgraduate School, 1990, and a Master of Science degree in space systems operations from the Naval Postgraduate School, 1990.

Col. Noriega served aboard Atlantis (May 15-24, 1997), which was NASA's sixth Space Shuttle mission to rendezvous and dock with the Russian Space Station Mir. During this mission Noriega logged a total of 221 hours and 20 minutes in space traveling 3.6 million miles in 144 orbits of the Earth.

Noriega was part of Space shuttle Endeavour (November 30 to December 11, 2000), which was

the fifth Space Shuttle mission dedicated to the assembly of the International Space Station. While docked to the Station, the crew installed the first set of U.S. solar arrays, performed three space walks, in addition to delivering supplies and equipment to the station's first resident crew. Mission duration was 10 days, 19 hours, 57 minutes, and traveled 4.47 million miles.

JOHN D. OLIVAS, PH.D.
ASTRONAUT (MISSION SPECIALIST)

Chosen by NASA as an astronaut candidate in 1998, Olivas currently serves as lead for the Special Purpose Dexterous Manipulator Robot, Mobile Transporter and the Mobile Base System. He previously worked at the Jet Propulsion Laboratory (JPL) as a senior research engineer developing tools and evaluating materials subjected to space environments, and as Program Manager of JPL's Advanced Interconnect and Manufacturing Assurance Program. Through his career, he has authored and presented numerous papers at technical conferences and in scientific journals and is principal developer of seven inventions.

Born in North Hollywood, California, but considers El Paso, Texas to be his hometown. Graduate of Burges High School, El Paso, Texas; received a bachelor of science degree in mechanical engineering from the University of Texas-El Paso; a masters of science degree in mechanical engineering

12.10 Astronaut John D. Olivas. Photo courtesy of NASA.

from the University of Houston and a doctorate in mechanical engineering and materials science from Rice University.

GEORGE D. ZAMKA, LIEUTENANT COLONEL, USMC ASTRONAUT (PILOT)

A graduate of the U.S. Naval Academy, Zamka reported for Astronaut Candidate training in August 1998. Before joining NASA, he flew the F/A-

12.11 Astronaut Lt. Col. George D. Zamka. Photo courtesy of NASA.

18 in 66 combat missions over Kuwait and Iraq in Desert Storm, and served as a test pilot at the Naval Air Test Center in Patuxent River, Maryland. Currently, he is assigned to the Shuttle Operations Branch of the Astronaut Office, where he serves as lead on Shuttle systems.

Born June 29, 1962 in Jersey City, New Jersey. Graduated from Rochester Adams High School, Rochester Michigan, in 1980.

He received a Bachelor of Science degree in Mathematics from the United States Naval Academy in 1984 and a Masters of Science degree in Engineering Management from the Florida Institute of Technology in 1997.

Special Honors

Navy Strike Air Medal (6), Navy Commendation Medal with Combat V, and various other military service and campaign awards. Distinguished Graduate, United States Naval Academy. Commodore's list and Academic Achievement Award, Training Air Wing Five. NASA Superior Accomplishment Award.

JOSEPH (JOE) ACABA ASTRONAUT CANDIDATE, MISSION SPECIALIST-EDUCATOR

Selected by NASA in May 2004, and currently undergoing training. Astronaut Candidate Training includes orientation briefings and tours, numerous scientific and technical briefings, intensive instruction in Shuttle and International Space Station systems, physiological training, T-38 flight training, and water and wilderness survival training. Successful completion of this initial training will qualify him for various technical assignments within the Astronaut Office.

Acaba taught 7th and 8th grade science and math in Dunnellon, Florida. He was born in Inglewood, California, and raised in Anaheim along with two older brothers and a younger sister. He now has three children of his own.

Both of Joe's parents were born in Puerto Rico. His dad moved to the States when he was about 10 and his mother moved when she was about 18.

"My dad is my hero. He came to the States with very little and worked hard to make sure we had what we needed," Joe says. "He instilled a real work ethic in me."

That work ethic has helped Acaba earn two degrees in geology. He earned a Bachelor's degree from the University of California at Santa Barbara and a Master's degree from the University of Arizona. After working as a hydro-geologist; someone who studies water that is under ground–Joe spent two years as a Peace Corps volunteer in the Dominican Republic, teaching the people about

12.12 Astronaut Candidate, Joseph Acaba. Photo courtesy of NASA.

the environment. "Once I did that, I knew that education was what I wanted to do. The only job that could take me away from teaching is being an astronaut," he says. "Being an educator astronaut is the best of both worlds."

Joe and his family thought it unbelievable that he was going to become an astronaut. When asked how he told his children he said, "It's been pretty neat. And, my daughter was actually in my class when I received the phone call, and my other students were dispersed throughout the classroom and the hallway. And so, once I hung up and I gained, or regained my composure, I was able to pull her to the side and tell her the call finally came in. It was an exciting time. And then, quickly after that, I rounded up the other kids and told them; and they just couldn't believe it. You're going to be an astronaut?" And, I said, "Yes, I am.

"I'm a fairly active teacher. I'm not an actor, but I try to keep the kids engaged. It's a great responsibility that I have, and I am very proud and honored to be here. The American standard is very high, and I look forward to working hard and to fulfilling my job. It's an honor and I'm glad to be a part of it."

SIDNEY M. GUTIERREZ, COLONEL, USAF, RETIRED ASTRONAUT RET.

Born June 27, 1951, in Albuquerque, New Mexico. Graduated from Valley High School, Albuquerque, New Mexico, in 1969; received a bachelor of science degree in aeronautical engineering from the U.S. Air Force Academy in 1973, and a master of arts degree in management from Webster College in 1977. Selected by NASA in May 1984, Gutierrez became an astronaut in June 1985.

In his first technical assignment he served as commander for the Shuttle Avionics Integration Laboratory (SAIL), flying simulated missions to verify Shuttle flight software. Following the Shuttle *Challenger* accident he served as an action officer for the Associate Administrator for Space Flight at NASA Headquarters. His duties included coordinating requests from the Presidential Commission and the U.S. Congress during the investigation.

A veteran of two space flights, he logged more than 488 hours in space. He was the pilot on STS-40 (June 5-14, 1991) and was the spacecraft commander on STS-59 (April 9-20, 1994). After his first flight, Gutierrez served as spacecraft communicator (CAPCOM) - the voice link between the flight crew and mission control– for STS-42, 45, 46, 49 and 52. In 1992, he became the Astronaut Office Branch Chief for Opera-

12.13 Astronaut Col. Sidney M. Gutierrez (Ret.). Courtesy NASA.

tions Development, overseeing ascent, entry, abort, software, rendezvous, Shuttle systems, main engines, solid rocket boosters, external tank, and landing and rollout issues.

In September 1994, Gutierrez retired from the U.S. Air Force and NASA, returned to his native home of Albuquerque, New Mexico, and joined Sandia National Laboratories. From September 1994 to March 1995, he served as Manager for their Strategic Initiatives Department. In March 1995, he became Manager of the Airborne Sensors and Integration Department in the Exploratory Systems Development Center. He also served as Chairman of the Governor's Technical Excellence Committee Spaceport Task Force.

Gutierrez serves on the Board of Directors of the Texas-New Mexico Power Company and Goodwill Industries of New Mexico, and is a member of the New Mexico Space Center's Governor's Commission.

The future is waiting. Photo courtesy of www.astronomy.com.

FUTURE
HEROES

■ ■ ■ ■ ■

13

Future Heroes

Note: The following is a compilation of articles written by Virginia Cueto and David Flores. For details please see Bibliography.

A LEGACY OF VALOR–
A NEW GENERATION CARRIES ON
A PROUD MILITARY TRADITION

Currently (2002), there are about 100,000 U.S. Hispanics on active duty, representing approximately seven percent of all active duty personnel. Latinos represent more than 6.2 percent of the Army, 8.1 percent of the Navy, 11 percent of the Marine Corps, and 4.4 percent of the Air Force, numbers that should continue to increase as all three branches of the Armed Forces step up their recruitment of minorities and Latinos.

But it is not just the ranks of enlisted men or ROTC programs that are increasingly bilingual. At all three U.S. military academies, where America's future military leaders are trained, the percentage of Hispanic-origin students is on the rise, and minority outreach efforts have been particularly successful among the Latino population.

13.1 Future Hispanic military leaders.
Photo courtesy of Hispanic Magazine.

Hispanics make up 6.7 percent of the corps of cadets at the U.S. Military Academy at West Point, the first of the academies to be established, in 1802. "This number is right on target," said Capt. Juan Carlos Ruck, a 1998 West Point graduate who now leads outreach efforts in the academy's Minority Admissions Office.

"Our goal is five to seven percent, to mirror the number of Hispanic officers in the Army Officer Corps," said Ruck, a first-generation American whose father emigrated from Peru at age 20.

13.2 Lt. Luis Gonzalez, USAF.
Photo courtesy of Hispanic Magazine.

The numbers are similar at the Air Force Academy in Colorado Springs, where Latinos represent six percent of the corps of cadets, and slightly higher at the Naval Academy in Annapolis, Maryland, whose class of 2005 accepted 109 Hispanic midshipmen, or about 10 percent of the class. While the academies actively recruit minorities, there are no official quotas, and Hispanic applicants must pass the same rigorous admissions standards as any other prospective student.

"Our job is to try and look like the society we serve," said 2nd Lt. Luis Gonzalez of the Air Force Academy's Minority Enrollment Office.

"While the academy's current student body is 18 percent minority, the school's goal is to eventually double that number to more closely reflect the make up of U.S. society," Gonzalez, a 2002 academy graduate, added.

But what motivates these young Latinos to seek a military career?

"There are many reasons why I chose to be here," said Midshipman Eldy Soto, a Mexican American from Houston finishing her senior year at the Naval Academy. "The first and above all is that I wanted to serve my country. I applied to the academy versus other universities because I had a chance to become an officer. The academy offered a challenge, an education, and a chance to lead."

13.3 Cadet Ricardo Cornejo, USAF. Photo courtesy of Hispanic Magazine.

Her sentiments are echoed by Cadet Ricardo Cornejo, a native Californian of mixed Nicaraguan, Mexican, and Spanish ancestry graduated from the Air Force Academy in May 2003.

"Of all the schools that had an interest in me, the Air Force Academy was by far the best opportunity for me," he said. "First, it was going to give me a chance to serve my country; second, it was going to give me a great education; and third, the whole experience, the challenges that I face here everyday, the discipline, I truly believe that that's something everyone should have the chance to do, and it's made me a better person, a better man for it."

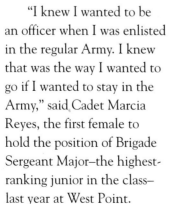

"I knew I wanted to be an officer when I was enlisted in the regular Army. I knew that was the way I wanted to go if I wanted to stay in the Army," said Cadet Marcia Reyes, the first female to hold the position of Brigade Sergeant Major–the highest-ranking junior in the class–last year at West Point.

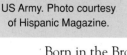

13.4 Cadet Marcia Reyes, US Army. Photo courtesy of Hispanic Magazine.

Born in the Bronx, New York, of Puerto Rican and Ecuadorian parents, Reyes is presently applying for a scholarship to complete post-graduate work in

England. "I'll probably end up branching into military intelligence and eventually I'm going to go to law school and be an Army JAG lawyer," she said.

Undoubtedly, the schools' top-notch education and scholarship programs offer an advantage that is hard to resist.

"With so many attractive options after graduation, I'm having trouble deciding which community service to select," laughs Midshipman

13.5 Midshipman Johann A. Guzman, US Navy. Photo courtesy of Hispanic Magazine.

Johann A. Guzman, a Baltimore, Maryland, native whose parents are from Puerto Rico.

"I was fortunate enough to win a scholarship called the Harry S. Truman Scholarship, allowing me to attend graduate school for two years after graduation. I am currently applying to Harvard, Princeton, Stanford, Georgetown, and Duke. Hopefully one of those will work out!" he said, although, as a future Naval Academy grad, he is considering whether to choose submarine service or flying.

For others, like West Point cadets Jorge Orlandini and Daron Moreno, a military career is a lifelong ambition.

"I always wanted to be in the military as a child," said Orlandini, born in Miami, Florida, to a Bolivian father and a

13.6 Cadet Jorge Orlandini, US Army. Photo courtesy of Hispanic Magazine.

Croatian mother. "I chose the Army because this is what I've always wanted to do. I honestly couldn't imagine myself doing anything else," he said. Moreno, a Mexican-American born and raised in Houston, Texas, agrees.

"I thought it was something that really, really fit me. Ever since I can remember, I've wanted to be a soldier. I came up here and thought that this place was the best way to go."

Service to their country and their communities is often a strong motivator, and many Latinos preparing to assume leadership positions list their Hispanic background as an asset in achieving their goals.

"I'm hoping to be able to fly, but…I would actually like to be a foreign liaison officer and work relations with some Latin American nations," said Air Force Academy cadet Jesus Raimundi III, a New York native of Puerto Rican ancestry. "I think it's very important in this day and age that there be good relations between allies. I'm a Latin American studies major, so it's a natural progression. I want to use my skills to help all the people that I can."

"While I was growing up, my mom and dad stressed family, courtesy and compassion about things," said Moreno, who plans on branching into the Infantry upon graduation from West Point. "I love dealing with people, and when you are a soldier and a leader, all you do is deal with people."

Orlandini, who spent his childhood in Bolivia before returning to the States as a young teen, cited the enormous contrast in opportunities available in the U.S. as an additional spur to choose to serve.

13.7 Cadet Daron Moreno, US Army. Photo courtesy of Hispanic Magazine.

"Living for six years in Bolivia then coming back here made me appreciate more, everything I have here. In Bolivia you have begging on the streets; you have 90 percent illiteracy rate; children die of common diseases. It was culture shock to come back here and see so many things that many people take for granted."

For these young leaders, being bicultural, far from diluting their commitment, is an advantage.

"Being Hispanic, especially being a *puertoriqueño*, a *boricua*, it's kind of an interesting situation," said Raimundi. "You are Hispanic and you are American. I'm very proud to be an American,

I'm glad to be in the Armed Forces. There is a long history of military service in my family," he adds proudly. "My grandfather served in WWII and Korea, and my brother also served, and now I'm serving.

"I just feel that it is great to make a positive contribution to what our great nation has to offer, and at the same time I do my best to represent myself well–not only as a cadet, or a member of the Air Force, or of my family, but also as a Hispanic in America, and to show people that we are out there doing positive things, and this is one of the many ways in which we contribute to this wonderful society," he emphasized.

Would they recommend other Latinos consider the rigors of a military academy?

"Absolutely," said Orlandini from West Point. "I feel really fortunate to be able to do what I'm doing right now. I'm proud I can do it. It's a wonderful experience. I've made the best friends I've ever had here, and I'm getting to do something I've always wanted to do."

13.8 Cadet Jesus Raimundi III, USAF. Photo courtesy of Hispanic Magazine.

"It is an incredible honor and a privilege to be attending the Air Force Academy," said Raimundi. "I wouldn't have been able to do it without the unending support of my parents, they've been absolutely wonderful about that. I would encourage any young people out there, especially young Latinos who are curious about pursuing the future, to consider the academies. The military academies are one of the best opportunities that they can have.

"My dedication and commitment to my country have grown from attending this fine institution," adds Midshipman Soto, whose interest in the military was initially spurred by curiosity about her grandfather's service during WWII.

13.9 Midshipman Eldy Soto, US Navy. Photo courtesy of Hispanic Magazine.

"My social skills have risen. I am the vice president of the Naval Academy's Pistol Club and the vice president of the Latin American Studies Club. I am a member of the Catholic Midshipman Club and the Semper Fi Club. I have set so many high standards for myself due to the atmosphere of the academy.

"As a young Hispanic, I have gone back to my community and high school to let the young kids know that everything is possible. They should know that an ordinary Mexican-American from the city can do it."

A Latino All-Star Quarterback

There are also Hispanic athletes in the military academies. Navy quarterback Aaron Polanco became a full-time starter on the 2004 U.S. Naval Academy football team and helped guide them to one of their best seasons in school history. Navy finished 10-2, and was ranked No. 24 in the final 2004 Associated Press Top 25 football teams. The Midshipmen had not won 10 games since going 10-1-1 in 1905, and had not ended a season ranked in the AP poll since 1963.

Polanco, who graduated from Wimberley High School in central Texas, capped his career with an MVP performance in the Midshipmen's 34-19 victory over New Mexico in the Emerald Bowl.

He rushed 26 times for 136 yards and scored three touchdowns, and he completed 3 of 6 passes

for 101 yards and another TD. Polanco, whose rushing total set a Navy bowl record, even caught two passes.

"It was a great season and a great bowl game for us," Polanco said during a brief visit to Wimberley this week. "The coaches taught us well and the players did what they were supposed to do, took things to heart."

Young Hispanics should take note of Polanco, who is among a handful of Hispanics who have played football at the Naval Academy. He is proof *que si se puede*. It can be done.

"I definitely take pride in

13.10 Midshipman Aaron Polanco, US Navy. Photo courtesy of CBS Sports.

that," Polanco said. "You want younger guys to follow in your footsteps."

Polanco's twin brother, James, was a junior defensive back also at the Naval Academy during the 2004 football season.

Aaron, who graduates in May 2005, plans to become a pilot in the Marine Corps. With the war in Iraq raging, he understands what lies ahead.

Final Thoughts

This book is not meant, in any manner, to be a thorough review of all the heroic and patriotic deeds contributed by Hispanic men and women in the military. There are obviously many more hundreds, if not thousands, of stories not yet told about Hispanics exceptional service to the United States armed forces. And these stories need not all be about saving lives or capturing the enemy. Merely serving a tour of duty is considered heroic by most Americans–Hispanic or not. I hope this book encourages more Latinos to share their military experiences with their families and friends.

Sharing experiences must be done in order to demonstrate to this country that Hispanics are more than illegal alien landscapers, dishwashers, or maids. Unfortunately, the predominant (English) media only gives the U.S. Latino community negative publicity; therefore, we must take it upon ourselves to generate positive information about our Latino family.

Our younger generations need to realize how much pride, courage, and dedication our Hispanic community has given to this country. However, joining the service is not the only manner this can be accomplished. We must share and learn of the Latinos in all the various professions. Many of them were able to go directly from high school to college and then graduate as doctors, lawyers, engineers, architects, teachers, police officers, computer specialists, reporters, mechanics, electricians, and so forth.

But, if a young person is not ready for college, then perhaps they can examine a trade or profession in the military. Four years of active duty may be enough experience to realize that getting a college degree is what is needed to reach a newly acquired goal.

So, if a decision to join the service is made, remember that we will always be here praying for you and your family. All that we ask of a service-member is to perform your duty honorably and protect those who can not do for themselves.

It will be then, when you will be seen as a patriotic
Hispanic Military Hero!

Bibliography

Preface

Mariscal, Jorge. "They Died Trying to Become Students." *Counterpunch Magazine*. April 18 2003.
http://www.counterpunch.org/mariscal04182003.html

Chapter 1 Sgt. Rafael Peralta

Filner, Bob. "A Salute to An American Patriot, Sgt. Rafael Peralta." U.S. House of Representatives.
http://www.house.gov/filner/enews/0105.htm

Kaemmerer, Travis J. Lance Corporal. "Marine sacrifices his life for others in grenade blast." U.S. Marine Corps.
http://www.ronaldreagan.com/ubb/ultimatebb.php/ubb/get_topic/f/12/t/000397/p/1.html

Marosi, Richard and Perry, Tony. "A Hero's Courageous Sacrifice-Marine Sgt. Rafael Peralta saved the lives of five others in his unit by smothering the blast of a grenade in Iraq." *Los Angeles Times*. December 6, 2004.
http://www.keystonemarines.com/article.php?story=20041206110952918

Chapter 2 History of Hispanics in the Military

"A Review of Data on Hispanic Americans." Directorate of Research, DEOMI, Defense Equal Opportunity Management Institute. August 1998.
https://www.patrick.af.mil/DEOMI/Observances.pdf

Contreras, Raoul Lowery. "Vilification by a Motley Few, A Hispanic View: American Politics and the Politics of Immigration." November 2002.
http://www.voznuestra.com/PoliticalWires/_2003/_May/11

Fernandez, Lionel, and Rochin, Refugio I. "U.S. Latino Patriots: From the American Revolution to Afghanistan, An Overview." Pew Hispanic Center. 2002.
http://pewhispanic.org/files/reports/17.3.pdf

Hispanic Contributions to America's Military. Las Culuras website.
http://www.lasculturas.com

Ide, SFC Douglas. "Saluting Hispanic Soldiers." *U.S. Army Soldiers*. September 1994. Volume 49, NO.9.
http://www.army.mil/soldiers/sept94/p52.html

Normand, Pete. "Juan Seguin Tejano Patriot." *The Texas Mason*. Brazos Valley Masonic Library and Museum Association. College Station, TX. 1986.
http://www.grandlodgeoftexas.org/seguin.html

"On the Battlefront-Latinos in America's Wars." *HispanicOnline*. HispanicOnline Staff. 2002.
http://www.hispaniconline.com/hh02/history_heritage_on_the_battlefront.html

Schmal, John P. "Hispanic Contributions to America's Defense." November, 1999.
http://www.houstonculture.org/hispanic/memorial.html

U.S. Department of Defense. *Hispanics in America's Defense.* Washington, D.C. 1990.

Villahermosa, Col. Gilberto. "America's Hispanics in America's Wars." *Army Magazine*. September 2002.
http://www.valerosos.com/HispanicsMilitary.html

Chapter 3 Medal of Honor Recipients

"Aguilera to Help Lead Remembrance for Emilio De La Garza." Indiana House of Representatives. News and Information. June 20, 2005.

"Aleutian Islands World War II." America USA, Hispanics in Americas Defense. 2001.
http://www.neta.com/~1stbooks/defen11c.htm

Associated Press. "Memorial to Hispanic Medal of Honor Recipients Approved in 2002." Los Angeles, CA. 2002.

Christenson, Sig. "Medal of Honor winner Benavidez dies." *San Antonio Express-News*. A Section Page 1A.
November 30, 1998.

Clinton awards Vista man Medal of Honor. Medal of Honor website. June 6, 2000.
http://www.medalofhonor.com/RudyDavila.htm

Cohea, Carol. "Gobernador Honors Its Own Local Hero." Daily Times Farmington, New Mexico. August 3, 2002.
http://www.medalofhonor.com/JoseValdez.htm

Congressional Medal of Honor Society website.
http://www.cmohs.org/

Danini, Carmina. "Family, friends honor WWII hero Adams." *San Antonio Express-News*. Metro / South Texas Page 1B.
April 6, 2003.

Danini, Carmina. "Rocco, 63, earned Medal of Honor in Vietnam–Army medic who saved three crewmen from a burning helicopter dies of lung cancer." *San Antonio Express-News*. Metro / South Texas Page 1B. November 1, 2002

"Family of Hometown Hero Presented with War Medals." Los Angeles Mission College. News Release. November 7, 2002.
http://www.lamission.edu/news/family_of_hometownhero_newsrelease.html

"First Lieutenant Baldomero Lopez, USMC." Who's Who in Marine Corps History. United States Marine Corps–History and Museums Division.
http://hqinet001.hqmc.usmc.mil/HD/Historical/Whos_Who/Lopez_B.htm

Flores, John. "The Ballad of Freddy Gonzalez–The Navy names a battleship for a Hispanic Marine 28 years after his death in Vietnam." *Hispanic Magazine.* November 1996.
http://www.mishalov.com/Gonzalez.html

Garcia, Kevin, and Carmina Danini and Scott Huddleston. "Lasting Legacy, WWII hero laid to rest; statue keeps memory alive in Brownsville." *The Brownsville Herald.* May 22, 2005.
http://www.homeofheroes.com/news/archives/2005/0522_lopez_obituary.html

Garcia, María-Cristina. "Macario Garcia." *The Handbook of Texas Online.*
http://www.tsha.utexas.edu/handbook/online/articles/view/GG/fga76.html

Garza, Alicia A. and Leatherwood, Art. "Alfredo Cantu Gonzalez." *The Handbook of Texas Online.*
http://www.tsha.utexas.edu/handbook/online/articles/view/GG/fgoqp.html

Goldstein, Richard. "Roy Benavidez Died at Age 63 on Sunday, 29 November 1998." *New York Times.* December 4, 1998.
http://www.mishalov.com/Benavidez.html

Gonzalez, John W. Lopez awarded Belgium's highest military honors–Symbols of valor earned for bravely in Battle of the Bulge." *Houston Chronicle.* July 8, 2004.

Gray, Richard. "Herrera's moment of unparalleled courage." *The Arizona Republic.* Sept. 25, 2005
http://www.azcentral.com/arizonarepublic/viewpoints/articles/0925herrera0925.html

Hahn, Laurie. "Real Heroes–Medal of Honor Recipients Write Students–Letters Are A History Project." *Times-Union Indiana.* December 21, 2002.

Halvorson, Barry. "Carrying on the name of war hero Roy Benavidez." *Victoria Advocate.* January 12th, 2004.

"He Gallantly gave His Life for His Country, age 22." *Tropic Lightning News.* November 24, 1966.

Huddleston, Scott. "Then & Now Redeemed by service–War hero Rocco's dedication to others has left its mark on city." *San Antonio Express-News.* Metro / South Texas Page 2B. November 10, 2002

Jose M. Lopez–Medal of Honor Recipient, Gallantry Beyond the Call of Duty. Hispanic America USA website.
http://www.neta.com/~1stbooks/m-s.htm

"Joseph P. Martinez Congressional Medal of Honor Recipient." The Aleutian's website.
http://www.hlswilliwaw.com/aleutians/Attu/html/attu-josephpmartinez.htm

"Korean War Congressional Medal of Honor Recipient–Pfc. Eugene Arnold Obregon, USMC." Medal of Honor website.
http://www.medalofhonor.com/EugeneObregon.htm

"Korean War Congressional Medal of Honor Recipient, Pfc. Fernando Luis Garcia, USMC." Medal of Honor website.
http://www.medalofhonor.com/FernandoGarcia.htm

Kozaryn, Linda D. "POW hero honored-Bush awards West Point '59 grad posthumous Medal of Honor." *American Forces Press Service.* July 12, 2002.

"Lance Corporal Emilio A. De La Garza, Jr., USMC." Who's Who in Marine Corps History.United States Marine Corps History and Museums Division.
http://hqinet001.hqmc.usmc.mil/HD/Historical/Whos_Who/DeLaGarze_EA.htm

"Lance Corporal Jose F. Jimenez, USMC." Who's Who in Marine Corps History. United States Marine Corps History and Museums Division.
http://hqinet001.hqmc.usmc.mil/HD/Historical/Whos_Who/Jimenez_JF.htm

Langdale, George W. *Wolfhounds of Sandbag Castle: A 96 Day Defense*. 1999.
http://www.kolchak.org/History/Korea/Langdale1999/Default.htm

Leatherwood, Art. "Miguel Keith." *The Handbook of Texas Online*. June 6, 2001.
http://www.tsha.utexas.edu/handbook/online/articles/view/KK/fkeyj.html

Lou, Linda. "The Alvord district readies the latest tribute to Ysmael Villegas, a middle school." *The Press-Enterprise*. Riverside, California. August 18, 2002.
http://www.alvord.k12.ca.us/Villegas/history/article.html

McLellan, Dennis. "Richard Rocco, 63, Ex Gang Member Won Medal of Honor for His Heroics in Vietnam War." *Los Angeles Times*. November 5, 2002.
http://www.medalofhonor.com/LouisRichardRoccoPassedAway.htm

Medal of Honor Recipients, Americans of Hispanic Heritage. Hispanics in Americas Defense. 1996.
http://www.neta.com/~1stbooks/medal2.htm

"Medal of Honor Recipient Master Sergeant Roy Benavidez." Psychological Operations website.
http://www.psywarrior.com/benavidez.html

Myers, James M. "David Bennes Barkley." *The Handbook of Texas Online*. June 6, 2001.
http://www.tsha.utexas.edu/handbook/online/articles/view/BB/fbabz.html

Myers, James M. Famous Hispanics in the U.S. Military website. 2003.
http://www.coloquio.com/famosos/usmilita.html

Nelson, Kate. "Friends say Richard Rocco gave all–and more." *Albuquerque Tribune*, November 4, 2002.
http://www.mishalov.com/Rocco.html

Orozco, Cynthia E. "Cleto L. Rodriguez." *The Handbook of Texas Online*.
http://www.tsha.utexas.edu/handbook/online/articles/RR/frobv.html

"Private First Class Edward Gomez, USMCR." Who's Who in Marine Corps History. Who's Who in Marine Corps History.United States Marine Corps History and Museums Division.
http://hqinet001.hqmc.usmc.mil/HD/Historical/Whos_Who/Gomez_E.htm

"Private First Class Ralph E. Dias, USMC." Who's Who in Marine Corps History. United States Marine Corps History and Museums Division.
http://hqinet001.hqmc.usmc.mil/HD/Historical/Whos_Who/Dias_RE.htm

"Puerto Rico Profile: Euripides Rubio." Puerto Rico Herald. September 24, 1999.
http://www.puertorico-herald.org/issues/vol3n39/ProfileRubio-en.shtml

Rivas, Lisa Harrison. "Final salute to a hero-Medal of Honor recipient is laid to rest. He requested his casket arrive in vintage truck." *San Antonio Express-News*. Metro / South Texas Page 1B. November 5, 2002.

Ross, Sonya. "Vietnam Medic Given Medal of Honor." *Associated Press*. February 8, 2000.
http://corregidor.org/heritage_battalion/moh/rascon.html

"Silvestre S. Herrera, Medal Of Honor, World War II." Home of Heroes website.
http://www.homeofheroes.com/profiles/profiles_herrera.html

Somos Primos website. "Celebrating Hispanic Heritage."
http://www.somosprimos.com/heritage.htm#Society

Sullivan, Deborah. "In Memory of a Hero East L.A. Man is Focus of Planned Monument to Latino Medal Winners."
Los Angeles Times. June 28, 1994.
http://www.neta.com/~1stbooks/m-vaa.htm

The Medal of Honor website.
http://www.medalofhonor.com

The Wolfhound History Project. 27th Infantry Regimental Historical Society. The Wolfpack.
http://www.kolchak.org

Vogel, Steve. "Captain Humbert Roque 'Rocky' Versace." The Medal of Honor website. May 23, 2002.
http://www.medalofhonor.com/RockyVersaceBiography.htm

Williams, Michael J. "Rudolph Davila, 85, was Medal of Honor recipient." North County Times, California.
February 8, 2002.
http://www.nctimes.com

U.S. Department of Defense. "Fact-Sheet, Hispanic-Americans and the U.S. Military in the Korean War."
Hispanics in Americas Defense, 1990.
http://korea50.army.mil/history/factsheets/hispanic.shtml

"Vietnam War Congressional Medal of Honor Recipient-Captain Humbert Roque 'Rocky' Versace." Medal of
Honor website.
http://www.medalofhonor.com/RockyVersaceBiography.htm

Chapter 4 Not Awarded a Medal of Honor

Baird, Mike. "WWII Marine shares Saipan story, Renowned vet Guy Gabaldon encouraged Japanese 'to live.'"
Corpus Christi Caller Times. May 26, 2005.

Gomez, Elena. "Marcelino Serna Became WWI Hero." *Borderlands–An El Paso Community College Local History
Project*. Spring 2004-2005. Volume 23:10.
http://www.epcc.edu/ftp/Homes/monicaw/borderlands/23/Marcelino%20Serna.htm

Kakesako, Gregg K. "'Pied Piper' returning to Saipan, The Chicano recipient of the Navy Cross will revisit the site of
a historic WWII battle." *Honolulu Star Bulletin*. June 6, 2004.
http://starbulletin.com/2004/06/06/news/index10.html

Olvera, Joe. "Three Chicano war heroes deserve Congressional Medals of Honor." *Hispanic Vista*. September 16, 2002.
http://www.hispanicvista.com/html/091602commentary.htm

Chapter 5 Hero Street
Culhane, John. "Hero Street USA." *Reader's Digest*. May 1985.

Chapter 6 Borinqueneers
Camacho, Luis Asencio, "A Borinqueneer Christmas Carol." University of Puerto Rico, Mayaguez Campus. 2004.
http://www.valerosos.com/aborinqueneerchristmascarol.htm

The Borinqueneers. El Boriqua Cultural Publication for Puerto Ricans.
http://www.elboricua.com/Borinqueneers.html

Villahermosa, Lt. Col. Gilberto. "From Glory to Disaster and Back." *Army Magazine*. September 2001.
http://www.valerosos.com/GlorytoDisasterandBack.html

Chapter 7 Squadron 201
Guevara, Lucy. "U.S. Latinos and Latinas & WWII Oral History Project–Mexican Airmen Join the War Effort." *University of Texas School Journalism*. 2000.
http://www.utexas.edu/projects/latinoarchives/narratives/02ESCUADRON_201.HTML

Uhler, David. "Escuadron 201." *San Antonio Express-News*. July 7, 2001.
http://www.somosprimos.com/spnov01.htm

Unander, Sig. "Strike of the Aztec Eagles." *Air Art Northwest*.
http://www.airartnw.com/index.html

Chapter 8 Fighter Aces
Air Education Training Command, History Office, Randolph Air Force Base, Texas.
http://www.aetc.randolph.af.mil/default.htm

"A Salute to Hispanic Fighter Aces." Hispanics in the Defense of the United States of America. 2001.
http://www.neta.com/~1stbooks/def1.htm

Flores, Santiago A. "Mexican-Americans in the Eighth Air Force." unpublished manuscript.

Flores, Santiago A. "Oscar F. Perdomo–The Last Ace In a Day of WW II." *WW II Ace Stories*. May 31, 2001.
http://www.elknet.pl/acestory/perdomo/perdomo.htm

Flores, Santiago A. "Richard Gomez Candelaria vs. Schulungslehrgang 'Elbe.'" Hispanics in the Defense of America website.
http://www.neta.com/~1stbooks/floresRGC.htm

Freeman, Roger A. "WWII Combat Europe Duty Above All: The Story of TSgt. Sator 'Sandy' Sanchez." *Mighty Eighth War Diary* (New York, 1981).

"Hispanic American Army Air Forces Heroes of World War II, The Ace-Oscar Perdomo." Air Education Training Command, History Office, Randolph AFB, Texas.
http://www.aetc.randolph.af.mil/ho/hispanic/his_perdomo.htm

"Hispanic American Army Air Forces Heroes of World War II, The Crew Chief–Jose Ramirez." Air Education Training Command, History Office, Randolph AFB, Texas.
http://www.aetc.randolph.af.mil/ho/hispanic/his_ramirez.htm

"Hispanic American Army Air Forces Heroes of World War II, The Gunners-Sator 'Sandy' Sanchez and Max Baca, Jr." Air Education Training Command, History Office, Randolph AFB, Texas.
http://www.aetc.randolph.af.mil/ho/hispanic/his_sanchez_baca.htm

"Hispanic American Army Air Forces Heroes of World War II, The Instructor–Edward Suarez." Air Education Training Command, History Office, Randolph AFB, Texas.
http://www.aetc.randolph.af.mil/ho/hispanic/his_suarez.htm

"Hispanic American Army Air Forces Heroes of World War II, The Strategist–Pete Quesada." Air Education Training Command, History Office, Randolph AFB, Texas.
http://www.aetc.randolph.af.mil/ho/hispanic/his_quesada.htm

Hood, MSgt Sarah. "B-17 to enter Air Force Museum." U.S. Air Force, Department of Defense.
www.af.mil/news/Mar1996/n19960325_960267.html

Official Biography. Major General Edward W. Suarez, [1962]. "Notes from Air Corps Fields." *Air Corps Newsletter*. July 1, 1935.

Scott, Mary. "The Last Ace of World War II." *Air Power History*. Fall 1989.

Sims, Edward. "Greatest Fighter Missions." Harper and Brothers. 1962.

Student Paper. "TSgt Sator 'Sandy' Sanchez: A Hero Forgotten." Gunter Air Force Base. 1996.

"The Story of TSgt. Sator 'Sandy' Sanchez." USAF History Museum.
http://www.wpafb.af.mil/museum/history/wwii/ce46.htm

Tillman, Barrett. "Hellcat: The F6F in World War II." Naval Institute Press. 1979.

Tillman, Barrett. "U.S. Navy Fighter Squadrons in WWII." Specialty Press. 1997.

Chapter 9 Servicewomen

Anderson, Karen. *Changing Women*. New York: Oxford Press, 1996.

Bellafaire, Judith, Ph.D. "The Contributions of Hispanic Servicewomen. Women In Military Service For America." *Women In Military Service For America Memorial Foundation*.
http://womensmemorial.org/Education/HisHistory.html

Ember, Melvin. *American Immigrant Cultures*. New York: MacMillan, 1997.

Documenting the American South. *Loreta Janeta Velazquez–The Woman in Battle*. The University of North Carolina at Chapel Hill.
http://docsouth.unc.edu/velazquez/summary.html

Servin, Manuel. *The Mexican-Americans: an awakening minority*. Beverly Hills, CA: Glencoe Press, 1970.

Whatley, Felicia U.S. Army Spc. *Florida National Guard Captains Rosalia & Rosana Maldonado, Two of a Kind–Sisters Share Similar Lives, Careers.* US Army Dept of Defense, Task Force Eagle Public Affairs. July 28, 2003.

Women Spies for the Confederacy.
http://womenshistory.about.com/library/bio/blbio_loreta_velazquez.htm

Chapter 10 American GI Forum and Dr. Garcia

Ayalin, Staff Sergeant Marc and Perkins, Sgt. Jimmie. Marine Corps bids farewell to highest-ranking Hispanic officer. Marine Corps Recruiting Command. September 17, 2004.
http://www.usmc.mil/marinelink/mcn2000.nsf/lookupstoryref/200492010841

Galloway, Joseph L. "American tale: Poor Hispanic rises to commander in Iraq." *Americans.net website.* June 2003.
http://www.iraqiwar.com/RicardoSSanchez.htm

Garamone, Jim. "Elwood R. 'Pete' Quesada." American Forces Press Service. September 11, 2000.
http://www.arlingtoncemetery.net/erquesada.htm

Guerra, Carlos. "A warrior returns to cheering throngs–and life at home." *San Antonio Express-News.* July 11, 2004. Metro / South Texas Page 1B.

Hispanics in the Navy. U.S. Navy website.
http://www.elnavy.com/us.navy?id=e.hn.admirals3

Holston, Mark. "Soldier of Fortune, Far from home, Lt. Gen. Ricardo S·nchez leads the effort to stabilize postwar Iraq." *Hispanic Magazine. December 2003.*
http://www.hispaniconline.com/magazine/2003/dec/CoverStory/

Rodriguez, Ken. "Resolute GI has two stars–and a plan for the West Side." *San Antonio Express-News.* October 29, 2003. A Section Page 3A.

US Southern Command Biography. *Maj. Gen. Alfred Valenzuela.* U.S. Army. January 22, 2003.

Williams, Rudi. *General Says Hispanics Underrepresented in Military; Services Trying to Attract More.* American Forces Press Service. October 10, 2002.
http://www.dod.mil/news/Oct2002/n10112002_200210112.html

Chapter 11 Generals and Admirals

Allsup, Carl V. "American GI. Forum of Texas." *The Handbook of Texas Online.*
http://www.tsha.utexas.edu/handbook/online/articles/view/AA/voa1.html

Averyt, Libby; Ron George, et al. *"Legacy endures in the hearts left behind."* Corpus Christi Caller Times and The *Associated Press.* January 22, 2002.
http://www.caller2.com/drhector/

Chapter 12 Astronauts

Acosta, Dean and Juhans, Renee. "NASA's First Female Hispanic Astronaut Shares Experiences." NASA Public Affairs Office. June 26, 2003.
http://www.nasa.gov/home/hqnews/2003/jun/HQ_03207_Ochoa_1st.html

Hudson, Terry. "Hispanic astronaut relishes being role model." *Tri-City Herald,* Kennewick, Washington. September 4, 2000.
http://www.tri-cityherald.com/news/2000/0904/Story4.html

NASA Johnson Space Center Astronauts. May 2005. NASA website.
http://oeop.larc.nasa.gov/hep/hep-astronauts.html

Chapter 13 Future Heroes

Cueto, Virginia. "A Legacy of Valor–A new generation carries on a proud military tradition." *HispanicOnline Staff.* 2002.
http://www.hispaniconllne.com/hh02/history_heritage_legacy_of_valor.html

Flores, David. "Area QB made most of chance at Navy." *San Antonio Express-News.* January 7, 2005.
http://www.mysanantonio.com/sports/stories/MYSA010705.1C.COL.FBCflores.80ff0e3e.html

Photo Credits

Chapter 4 Not Awarded a Medal of Honor

Index